P9-CJZ-973

SNAKE LAKE

JEFF GREENWALD

SNAKE LAKE

COUNTERPOINT
BERKELEY

Copyright © 2010 by Jeff Greenwald. All rights reserved under International and
Pan-American Copyright Conventions.

Author's Note: *Snake Lake* is primarily a memoir, reflecting my life in Nepal and the U.S.
in 1990. The identities of several friends and lovers, however, have been concealed, and
their roles in the story recast. The other events in the book—pertaining to Nepal's political affairs, my Buddhist studies, and my family—are as accurate as my research
and memory allow.

Library of Congress Cataloging-in-Publication Data

Greenwald, Jeff
  Snake lake / by Jeff Greenwald.
    p. cm.
  Hardcover ISBN: 978-1-58243-612-8
  Paperback ISBN: 978-1-58243-649-4
  1. Nepal—Description and travel. 2. Greenwald, Jeff, 1954—Travel—Nepal. 3.
Kathmandu (Nepal)—Description and travel. 4. Greenwald, Jeff, 1954—Friends and as-
sociates. 5. Nepal—History—Civil War, 1996-2006. 6. Nepal—Social life and customs.
7. Nepal—Religious life and customs. 8. Greenwald, Jeff, 1954—Family. 9. Brothers—
United States—Biography. I. Title.

  DS493.53.G75 2010
  915.49604—dc22
                                            2010017804

Interior design by Megan Jones Design
Cover design by Domini Dragoone
Cover image: Buddha statue courtesy Curio Concern, Kathmandu.
Printed in the United States of America

COUNTERPOINT
1919 Fifth Street
Berkeley, CA 94710

www.counterpointpress.com

Distributed by Publishers Group West

10 9 8 7 6 5 4 3 2 1

JEFF GREENWALD

SNAKE LAKE

COUNTERPOINT
BERKELEY

Copyright © 2010 by Jeff Greenwald. All rights reserved under International and
Pan-American Copyright Conventions.

Author's Note: *Snake Lake* is primarily a memoir, reflecting my life in Nepal and the U.S.
in 1990. The identities of several friends and lovers, however, have been concealed, and
their roles in the story recast. The other events in the book—pertaining to Nepal's political affairs, my Buddhist studies, and my family—are as accurate as my research
and memory allow.

Library of Congress Cataloging-in-Publication Data

Greenwald, Jeff
  Snake lake / by Jeff Greenwald.
    p. cm.
  Hardcover ISBN: 978-1-58243-612-8
  Paperback ISBN: 978-1-58243-649-4
  1. Nepal—Description and travel. 2. Greenwald, Jeff, 1954—Travel—Nepal. 3.
Kathmandu (Nepal)—Description and travel. 4. Greenwald, Jeff, 1954—Friends and as-
sociates. 5. Nepal—History—Civil War, 1996-2006. 6. Nepal—Social life and customs.
7. Nepal—Religious life and customs. 8. Greenwald, Jeff, 1954—Family. 9. Brothers—
United States—Biography. I. Title.

  DS493.53.G75 2010
  915.49604—dc22

                                    2010017804

Interior design by Megan Jones Design
Cover design by Domini Dragoone
Cover image: Buddha statue courtesy Curio Concern, Kathmandu.
Printed in the United States of America

COUNTERPOINT
1919 Fifth Street
Berkeley, CA 94710

www.counterpointpress.com

Distributed by Publishers Group West

10 9 8 7 6 5 4 3 2 1

for Jordan

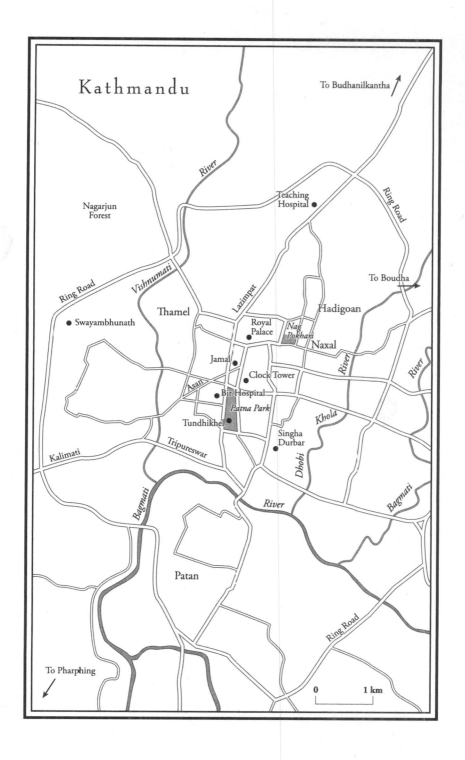

CONTENTS

Who is brave enough to remove the bell from the neck of the fierce snow lion?

The one who tied it there in the first place.

—Buddhist riddle

SNAKE LAKE

PART I

Before

1

Urban Bardo

THE BRAWL BEGAN with an eggplant. Maybe the *sauji*'s scale was off by a few grams, or his change short a few paisa; maybe the woman in the pale blue sari had miscalculated. But her outraged shouts caught the attention of six local boys, who stood smoking unfiltered Gaidas in a nearby doorway.

The Indian merchant shouted back, his brooding face screwed into a mask of indignation. The teens sidled up beside the shopper, adding their own racial insults to the mix. Their voices carried down the alley, inciting a state of alert. Guava and tamarind vendors, freshly arrived from the Indian border, glanced nervously up the lane, counting out change with fresh precision. The housewives and *didis* pretended to ignore the altercation, but held their purses more tightly against their bellies.

The *brinjal* seller was on his feet now, yelling at the teens. He was a thin man with a square face, a few years older than the boys but much smaller. He grabbed an eggplant and raised it high, meaning to display the fruit's tender flesh, expound upon how difficult they were to transport. But his gesture was misread—and before anything could be explained, one of the boys seized one of the purple fruits and pitched it with tremendous force into the little man's chest. It burst against his shirt like a balloon. The seller shrieked with rage and groped for the hardwood stick reserved for pariah dogs and greedy cows. The teens charged, grabbing his cart by the corners and heaving it over.

Eggplants and lead weights rolled at drunken angles down the filthy street. As the shoppers scattered, sellers leaped to defend their wares. Most of their stands were spared—but the hooligans toppled a pyramid of tangerines, and kicked over a basket of onions before skipping away.

THE INCIDENT MIGHT never have registered if the taxi driver hadn't been chewing pan. We were stopped at a traffic light on Kalimati Avenue: the ugliest road in Kathmandu. My driver cleared his throat and tilted his head out the window.

"Fight," he observed, and spat red spittle.

"What? Where?"

There was an alley on our right: a sloping chute angled between precarious brick tenements. Women were fleeing the lane, moving awkwardly in their saris. Oranges and potatoes fled with them, rolling across the sidewalk and into Kalimati's gutter, where they were snatched up by a gathering crowd of pedestrians and dogs.

I felt a certain thrill. "Who is fighting?"

"Everyone fighting." He craned his neck to see over the crowd. "Always fighting. In Nepal, too much fighting. Over there, market, many Indians. Too many Indians in this place." He spat again.

Further up the lane I could see the unmistakable aftermath of chaos: overturned carts, scattered produce, men waving their arms like agitated mantises.

I opened the taxi door and shouldered my daypack. "I'll get out here."

"Better you stay in car. Very danger here. Maybe shooting, also. If police come, maybe shooting." He squinted as I pulled a large bill out of my pocket. "Sorry . . . no change."

"Never mind."

"Sir?" The driver held my sleeve.

"*Hajur*?"

"You are a very lucky man."

"Why is that?"

"You can leave Nepal."

I grinned at the irony. "Drive safely," I said.

THE SITUATION HAD calmed by the time I arrived. The produce sellers were reclaiming their wares, arguing among themselves in rapid, overlapping Hindi. I spoke with a few bystanders, but there wasn't much of a story. Tensions between Nepalis and Indians had been escalating for months, and incidents like this were common. But the locals needed vegetables, and Indians needed to sell them. In a few days the street market would be open again, with a bored soldier leaning against a utility pole. Or maybe not; another half hour passed, but the police never arrived.

Back on Kalimati, I held my breath as a convoy of diesel trucks roared by. Gravel dust swarmed above their beds with every bounce. A pall of black soot hung above the ground. Taxis navigated the miasma like devils on the fly, weaving erratically to avoid cows, bicycles, and pedestrians.

I was standing just before an uphill grade. Along the roadside, boys and men in tattered and grimy rags hauled huge, flat carts loaded with pipes, lumber, rebar, or tin roofing. Their bare feet left shallow prints in the asphalt as they pulled the wagons with woven hemp ropes. Twenty yards up the rise, the grade became steeper; half of the pullers on each cart would drop their ropes and run behind to push, their backs bent at right angles to the road. Beneath leathery skin, the sinews of their calves bulged like balls of twine. They moved so slowly I could almost feel them breathe, hear the breath hiss out between their lips, sense the ache in their ruined lungs. Their labors were never-ending. Once these loads were delivered they would collect their pay and buy themselves just enough food and *chiya* to fuel the next uphill push.

A stream of foot traffic coursed along the sidewalk, moving in both directions. Men in baggy *darwa-surwals*, their black woolen vests absurd in the afternoon heat; women in bright polyester saris; kids chasing metal hoops through the gutters, their threadbare clothes the weakest link in a decade-long chain of hand-me-downs. All beneath a soundtrack of ceaseless diesel thunder, the blaring of Hindi movie soundtracks, Radio Nepal soap commercials, car horns, bicycle bells, barking, braying, shouts.

ONE MEMORY DOMINATED my thoughts every time I found myself on Kalimati. Years ago, when I was green around here, I'd bicycled down this avenue with a seasoned traveling buddy named Paul Janes. Janes had prematurely thinning hair and pale blue eyes, the youngest son of a Texas panhandle preacher. We'd stopped at this very point on Kalimati, straddling our bikes, and squinted up the filthy, congested road. Paul raised his eyebrows, and shook his head.

"*This is it,*" he said.

I turned toward him. "What's *it*? What are you talking about?"

"*This,* man! Kalimati! I know it." Paul gazed up the road with theological dread. "One day, we're gonna arrive in hell," he whispered. "You and me. We're gonna drop down that long, slimy chute and land bare-assed on the griddle. Then we're gonna stand up, and look around us. You know where we'll be?"

"Where?"

"Right here, man. Kalimati. Wait and see. *This is it.*"

WHETHER OR NOT Kalimati would prove to be hell itself remained to be seen. But it certainly qualified, in the here and now, as a bardo.

Not, of course, as *the* Bardo. The Bardo—capital *B*—is the spooky purgatory mapped out in *The Tibetan Book of the Dead.* In that ancient treatise (one of the first great travelogues), the Bardo is defined as the terrifying obstacle course that awaits the soul between death and rebirth. While migrating through this zone, our final spark of consciousness faces all manner of demons and obstacles: pits of fire, multiheaded cobras, rabid weasels. But these demons are all self-generated. It is during this crucial test that the trained mind can attain liberation—or control the circumstances within which it will be reborn.

In a broader sense, though, any difficult passage can be considered a bardo. Life, for example, is the bardo we navigate between birth and death. And there are bardos within bardos. Enduring a root canal, for instance, is a kind of bardo. A bout of dysentery is a bardo. Facing gridlock on the San Francisco–Oakland Bay Bridge, standing in a grocery line behind an old man counting out pennies, and paying off a student loan as an unemployed ·English major all are de facto bardos.

At this moment, Kalimati was the latest in a series of brief, personal bardos—this one transporting me to an appointment at the Kalimati clinic.

The clinic was one of the few places in Kathmandu where I could get an injection with confidence. It was run by Western nurses: people who believed in germ theory and practiced the option of sterilization. It is very important to seek out such enlightened caregivers in Asia. Otherwise, one runs the risk of contracting ailments far worse than hepatitis B: the debilitating liver disease that I was attempting, through a stringent schedule of gamma globulin shots, to avoid.

Fifteen minutes later I descended from the clinic with a limping, but relieved, step. Common sense dictated I walk or jog the four miles home, exercising my hindquarters in order to stave off soreness from the injection. Laxmi would be waiting, a lunch of noodle soup and home-baked bread at the ready. But for some reason (to flaunt my fresh immunity to the local germs?) I detoured into a tea shop and ordered a glass of *chiya*.

The *bhojanalaya* was dark and musty. A few flies circled in the air. There were no lights, and scant illumination filtered through the windows. The cement floor had been recently mopped; there were streaks of wetness and the sharp smell of bleach. Posters of current pop idols—Bruce Lee, Bob Marley, Phoebe Cates—were tacked to the walls.

The table by the kitchen was occupied by a little girl, drying metal plates with a dirty towel. I chose a spot near the windows, the better to see what I was drinking.

"*Khaana khaanuhuncoha?*" A woman in her late thirties turned from the glass cabinet above the cash box and addressed me in Nepali. "Will you eat?"

"*Hoina . . . duud chiya matrey dinus. Cheenie chaindaina.*" No thanks. Milk tea, please. No sugar.

"*Haus.*" The woman set down her rag and walked through a curtain of plastic beads into the kitchen, returning a moment later with my order. "*Biscoot khaane?*"

"*Haus.*" She brought a packet of arrowroot biscuits. They were good and crisp, as they should be in February—a far cry from the waterlogged wafers that had constituted my very first purchase in the Kingdom of Nepal, more than ten years ago, during the heart of the monsoon.

TEN YEARS AND seven months ago: That was July 1979. It already seemed like ancient history. Nepal in 1979 was unknown to me, a place that had never crossed my radar. I'd been lured to Asia by a gorgeous woman I'd met in Athens, a medical school graduate on her way to Kathmandu to study ayurvedic medicine for six months before starting her internship. After a month together in Greece we parted, vowing to meet in Nepal. But in the time it took me to scrape up enough money for an onward flight, she'd fallen in love with someone else. Her Dear John letter reached me in Cairo. I'd held a match to my ticket, but finally succumbed—not to hope, but to sheer momentum.

Cairo to Bombay, Victoria Station to Patna. I'd arrived in Kathmandu by overnight bus, during the thick of the rainy season. Though the ground was a sea of mud, the magic of Kathmandu filled the air like ozone. I loved the monsoon. It was a miracle, a dual baptism in water and fire. After each lightning storm the sky broke open, and rainbows arched between impossibly green hills. Then the clouds coalesced, and with a clap of thunder the rains fell again. It was as if the whole valley were being washed clean, over and over again. With my broken heart, Nepal was the right place to be: a green world.

Mornings I followed the trains of pilgrims walking in bare feet or rubber thongs up the empty avenues, watching with curiosity and delight as they offered flowers and coins to Ganesh, the elephant-headed remover of obstacles and lord of auspicious beginnings. There were always drums beating from someplace, tablas and horns and bicycle bells, the grating scream of ravens, arguments and laughter. Yet, somehow, Kathmandu was also the *quietest* place I'd been. Between every sound was a beat of pure silence, so pure that the temples and pedestrians seemed like brilliant, abstract stitching on a sheet of air.

I'd never expected it to be so *cinematic*. Every sight, large or small, was a flawless frame in a motion picture. A sacred cow poised in a carved wooden doorway, three schoolgirls in bright purple uniforms, a street stall selling pistachios and masks. I shot picture after picture: a beggar with a melted face, the hallucinatory displays of the glass bead district, butchers' shops displaying the fly-blown heads of freshly slaughtered goats.

My senses awakened with a vengeance. Smell, especially: juniper incense, tobacco and ganja, cow shit, jasmine, frying honey, kerosene and eucalyptus. I spent my afternoons at the Yin Yang Coffee House, filling my journal with a wild energy fueled by hashish, ginger tea, and french fries. As I rode home on my rented Hero bike, the thunderstorms turned the streets and alleys into a slush of cow manure. Primitive electrical lines spat and shorted, with blue and red explosions, above my head. On clear evenings I'd watch the sunset from the roof of the Kathmandu Guest House, waiting for the fruit bats to drop from the trees and soar over the grounds of the Royal Palace. I could follow their path across the valley—which was still, in July 1979, a patchwork of emerald paddies, uncluttered temples, and white palaces.

It was like no place I'd ever been, no place I'd even imagined. Yet it was so familiar that on my very first afternoon in Nepal, I sat on a cane chair in the garden on the Kathmandu Guest House, opened a package of soggy arrowroot biscuits, and—surrounded by flowers and a grinning plaster Buddha—wrote down the words I'd waited all my life to write: *Welcome home.*

BUT BARDOS LIKE Kalimati were part of the scene, too. The avenue connected the country's capital with all points west and south, including India. Since nearly everything that came into Nepal was imported from India, Kalimati remained a congested conduit for diesel-spewing lorries and buses.

For decades, the friendly relationship between Nepal and India was one of the few reliable facts of South Asian politics. The two countries have more than a border in common; they share cultural and religious bonds dating back thousands of years. Siddhartha Gautama—the historical Buddha, who traveled and taught in India during the fifth and sixth centuries BC—was born in southern Nepal, in a small kingdom called Kapilavastu. The long friendship was also sanctified by two treaties, giving landlocked Nepal special trading status. Nepal was able to export goods to India virtually tax

free, and to import petrol, medicines, and other critical goods without paying high tariffs.

India's concern for its poor neighbor wasn't purely altruistic. The
Kingdom of Nepal, a vaguely rectangular country roughly the area of North
Carolina, is wedged between India and China. In a geographic irony, the
Himalaya on Nepal's northern border, formed by the violent collision of
the Tibetan and Indian plates, is all that is holding the Chinese and Indian
armies apart. If Chinese troops were to gain control of Nepal's high passes,
only rolling foothills and dry scrub would stand between them and New
Delhi.

A reasonable fear, or groundless paranoia? It mattered not. Even though
the treaties didn't spell it out, it was understood that Nepal's privileges came
at a price. India's concerns were Nepal's concerns. The two nations would
enjoy free trade, open borders, and a cozy solidarity against the Chinese
threat.

Imagine, then, India's astonishment when, in the late 1980s, Nepal
blithely permitted China to build a road right over the mountains, and
smack into Kathmandu. Once the road was completed, Chinese factories
began to spring up on Nepal's southern plains, striking distance from the
India border. This deviant display was followed, only a few months later,
with news that Nepal had violated a secret treaty with India—in force since
1965—by purchasing arms from Beijing. The tanks and guns were no threat
to either neighbor—but for India's prime minister, Rajiv Gandhi, this was
one more act of betrayal.

In March of 1989, the India/Nepal treaties came up for review. This
might have been an opportunity for Nepal's King Birendra, one of the
world's last absolute monarchs, to reassure Gandhi of Nepal's political
fealty. The king did nothing of the sort. In an act of stunning hubris, Nepal's
parliament refused to sign the documents. Their needs had changed; it was
time for a new, improved treaty that recognized Nepal's new power and
position.

India nodded sagely and said nothing. The treaties expired. Rajiv
Gandhi closed thirteen of India's fifteen border crossings with Nepal and
raised the import taxes on Nepali goods thirtyfold. He then sent inspectors

to Nepal's shipping docks at the Port of Calcutta. The facilities were deemed unsafe, and padlocks snapped into place.

It was as if New Delhi had clamped a pillow over Nepal's face. Medicines vanished from the Kathmandu pharmacies. Gasoline was rationed to a trickle. Manufacturers could no longer get the materials they needed, and production on everything in the kingdom, from jewelry to hydroelectric dams, ground to a halt. Fruits and vegetables instantly quadrupled in price. An Indian merchant whose stall was located in an alley just off Kalimati announced an extortionate price for spinach. Less fortunate than this afternoon's eggplant *wallah*, he was beaten to death by an angry mob.

I'D COME TO Kathmandu five months ago, in the fall of 1989, finishing up a book. As the mess with India heated up, I started reporting on the crisis for the *San Francisco Examiner*. Even now, things were in steady decline. The conflict with India was still unresolved. Gasoline and medicines remained scarce, although the moneyed few (and all foreigners, of course) could tap into the black market. For the majority of Nepal's population, though, the crisis was intolerable. Rice and rubber, cookware and cloth—anything Indian, which was pretty much everything—had soared in price.

Something was happening, unique in the kingdom's long history: The Nepali people were getting fed up. Not just grumbling and mumbling fed up, but angry and dangerous fed up. Nepal was a kingdom on the verge of a nervous breakdown.

The ministers didn't care; they were too busy draining aid money into their own pockets and feathering their own nests. India didn't care; Rajiv Gandhi wasn't going to budge until his adversary cried "uncle." As for the king himself, well, no one dared guess what Sri Panch Maharaja Birendra Bir Bikram Shah Dev was thinking. He seemed to pass the days in a royal coma, spouting empty epithets in *The Rising Nepal* and remaining majestically aloof.

No one was minding the store. And as Nepal's people absorbed this fact, so too did they become aware of recent events in the Philippines, Soviet Union, and especially Romania—where a similarly clueless leader had lately been perforated by his subjects. Tired of spending five hours waiting in line for a jerry can of kerosene, sick of the crazy inflation that had pushed the price of a kilo of sugar to a full day's wages, students, merchants, housewives, schoolteachers, and even government workers were beginning to speak the unspeakable.

Did I want to go back to America? The truth was, I was ready for a break. I'd been in Nepal for more than 150 days and missed the small comforts of central heating, California wine, and potable tap water. I was tired of showering with a snorkel. March 6 would be my thirty-sixth birthday, and my girlfriend—a term that seemed more theoretical with every passing week and increasingly lukewarm letter—had expressed her intention to wait until that day, and not a day longer, for my return.

But revolution was in the air. The fever had a grip on me. January and February had seen a continual series of protests and strikes, each one larger and more passionate than the last. They were the growing expressions of Jana Andolan: a People's Movement that had begun with student uprisings almost one year ago. At any moment, the *deesha* could hit the fan. And I'd be here when it did, filing front-page stories.

I FINISHED MY tea and paid the *sauni*. Outside, the glare off the asphalt clenched my pupils down to dots. Kalimati's baseline cacophony was matched by the ululating shriek of a car alarm (issuing, I noticed, from a moving vehicle; the driver looked pleased). Traffic, courtesy of the black market in petrol, had stabilized at about 50 percent. It was hard to imagine where the missing half, when it showed up, would fit.

I reached into my jacket pocket and was momentarily puzzled when my hand found a small, round object: a tangerine I'd picked up on my way out of the vegetable seller's alley. It looked okay, despite a spate of recent abuse. I cupped it in my right hand and flagged a cab with my left.

I was staying, then. Here for the duration. It wouldn't be easy, and it wouldn't be pretty. There would be some nasty scenes: broken windows, cracked ribs, maybe worse. And even if the Nepalis took to the streets en masse, demanding self-determination, there were no guarantees. The kids in Tiananmen Square knew all about that.

But what if they *did* pull it off? What would follow centuries of absolute rule and decades of wholesale corruption? Democracy, one hoped. Prosperity. Liberation! Because that, presumably, is what bardos, including *the* Bardo, are all about. At the end of its painful journey, if the soul plays its cards right, there's a payoff: the chance to leap off one's rusted, creaking cart and fire up the warp engines.

No one could say where Nepal was going, but it was bound to be an interesting ride.

I peeled the tangerine, and tossed the rind to a waiting cow.

2

Fear of Shoes

I N CHAPTER 9 of *Cosmos*, Carl Sagan describes the end of the world. A two-page spread, accompanying the text, reproduces a series of four paintings. Each illustrates a phase of the Earth's annihilation, due to the inexorable heat-death of the sun.

Of all these images, the first is the most eerie and disturbing. The painting portrays an idyllic, sun-washed coastline, ripe with trees. The sky is peppered with clouds, and islands dot a perfectly blue sea. *Several billion years from now*, the caption reads, *there will be a last perfect day.*

For the Kingdom of Nepal—and for myself, for strangely similar reasons—February 17, 1990, was one of those last, perfect days. Pilgrims and children crowded the entrance to the Chabahil Ganesh shrine, tossing rice at the brass image of the elephant god. Men strolled down Mahankhal, their arms linked. Dogs nosed lazily through wrappers and rinds, somehow aware of the rhythms of a Saturday. Strains of Bryan Ferry's *Bête Noire* pulled like an undertow beneath the soundtrack from *Coolie*, blaring from households on opposite sides of the street.

I walked my rented bicycle through the gate to the Boudhnath stupa, turned left, then rode clockwise around the massive white dome. A plastic bag of tangerines dangled from my handlebars, jerking as the bike bounced along the cobblestone road. The wide, circular path surrounding the shrine was an important *kora*: a devotional path, followed clockwise around a holy mountain or Buddhist monument. The ancient white dome of Boudha itself—symbolic of a lotus, an egg, and/or Buddha's overturned begging bowl—rests upon a three-tiered plinth. The entire site, viewed from above, is revealed as a giant earthwork: an elaborate geometric mandala.

There were constant distractions. The route circling Boudha has evolved into a hodgepodge flea market, an open-air bazaar crowded with statues and textiles, incense and conch-shell horns, Tibetan bells, Amitabh Bachchan posters, antique beads, army boots, and porcelain dishware. Beggars lean against the stupa's circular outer wall, waving wasted limbs beneath long rows of prayer wheels. Mendicants recite sutras from tattered manuscripts, nodding like Hassids. Here is samsara, the earthly realm, in microcosm: an infinite tattoo of pain and color, spread out beneath the four pairs of Buddha-eyes that gaze down, as colorful as a child's finger painting, from the golden square finial atop the high, white dome.

Overwhelming as the scene was, it was just warming up. Lhosar, the Tibetan New Year, was only eight days away.

I veered away from the kora, made my way down a muddy lane slick with banana peels, and arrived at the entrance to the Ka-Nying Shedrup Ling Monastery. The abbot of the monastery, Chokyi Nyima Rinpoche (*rinpoche* being an honorific title meaning "precious gem"), gave public talks about Buddhism every Saturday morning. They were scheduled for 10 a.m.; I was about ten minutes late.

No big deal, I figured; if the place operated on Tibetan time, I was still comfortably early. But after climbing the three flights of stairs leading to the lama's chambers, I saw that the waiting area was empty. Everyone was already inside. Against all odds, the Saturday teaching had begun on time.

There was something intimidating about the sneakers and flip-flops and hiking boots piled to the right of the heavy maroon curtain that served as a door to the meditation room. I could see Dr. Dan's black motorcycle boots, placed neatly against the wall, but most of the footwear was unfamiliar. The men and women who owned it were presumably regulars, earnest practitioners of Tibetan Buddhism. They were students who knew Chokyi Nyima Rinpoche intimately, and guarded their insider status.

But the fact of an ally in the room was comforting. My visit, after all, had been Dr. Dan's idea. An internist from Miami, Daniel Kauff had moved to Nepal in 1983 to volunteer with the Himalayan Rescue Association. When his tour with the HRA ended he'd organized Kathmandu's first Western-style clinic and published several papers on the etiology of bacterial dysentery. His involvement with Buddhism began three years ago, when he set up a free weekend clinic for Tibetan monks. This had involved working closely with Chokyi Nyima. Although Dan initially had little interest in the dharma, he'd found himself drawn in by the young Rinpoche's humor and insight.

Chokyi Nyima, for his part, was fascinated by the empirical diligence of Western medicine, and by the fact that a professional caregiver from one of the wealthiest countries in the world could also be quite neurotic. The two men became friends. Over the course of just a few months, their meetings evolved into spiritual Q&A sessions.

"It was such a unique and unlikely friendship," Dan confessed, "that I considered writing a book about it: *The Rinp and I.*" As time passed, though, and Dan's respect for the lama increased, he abandoned his thoughts of turning their rapport into a vehicle for comedy.

Dan had prevailed upon me to visit Chokyi Nyima several weeks earlier, after reading the manuscript for a book I was writing about Buddhist art.

"You talk the talk," he observed, "but when are you going to walk the walk? No offense, but your writing would be far more credible if you had a broader understanding of the dharma." I couldn't argue. Though I felt an intuitive understanding of Buddhism and comprehended the basics (I knew, for example, that *dharma* literally meant the "law," or practice, of Buddhism), I'd seldom attended any formal teachings.

COGNIZANT OF THE requisite formalities, I carried a few small gifts for the Rinpoche: a bag of tangerines, purchased outside the Boudha entrance gate, and a *kata*, the traditional silk scarf that one presents to high lamas and other respected personages. Possession of these props would be enough, I hoped, to place me a notch above the lowest stratum of curiosity seekers.

My Reeboks joined the pile of shoes by the door. I parted the woolen curtain and stepped into the meditation room.

The light was marvelous. It filtered through the yellow curtains hanging over the windows, giving the broad, rectangular space a buttery warmth. There were about thirty-five Westerners inside. They sat attentively on the round cushions and thick Tibetan carpets covering the floor. A low sofa rested against the wall below the yellow curtains. Against the facing wall stood a huge wooden altar, a sort of high hutch with glass doors and shelves. It contained dozens of small statues, all flanking a golden Shakyamuni Buddha with sly, almost mischievous eyes. Among the smaller statues I recognized Tara, the goddess of compassion; Padmasambhava, the saucer-eyed wizard who had brought Buddhism from India to Tibet; and Manjushri, master of discriminating wisdom, with his flaming sword poised in the air.

Chokyi Nyima sat on a comfortable cushion on a slightly raised platform. He wore a dark maroon robe, which passed over his left shoulder. A red silk vest and yellow undershirt were visible beneath the robe's swoop. His head, I noticed immediately, had an unusual shape. It was somewhat oblate, flattened out at the top and bottom, like an ostrich egg on its side. On a small table before him sat a Tibetan bell, a silver altar-box, a *dorje*, and a pile of red blessing cords, which he knotted as he spoke.

When he noticed a stranger had entered, Chokyi Nyima stopped speaking and fixed me with an appraising eye. As if on cue, every other eye in the room turned to regard me as well. I stood very still, feeling like someone who intended to steal a honeycomb and had just been noticed by the bees. My kata hung over my slightly outstretched hands; the bag of tangerines dangled from my forearm.

Serious dharma students, I knew, prostrated themselves three times before approaching a high lama. This I could not do. I could never reconcile such an action with the images I'd absorbed in Hebrew school: heroic Jews forfeiting their lives by refusing to bow, for any reason, to a mortal king.

The Rinpoche studied me for a moment, smiled, and beckoned me forward with a staccato of nods. I walked forward resolutely. But as I approached the dais I realized that I was towering above him. This didn't seem appropriate, either. So I dropped to my knees, set down the tangerines, and—before he could resist—draped the silk kata around Chokyi Nyima's neck.

There was muffled laughter from the assembly. I remained calm, folding my hands in my lap as Chokyi Nyima regarded me with a highly amused expression.

"Do I know you?" His voice was frank with a high, slightly comedic pitch.

"No, Rinpoche. We haven't met."

"I see." More tittering from the audience. He reached into the bag of fruit and handed me one of my own tangerines. "You can sit down now," he said.

I stood up and turned around. Everyone seemed amused, but I read no malice on their faces. I spotted Dan, who tapped a place next to himself on the low sofa. As I sat, tucking my legs into a sort of trampled lotus posture, an attendant monk placed a porcelain cup on the carved wooden table in front of me.

"It's tea," Dan whispered. I nodded, letting it cool.

"Don't you like tea?" Chokyi Nyima called out, still attending my every move.

"I love tea," I replied, sipping from the fragile cup and burning my tongue. "Mmmm. Very fine tea. Very fragrant. Thank you."

Chokyi Nyima nodded, and seemed satisfied enough with my well-being to return his attention to the room at large. But his cell phone rang; the lama plucked a handset from his robe, pushed a button, nodded, and spoke in rapid Tibetan into the receiver.

Dan leaned toward me. "Do you know why everyone was laughing?"

"I did something stupid?"

"I wouldn't say stupid. Different. Charming, actually. You put the kata around Chokyi Nyima's neck."

"And?"

"That's wrong. You're supposed to hand the kata to the *rinpoche*. He blesses the scarf and puts it around *your* neck. That's the way it's done. So, basically, it was like you were giving *him* a blessing."

I felt the blood drain from my face. "He wasn't insulted?"

"Not at all." Dan leaned in closer, placed a hand on my shoulder. "And I'm pretty sure you made an impression."

I GLANCED BACK toward the head of the room. Chokyi Nyima had concluded his telephone conversation and was sorting through a pile of papers on a lacquered tray. He was humming softly and had tucked the ends of my kata scarf into the V-neck of his yellow undershirt.

"So," he said, slapping his palm on the stack of paperwork and looking up abruptly at the assembled group. "Where were we?"

"Buddhism," someone volunteered. It must have been a joke, though no one laughed.

"Ah yes. Buddhism!" The Rinpoche scanned the room with a droll countenance. "Always Buddhism! Never talk less than Buddhism here. Only Buddhism! Such high mind! Such great mind! Oooooo! Very, very good!" He adjusted his robe with a practiced gesture and smiled winningly.

"So. What is Buddhism? First, here's what I'd like to say: In this world, there are many types of religion. On the one hand, Buddha dharma is a religion. But Buddha dharma is not the same as other religions. We shouldn't include it in the religion section! Understand?" There were many nods, and a few affirmative grunts.

"What I think—and also true!—is that religion is on one side, and science, physics, chemistry, on another side. Buddha dharma is in the middle! Buddhism is a religion, but Buddhism is not really a religion. Buddhism is a science, but Buddhism is not really a science.

"So what is Buddha dharma? Hmmm?" The Rinpoche lowered his voice and spoke slowly. "Buddha dharma is common sense: Truth.

"Other religions are also searching for Truth. Science, also, is searching for Truth. Each has a different way of searching, and each has a different idea of what makes Truth.

"Now, one problem is God. Some people are sure there's a God. Hundred percent sure! Some people say no, there's no God; believing in God is wrong. This is not a small contradiction! What I think is, there's no need to contradict. But first we must ask, what means 'God'? Hmmm?" He cupped his ear expectantly.

Hands were raised, and opinions offered. God is energy; God is love; God is Jesus Christ. God created the Universe. God is dead. God is that which protects us. God is an old man with a white beard, wrathful but just. God is George Burns. The group broke into laughter and scattered conversations.

"Okay." Chokyi Nyima raised his hand for silence. "If you believe God means something solid, powerful permanent, controlling the universe, then it's a little strange. Who made him? Why does he behave as he does? When he's happy, he helps; when he is not happy, he punishes. He's sort of a nasty man! If, on the other hand, God is a kind of truth—a kindness, a peace, existing beyond ideas—perfect! Then there's nothing wrong! If you understand that way, it makes more sense, and it's also quite logical.

"A different way of believing," the Rinpoche continued, "makes a different way of understanding. And the best understanding is the most logical understanding. When something is logical, we have no choice but to believe. So: Logic is the best religion. Do you understand? If an argument can be defeated, it is not the best! If you cannot defeat it, then . . . what? Automatically, without choice, it's the best. Okay? Make sense?"

His words recalled a memory, a scene I'd once witnessed in Lhasa. Dozens of novice monks filled the courtyard of Sera Monastery, engaged in a debate class. They paired off, arguing philosophy in high, shrewd tones. One monk played the devil's advocate, and the other replied. Each point of logic was underscored with histrionic gestures: The monks smacked their palms together, tossed their robes over their shoulders, and swung their prayer-bead rosaries in yo-yo-like loops. Debating skills are an integral part of Tibetan monastic training. If Buddha's teaching is robust enough to withstand objective scrutiny, the thinking goes, any doubts or denials can be met with rational, watertight replies.

The Rinpoche cleared his throat and shifted forward on the dais. "So. Thinking logically, here is what Buddha says.

"First: Everything—trees, birds, rocks, even world, even whole universe—is *impermanent*.

"Second: The mind, jumping between hope and fear, creates *suffering*.

"Third: *emptiness*. All phenomena are essentially empty; nothing actually exists, or has solid form.

"Fourth: *egolessness*. Even the ego does not exist! There is no *I*.

"This what the Buddha taught. But do we trust him? Hmm?" The Rinpoche scanned the room, eyebrows raised. "Okay. First, we listen. Then, we test: like science."

I listened to this teaching, enthralled. It was one thing to read about Buddhist philosophy in texts, or on the little cards describing Buddhist statues in museums; it was a completely different experience to hear a lively, charismatic lama explain the teachings with humor and conviction. Most of all, though, the emphasis on logic fascinated me.

And on general principles, the notion of a spiritual philosophy that could be tested (and dismissed if proved untrue!) appealed to me immensely. Science had always been my strongest subject, and direct experience was its lodestone. When we were kids, my brother, Jordan, and I had combed the nearby woods for dead birds and squirrels, dissecting them with scalpels from the local hobby shop. It wasn't enough to read about hearts, brains, and intestines; we needed to *see* them. Not only that; we had to pickle them, preserving the choicest organs in baby food jars on our bedroom bookshelves.

"First, Buddha says, impermanence. True, or not?" The lama peered around the room. "Whichever way we examine, we have no choice but to believe about impermanence! Why? Because everything is changing. Always. Everything is changing, very subtly, moment to moment. Everything is impermanent."

I nodded, knowing this to be true. I'd read about it in physics books and seen it at work on my 1979 Datsun station wagon. Nothing, large or small, lasts forever. According to the laws of entropy, the entire universe is in a state of slow death: cooling, inexorably, toward absolute zero.

Chokyi Nyima continued, as if reading my mind. "The whole world will change. Even the sun. Even the moon. But our inner world—our thinking, hoping, fearing, all our emotions—also changes. Every day, many changes. There is nothing, *nothing*, that does not change. Right? Hmm?"

There was a brief interruption. Two Indian children walked right in, and casually approached the Rinpoche. The eldest, a young girl, carried a bouquet wrapped in cellophane. "Oooo!" Chokyi Nyima cried. "Really good flowers! But where is a vase?! Really good flowers need a vase!" He bounced up from his seat and abruptly left the room. Dan turned toward me.

"What do you think?"

"He's wonderful," I said. "Very cute. Is that it?"

"I don't think so. This kind of thing happens all the time."

Indeed, Chokyi Nyima returned a moment later with a porcelain vase. The tightly bunched stems cleared its narrow throat with a pop, splattering water everywhere. The Rinpoche set the vase on his table with a grin, placed his hands over his knees, and leaned forward again.

"So? What next? *Suffering*.

"To suffer means, what? Buddha says, where there is ego, there is emotion. Therefore there are also negative emotions, and hope and fear. True?" His rhetorical question hung in the air. "We have no choice but to believe about suffering! Suffering is here. *We* have suffering. Ego creates the dualistic mind, and a dualistic mind means *you* and *me*. And from this idea of 'you' and 'me' come hope and fear, and many other negative emotions.

"We know about suffering and impermanence very well," the Rinpoche concluded. "We all have direct experience, so we don't need to doubt these two points. We have some kind of *trust* in them. On the one hand, trust is faith; but it's not blind faith, because it can be tested."

So far, I had followed his train of thought without a hitch. There was no need to apply the scientific method to impermanence, or to suffering, two facts that no one who'd ever owned a goldfish, or a human heart, could deny. But I was curious to know how the Rinpoche would "prove" the notion of emptiness. String theory, which holds that matter is a tangle of formless, energetic vibrations, had come to this notion fairly recently. Buddhist philosophers must have their own way of describing this abstract idea.

"Okay. Everyone okay? Everyone sharp?" Chokyi Nyima surveyed the room, clearly aware that the easy part of the teaching had come to an end.

"Next, Buddha says, everything is *empty*. Nothing is real!" The lama's eyebrows flew up. "Now there's trouble! Now we have trouble! But one good thing: Buddha says, 'Please check well! Don't trust only me. Don't trust only what I say. Check yourself, to see if this makes sense or not.' So, we are

allowed to check! We are happy to check! Even if we trust Buddha, even if
we respect the dharma, Buddha said, 'Check.' So, we check. We examine.

"The problem is this: Everything *seems* to exist. We say that everything
is empty, but we have no direct experience of that. We need to have some
kind of proof. But what is our proof? So far our proof is seeing, touching,
hearing, feeling. This table . . ." He moved the vase of flowers onto the floor.
". . . is *here*. I see it; that's proof it exists." Chokyi Nyima leaned forward
and banged the wooden surface with his fist, rattling his teacup. "Touching:
second proof. And sound." He banged the table again. "Third proof. And
hurting!" He smacked the table sharply with his palm. "Aieee! Fourth proof
that table exists!

"So! There's many proofs that table exists. But these proof are very,
very *low* proofs. Very, very, very *gross* proofs. Why? Hmmm?" He waited
for an answer, but received none. "Because they rely on our senses.

"But there are other proofs; proofs that will show that the table does
not exist. How? If we really check well, we find . . . what? That all things,
all objects, are created of atoms. But the smallest atom itself does not exist!
Why? *Because everything that exists has at least six sides*: east, west, north,
south, up, down. To have size, must have sides. If no sides, then no size.
And the atom, if we try to examine, ends up being size-less; point-less. Even
the physicists say so: An atom does not really exist. Only if you look for it,
then it seems to exist!"

Though not entirely convincing, I did find these observations intriguing. They recalled Fritjof Capra's *Tao of Physics*, a reminder that Western
scientists were not the first to plumb the subatomic world.

I was also aware that this teaching, all the Saturday teachings, were
a superficial introduction to a subject that might take a lifetime, or many
lifetimes, to master. This morning's session was not designed to enlighten,
but to stimulate. It was working; I was already thinking of this as the beginning of something, the first of many teachings that I would attend over the
coming months.

"Finally," Chokyi Nyima continued, "The Buddha says, *egolessness*.
And this, maybe, is the most difficult of all. Because we really, really think
'I' exists. We are *very* sure 'I' exists. We think the ego is *me*, *I*. And that *I am*

here . . ." (he pointed to himself) ". . . and not there." (Pointing to a woman at the front of the room). "Isn't it?

"But where am 'I'? Can we pinpoint 'I'? We think the body is 'I.' But no; the body is not *me*; it's my body. Is my name me? No; my name is not *me*; it's my name!" He glanced around eagerly, clearly enjoying this riddle. "I know! My *mind* is me! But wait... my mind is not *me*. It's my mind. It *belongs* to me, but it is not *me*! So what's me?!" Heads shook throughout the room, a silent chorus of befuddlement.

"It's complicated," Chokyi Nyima admitted. "But true! My body is not *me*. My name is not *me*. My mind is not *me*. These three things are *mine*.

"But where is the owner? We cannot find the *me* to which these things belong! Yes? No? Right? *You!*"

Chokyi Nyima looked directly at me, tugging the silk kata I'd given him with both hands. "You, with the neck like a giraffe! What is your name?"

"Jeff." The room rollicked at my expense.

"*Jeff.* Even sounds like giraffe. No? Jeff. Gireff. Jaff. Giraffe. Right? Right? Ha ha ha! Very good!" He slapped his leg with delight. "If I say Jeff—or Giraffe!—you think, *me*. Oh, oh! Me! You don't think, 'Jeff is my name.' You think, 'Jeff is *me*. Me and Jeff are one.' Same with the body. *My* body. Also, same with thinking. *My* mind. Today my mind is happy; today my mind is not happy. Isn't it?" I nodded dumbly. "So it seems there *is* a me in there somewhere—hiding. But where? Can we find it? No! Very strange! Very complicated! But we cannot find! *Whose* name? *Whose* body? *Whose* mind? Who?!"

I was unable to reply. Fortunately, I didn't have to. The monk who had poured my tea approached the lama and whispered something. Chokyi Nyima looked at his watch, nodded, and turned back to his students.

"Today we talked so many things," he concluded. "Talked God; talked Buddhism. Talked logic; talked faith. But most important, we talked about the basic conditions: Impermanence, Suffering, Emptiness, Egolessness. Hmm?"

No one could disagree.

"So, please: Think well; examine well. Test well! And we will discuss more, later. Okay?" He adjusted his robes again. "Finished. Now, necessary to perform *puja*." He tapped his wrist. "Good watch. Very important. These days, we can time our puja exactly. Start at the exact right second. *Split* second," he added wryly. "What did we do before watches? Maybe everything went wrong! One second early! Split second late! Oh! Oh!"

He stood up, but his students remained seated.

"Lhosar, Tibetan New Year, is coming. Many pujas! So next Saturday, no teaching." There was a collective sigh of disappointment. "Maybe Monday. Call and see." He looked at me. "You have my number?" I shook my head. "No? Get it from this monk. Giraffe is always welcome. Free from the zoo, always welcome! Right? Ha ha ha!" With that, he left the room.

"You're a hit," Dr. Dan said.

We left to find our shoes. A few students cast me amused smiles. My own feelings were bittersweet. Though it was flattering the Rinpoche had noticed me, I couldn't pretend to enjoy hearing my schoolyard nickname revived.

3

Black Armbands

THE MORNING WAS clear, cold, and fogless. Barefoot devotees filled the sidewalks, returning from their morning pujas at the neighborhood shrines. A small crowd thronged the vermilion-smeared Ganesh next to the Candy Cane Cold Store, lighting incense and offering flowers and fruit.

I hit a pothole, and my Nikon bounced against my back like a sharp-nosed papoose. After a short uphill climb, Maharajganj Teaching Hospital appeared to my left. It was a high brick edifice with few architectural pretensions and a dry, trampled lawn. Dozens of doctors, nurses, and orderlies stood in front of the main entrance, holding signs. All wore stethoscopes—as if prove, touchingly, that they really were doctors. An instant later I guessed the real reason: The stethoscopes were stage props, for the benefit of the press. Trained in the Western world, these doctors understood the power of images. Though it was unlikely many newspapers would run a story on the strike, a captioned photo might make the cut.

News of this historic strike, the first by the doctors and staff of Nepal's most prestigious hospital—by *any* urban professionals in Kathmandu—would appear in the *San Francisco Examiner* within twenty-four hours. Filing that report was my job—though at the moment, it felt more like a privilege.

The events that provoked the doctors' action had stunned the entire valley. They'd begun two weeks ago, when thousands of university students in Pokhara, a lakeside town in central Nepal, gathered to celebrate Nelson

Mandela's release from prison. Armed police troops arrived. The scene descended into violence: Six teenagers were shot, and hundreds arrested.

And last Sunday—February 18, "Democracy Day"—the crisis reached a head. The holiday was created to honor Tribhuvan, the present king's grandfather: a worldly ruler who'd pledged reforms, but died before he could deliver. Far from celebrating his legacy, the day was a flash point for passionate demonstrations across the country.

Undaunted, the police had cleared the streets for the official parade. A cardboard cutout of the waving King Tribhuvan bounced along Durbar Marg in a horse-drawn cart, its right arm pulled up and down by a string. When the figure was pelted with stones, the troops charged the crowd. By nightfall, half a dozen demonstrators and a policeman lay dead.

I PARKED MY bike by a wall where, in the event of another riot, it might be protected from bricks and tear gas canisters. Shrugging my left shoulder forward swung the Nikon around my torso and into my hands. There was an interesting photo shaping up near the police truck. I could get the silhouetted soldiers, wearing olive green riot gear, in the foreground. The doctors, dressed in white lab coats and holding their protest signs aloft, formed a human chain beyond.

This would need a long lens: I wanted everything flat and sharp. Moving toward the anemic flower bed that would provide my angle for the photograph, I saw I wasn't alone. A determined, dark-haired woman wearing a khaki photographer's vest and three cameras slung around her neck beat me to the position. She pulled a shot, grimacing as she focused. I guessed she was with Reuters, or the AP; she had the earnest, entitled posture of someone who intrudes on other people for a living.

It would look like I was stealing her shot, but there wasn't a lot of choice. She bristled when she saw me, but it was more a "don't-bother-me-I'm-busy" scowl than a territorial snarl. She was quite pretty, I thought. Or, if not pretty, attractive—if you went for women with lipstick stains on the backs of their Nikons. I liked her shoes: red Converse All Stars with yellow laces, a dash of color in her otherwise functional uniform.

I felt an urge to make conversation, but decided to let her be. We had pictures to take and, for my part, interviews as well. I snapped a 135-millimeter lens onto my camera's bayonet mount, narrowed the aperture, and advanced the film with my thumb. The lever moved without resistance, and when I looked at the frame counter I realized why: There was no film in the camera. My vivid memory of loading a camera the previous night was accurate—but I'd loaded my point-and-shoot, not my Nikon. The clam-shell Olympus was still sitting on my night table, atop a pirated edition of *The Bonfire of the Vanities*. I was screwed.

There was nothing to do but ask the woman. She performed a quick double-take as I approached.

"Hi, excuse me. Can I ask you a favor?"

"What might that be?" She gave me a slightly wolfish appraisal, then glanced at the settings on her camera.

I took her in. She was on the tall side, slender but sturdy, with vivid hazel eyes and thick chestnut hair looped through a dark green scrunchie. Up close, high cheekbones and a wide, animated mouth lent her face a larger-than-life, celebrity quality. I felt I'd seen her somewhere—on a news broadcast, or a late-night comedy special. Or maybe I'd just sat across from her at Mike's Breakfast. People start to look familiar fast in Kathmandu.

"I'm shooting *f*8 at 125," she offered, "if your meter's broken."

"No," I said. "You'll never believe this, but I forgot to load my camera. Or bring extra film. Incredibly stupid."

"It happens." She grinned. "Or so I've heard."

"Right. So . . . Have you got an extra roll I can borrow? Or buy?"

"Or beg?"

"I am begging."

"Black and white, or color?"

"Black and white would be perfect."

She fished through the pockets of her vest, probing half a dozen before she found a stash of Plus-X. "Here, take two."

"Thanks a million. Listen, let me pay you for these."

"Forget it. I appreciate the opportunity to even out my karmic debts."

"I'm going to run over there and load this," I said, raising my chin toward the shadow of a brick wall. "Will you be here awhile?"

"I live here. My name's Grace." She extended her hand, which was small and cool.

"Jeff."

"Yeah. I've seen you around. Didn't you write that book, with the great title? What was it?"

"*Mr. Raja's Neighborhood.*" Recognition is the ultimate aphrodisiac. I was suddenly eager to know this woman. "I'm surprised you've read it."

"I haven't," she shrugged. "I just like the title."

This seemed the appropriate moment to end our conversation. I made the ritual noises and moved away to load up.

THE MORNING PASSED without incident. The doctors walked in a wide circle, joined by scores of laypeople and patients, and chanted political slogans. The soldiers slouched in their flatbed truck, smoking cigarettes and annoying each other with their bayonets. I shot a full roll and decided to call it a day, as far as picture-taking was concerned. There wasn't a big story here—no violence—but there was someone I wanted to meet before I left.

He was leaning against a brick column near the hospital doorway, talking to a local reporter. Dr. Mishra was unusually tall for a Nepali, with graying hair and a calm, paternal air. He wore a quilted black *topi*—the traditional soft, brimless Nepali hat—and fiddled with the bell of his stethoscope. A cardboard sign tacked to a stake leaned on the wall behind him, upside down, like a discarded shadow puppet. The reporter paused in his questioning as I approached, acknowledging with a nod the priority given to foreign press. Such behavior had initially embarrassed me, but I had learned to accept it gracefully.

"*Namasté.*" I pressed my palms together in the traditional greeting and introduced myself. "It's a pleasure to meet you, doctor. I'm impressed that you arranged this strike."

"Thank you, yes. I'm sorry we meet under these circumstances, but welcome." We shook hands. "And this gentleman, as you may know, is Mr. Kunda Mainali, editor of the *Shaligram.*"

"City desk only," Mainali amended, laughing. I liked him on sight. "A pleasure to meet you. Are you from the States?"

"Yes, how did you know?"

"I spent two years studying journalism in New York."

"Columbia?"

"Hunter." The reporter seemed apologetic, as if he had failed in his studies and landed Nepal as a hardship assignment.

About fifty yards away, Grace was photographing the soldiers. They struck macho poses, their rifles angled suggestively. Mainali glanced in her direction. "You are a friend of Grace?"

"We just met. How do you know her?"

"She and my wife are good friends. She's quite a character."

"Oh?" I didn't know whether he meant Grace or his wife, but felt myself in danger of being sidetracked. "Well, I hope to see her again . . ." Grace looked back toward us and gave a little wave, its intended recipient unclear. Both Mainali and I lifted our hands tentatively.

"Dr. Mishra," I asked, pulling out my notepad, "can you summarize the reasons for this unprecedented strike?"

"Well, you know, it has everything to do with Bhaktapur. Have you been there?"

"Yes. Many times." Bhaktapur, one of three "sister cities" in the valley, was a rustic woodworking village just east of the capital. It was less developed than Kathmandu, but far more political.

"Two days ago, when Bhaktapur had their wildcat strike, the police tried to force the merchants to open their shops. When the merchants refused, and students began throwing the stones, the police fired on the crowd.

"So that is the background. Yesterday, as you know, the people demanded that the police return the bodies of the demonstrators who were shot."

"I heard. Was that so they could be cremated within the appropriate time?"

The doctor shook his head. "Not only that. Aside from the religious concern, there was a humanitarian question to be addressed. I treated some of the victims, and I believe that the troops used dum-dums: lead bullets that flatten on impact, causing terrible wounds. Only a further examination of the corpses could prove or disprove such a charge. But the palace refused. And so we called this strike."

"Were there any risks associated with today's action?"

"There are always risks." Mishra narrowed his eyes at the soldiers. They were tossing an orange among them, completely uninterested in the demonstration. "But for doctors, the risks are not so great. If they throw us in prison, then what? Already, there are not enough doctors." He nodded toward the soldiers. "They will not willingly arrest us, not without orders. Because at some time, I think, they might get sick also! The greater risk, I think, is for this gentleman here, isn't it?" He placed his palm on Kunda Mainali's shoulder. "What do you say?"

"That is probably so." Mainali, also a tall man, appeared to be in his mid-thirties. Like Mishra and most of the other demonstrators, he wore a black armband. The journalist had clear, gray eyes and a cold sore on his upper lip. When he smiled it caused him visible pain. "If I were to publish the story of this demonstration, they would throw me in prison. In that way, you see, the lack of press freedom is good value for the palace; it's similar to banning the demonstration itself." Mainali grinned, and grimaced. "Protest all you like, no one will know about it!"

"That's not strictly true," I said. "The *International Herald Tribune* is in Nepal; so are *Time*, and *Newsweek*, and *Asia Week*. *I'm* here. Then there's the BBC, Voice of America, Reuters . . ."

"Yes, yes, yes," Mainali nodded. "The educated minority will hear about the strike." Mishra grunted in agreement, sensing what was to come. "But most of the people in this country don't speak English. The *Shaligram* is published in Nepali, yes. But this is a story we dare not print. And even if we do print it, many people don't even read Nepali! They speak Sherpa, Tamang, Limbu, Rai, Tharu, every dialect you can name. It's easy to forget, but the people affected by these actions live not only in Kathmandu, but all over Nepal. As you can imagine, gaining any kind of *consensus* in this country will be extremely difficult."

It was 10 a.m. Wednesday in Kathmandu, which made it 8:15 p.m. Tuesday in San Francisco. The foreign desk would be open until 1 a.m., which gave me four hours to file. I asked a few more questions of Dr. Mishra and walked toward the army truck. The day was warming up. Grace had taken her vest off, and was surrounded by a band of soldiers. They had worked out a pretty good system One or two would talk to her, diverting her attention, while the others locked down her blouse.

When she saw me coming she pulled a folded slip of paper out of her pocket. "Here's my number," she said, stuffing it into my shirt pocket. "Thought I'd save you the trouble of asking."

"That's very considerate. Are you free for dinner, or has one of these guys already invited you over to the mess hall?"

"Very funny. Actually, they're great. This sergeant's sister-in-law was in my class at the English Language Institute, two years ago. Small world, I guess."

"That's nothing. Dr. Mishra's uncle's best friend once sold a Tibetan carpet to a woman who babysat for my second cousin's Spanish teacher."

"Smartass," Grace said. "Call me after four."

4

Lotus Land

AT THE CORE of my being was a delusional notion, firmly rooted, that half the people in San Francisco spent the better part of each day waiting, in unbearable suspense, for the next news flash about the political situation in Kathmandu. But who in the Bay Area gave a damn about Nepal, except the Nepali community itself (150 people, maybe), the employees of the half-dozen local trekking companies (a similar number), and the people who'd actually *been* here?

But it had a grip on me. Since 1979, with each subsequent visit to Nepal I found myself more thoroughly ensnared by its culture and religious traditions. The palettes of Hindu and Buddhist philosophy had mingled here for fifteen centuries, interwoven but distinct, like colors on marbled paper.

Geographically, the story of the Kathmandu Valley began shortly after the dawn of human history. In those days, the area was a vast inland lake—"seven calling distances across," the ancient texts say—inhabited by a race of sophisticated snake gods, called *nagas*. One day a saint named Bipaswi, one of the first in a long line of human buddhas, climbed to the summit of Nagarjun, a fin-shaped hill on the valley's northwest rim. Bipaswi plucked a seed from within his robe and tossed it into Nag Hrad: "the tank of the serpents." Soon a miraculous lotus, with emerald petals and diamond pistils, blossomed on the lake's surface. The flower emanated a fierce radiance that hummed like a hive and illuminated the mountain flanks a hundred miles north. As the luminance had no earthly source, it was called *swayambhu*: the self-existent.

Centuries passed, and pilgrims from all over Asia traveled to the lake to pay homage to this amazing lotus and meditate within its novalike nimbus. One of these was a saint named Manjushri: the bodhisattva of pure wisdom. After surveying the scene, Manjushri decided to finish Bipaswi's work. He trekked around the ridges bordering the lake, raised his scimitar, and with a mighty blow cut a gorge in the southern hills. As the waters drained away, the circular valley gleamed like an emerald carpet: a mandala of otherworldly beauty, suspended between the plains of India and the peaks of Tibet.

And so it remained, more or less, until the first Toyota taxis arrived. These were joined by diesel buses, and two-stroke Tempos spewing toxic fumes. Cement factories rose among the valley's southern rice paddies, upwind of the city, churning out enough particulate matter to cover the trees with a fine patina of lethal white dust. Caustic chemicals from Tibetan carpet factories flowed into the Bagmati and Vishnumati, until the rivers became so polluted that children playing on their banks suffered chemical burns. Cheap concrete apartment buildings replaced carved wooden homes, and the gaps between these earthquake deathtraps were filled with billboards hawking whiskey and cigarettes. Meanwhile, the population exploded. In the decade since my first visit, Kathmandu had tripled in size.

Yet the magic of the place survived. It was choked and abused, but not even the ragged breath of industry could wilt it completely. There were always hidden realms, new discoveries to be made. The nearby foothills were still lush with pines and rhododendrons, while the sacred temple retreats of Boudha and Pashupati remained oases of calm.

And so I continued to visit Nepal, year after year. Arriving with my cameras and trusty Smith Corona, I installed myself in a spare, sunny sublet in the Naxal district. The venerable old neighborhood was five minutes from the shops on Durbar Marg, and a two-minute walk from Nag Pokhari: one of the mysterious "Snake Lakes" scattered through the Kathmandu Valley.

PARAKEETS SWARMED OVER the front lawn of my small compound. Laxmi, dressed in a purple sari with little gold dingbats, was hanging the laundry.

My didi had washed the sneakers I'd left, accidentally, next to the laundry basket. They lay on the grass, tongues protruding, preternaturally white.

I loved the word *didi*; the literal meaning was "sister," but it was also applied, universally, to women who served as housekeepers and cooks. During my early visits, I had viewed the arrangement cynically. I soon understood that these domestics earned about as much as high school teachers— and that working in a Western-style home, for people who made reasonable demands and had no caste-consciousness, was a cherished job. It worked for me, too. In Kathmandu, where washing machines were unheard of and finding an edible chicken might consume an entire afternoon, the relationship was an enormous asset.

"Laxmi, no lunch for me today . . ."

The Shresthas' eager Doberman began to bark from the roof, followed by an angry shout from inside the upper flat. Captain Shrestha himself, I guessed. The dog probably wouldn't listen to anybody else.

"Yes . . . all right . . . dinner?" She had the quietest voice, no more than a whispered squeak.

"Dinner," I repeated. "Yes. Can you make your lasagna? It's delicious."

This was a kindness. Compared to my previous housekeeper, who had mastered dozens of Western dishes, Laxmi was a disaster. Her quiche was soupy, her eggs oily, her brownies gritty with granulated sugar. A drumstick of her fried chicken, dropped from a height, would bounce like a rubber ball. The first time she cooked lasagna, working by sight from an English-language cookbook, she neglected to add cheese, vegetables, or tomato sauce. I was served a brick of baked pasta, doused with a film of catsup. At that point I'd paid Laxmi two weeks' advance wages and sent her off to apprentice with my friend Radha: a competent cook who'd agreed to teach my didi the basics. During that week Laxmi absorbed the concept of lasagna and came to grips with a dozen other simple, essential dishes. Though her chicken remained elastic, I began to suspect that this was less a function of Laxmi's cooking than a genetic adaptation of the local fowl, which had developed the ability to be struck repeatedly by taxis and bicycles without suffering visible harm.

My housekeeper smiled shyly in response to my praise, revealing a
heartbreaking overbite.

I tapped my shirt pocket, making sure I'd remembered the floppy disk:
eight hundred words on the doctors' strike. The time difference between
Kathmandu and San Francisco would serve me well. If I filed my story by
noon, it would arrive in time for the Wednesday edition.

My fixation on Nepal's fate struck me as a brittle obsession. As far as
I was concerned, this oppressed little monarchy was my personal Soweto,
my own private Bucharest. But what if nothing happened? Critical mass
is impossible to predict when you're dealing with unknown combustibles.
What if the royal family, with the army's help, crushed the democracy movement? Who would really care? Development dollars might slow down, but
not for long. Funds would continue to flow in, funneled into the pockets of
panchayat ministers. Heroin would continue to flood Kathmandu, enriching an unnameable few. The best and the brightest would wrangle visas
and leave for Europe, Australia, America. While other South Asian nations
advanced into the twenty-first century, Nepal would remain a medieval fief-
dom, steered by an antique monarchy.

How much more abuse was required before the Nepalis shook off the
yoke of subservience?

For the moment, that question was irrelevant. My only concern was
filing my story. That meant going downtown to the single computer store,
printing a hard copy from my diskette, and riding to the Blue Star Hotel to
fax it off. But that final step was risky. Many of the major hotels were refusing to send out antigovernment dispatches. My best bet would be to drop
by Coal and Clarice's place. My friends had a printer as well as a fax, and
could be relied upon for a celebratory drink.

That was it, then. I'd have a small morning: hang out with Coal, fax
my story, and drop by American Express to pick up my mail. From there, I
could walk to the Nanglo Café.

The fog had burned off, but the air was so dusty that riding my bicycle
would invite respiratory failure. As our front gate slammed, the Shresthas'
Doberman went off like an air raid siren, crouched at the roof's edge. I
barked back—a move calculated to drive the dog insane—and was joined

by a pack of kids playing on the roof of the car park. Amid this chaos I departed, trotting a hundred yards to the neighborhood taxi stand.

There were no cabs. I sat on a low brick wall beneath a sacred ficus tree, watching a nearby tailor at work on a treadle sewing machine. A few yards away, protected by a low, green fence, was my favorite shrine: the brick-lined pool of Nag Pokhari.

The story of these dark, mysterious pools fascinated me. For centuries, the people of Nepal had worshipped nagas: snakelike demigods whose kingdom fills a warren of subterranean caverns and canals. Eons ago, when Manjushri drained the valley, the naga kings moved their palaces into these aquifers. From their hidden kingdom they continue to protect Nepal's rivers and households, regulate the monsoon rains, and guard the Earth's store of gems, minerals, and underground treasures. Their presence is ubiquitous, and pains are taken to appease them. Though benevolent by nature, these creatures can also be wrathful, sinking their fangs into those who trespass upon their territory.

There was a splash from the lake, and I craned my neck. But whether the noise had come from something jumping out or falling in, I could not tell.

5

Mail Call

"NEAT, OLD FELLOW, or on the rocks?"

"Rocks, please. You boil and filter your ice cube water, right?"

"Can't be bothered." Coal held a tumbler at eye level and poured out three fingers of Bushmills for himself. "With the water shortage and all, we generally use old bathwater. But neither of us have been taking baths recently, as I'm sure you can tell. So Clarice just pees into the tray. A few drops of bleach get the color out. It's quite amazing. You'd never know." He cracked the freezer door, extracted an ice tray, and smacked it on the countertop.

Nepal's political troubles called for whiskey, a neocolonial tradition that we never challenged. When the natives get restless, expatriates drink, and in this timeless spell of prerevolutionary calm we did so with conviction.

Coal and Clarice weren't my only friends in the kingdom, but they were the friends I saw the most. Originally from England, they'd begun their peregrinations in Nairobi—a dry and difficult city where they had founded a secretarial school. The foreign community in Nairobi was relatively small, and before long it became claustrophobic. Coal's accountant took a vacation in Nepal; he and his wife returned with Marco Polo–like tales of exotic temples, stupendous vistas, and plentiful hashish. Coal and Clarice visited the following autumn, planning to spend a few days in Kathmandu and take a short trek in the Annapurnas. Two months later they returned to Africa, closed the school, and changed continents.

Coal's dream, when we'd met four years ago, was to be a novelist. He'd been plodding through the first draft of a spy thriller. Attempts to support himself by freelancing for magazines quickly created a cash flow problem. After succeeding so well in Africa, the situation was humiliating. He abandoned the novel, deciding that he was a better businessman than a writer. He began designing clothes—skirts, dresses, and coats—and proclaiming his plan to launch an export business. People rolled their eyes, but Coal was a man of considerable talents. His designs were innovative and flattering, his models were sexy, and every rupee he made was rolled back into hiring the best tailors in town. Friends back in England agreed to represent his line. He stuck with it. Within two years the business was a success, with thousands of garments flying off to London, Barcelona, Sydney, Berlin, and Dublin. Coal became rich. It suited him.

Clarice lacked Coal's ambition, but found her own niche within the expat community. She opened a yoga studio, luring travelers with flyers posted outside the Lonely Planet–endorsed hotels. It was a modest business. The classes, though cheap by Western standards, seemed expensive in Nepal. Some mornings, only two people showed up. Clarice didn't care; she was doing what she loved. She was in her early forties, lithe and beautiful, one of the most poised women I'd ever met. The fact was, I had a mad crush on her. Two or three times I'd dropped by the Tangal cottage, and found her alone. The encounters had turned me into a babbling adolescent.

But today Clarice was at a baby shower. I sat down at the kitchen table while Coal emptied a bag of potato chips into a wooden bowl. Saraswati, their didi of four years, had prepared a curry. It simmered on the propane stove.

I looked around for Coal's shortwave radio. "Can we listen to the BBC?"

"Afraid not. It's in the shop. Yogini knocked it off the table. I tell you, it's like being on a desert island without it. Ouch! *Fuck.*" Coal took off his glasses and disentangled a strand of hair from the nose guard. He had a melodious British accent and reassuring good looks, with thinning hair and an expression of faint amusement, as if his brain were supplying a constant stream of witticisms, only a fraction of which might find their way into speech.

"Amazing how one needs, one absolutely *requires*, that daily dose of panic and propaganda. It's an addiction; it truly is." He perked up. "Speaking of news, I hear you met Grace."

"You know her?" I felt blindsided.

"Naturally. She's shed her clothes for me on many occasions."

"Are you serious?"

"Completely. We've worked together on two of my catalogs. She's also modeled my hats. Nice head, don't you think? Or have you not found out yet?"

"Did you sleep with her?"

"Not a wink."

He beheld my distressed expression. "She's not my type. I prefer the *apsara* look. You know: tall and leggy, narrow hips, breasts like ripe papayas."

"Like Clarice."

"Indeed."

"Do you still see her?"

"Every night; she's my wife."

I ground my teeth. "Grace."

"Of course. We're good friends. Actually, it's astonishing you've not met her earlier. Even more astonishing that we never introduced you. In any case, you can relax. We've never had sex. And I gave you a glowing endorsement."

"When did you talk to her?"

"About two hours ago. She came by for tea, right after the strike." His lips parted in mock amazement. "Why, she sat in the very chair you're sitting in now. Uncanny, isn't it?"

A series of beeps issued from the bedroom. "Finished," said Coal. I got up to retrieve my fax. When I returned, he was leaning back in his chair with a distant expression. "I saw the most amazing thing at Boudhnath this morning," he said. "It changed my life. I kid you not."

"Tell me."

"Do you know that gate—not the big gate that feeds onto the main kora, but the small, metal one that takes you up onto the shrine itself?"

I nodded. "It leads into a little courtyard, with the statues. Near that room with the giant prayer wheel."

"Right. Well, I was strolling around the kora, minding my business, when a middle-aged Tibetan woman came out of the gate. She was dressed in her finery: gold and coral necklace, turquoise earrings, a lovely *chuba*, the works. She was with a friend. They were laughing loudly and walking very fast, when a guy on a bicycle came out of nowhere and ran right into her. *Wham!* Just like that. Bowled her over like tenpins. She went rolling into the gutter, and came to rest in a heap of cow shit and banana rinds."

"Jesus. Was she okay?"

Coal stood up and opened the door leading into the yard. Yogini, a black Lhasa apso, trotted in. "That's the amazing thing," he said. "She simply picked up and carried on, as if it had never even happened. She'd been laughing when he hit her, and she was laughing when she stood up. And listen to this: *She never even looked at the guy who hit her.* Not once. Can you believe it? Can you imagine if the same thing had happened to me? I'd be livid, dragging the bloody idiot off his bike." He lifted the Bushmills. "More whiskey?" He divided the last few inches of liquor between us.

"So I watched this whole scene. And when it was over I think I understood, for the very first time, what it means to be enlightened. Not as a rinpoche, not as the Buddha, but as an actual person who has to wash clothes and shop for onions and find a taxi when it's pissing down rain." He looked at me expectantly, seeking permission to finish his epiphany.

"And?"

"All right, here it is: Enlightenment is *stability*. That's it. It means living so totally in the *now*, in the moment, that whatever misfortune befell you five days ago, or five seconds ago, is irrelevant. You just don't hold on to it. I tell you, this woman . . . the moment the accident ended, it passed right out of her mind. She let it go and carried on. That, in my considered view, is enlightenment. Don't you agree?"

I shrugged. "She's probably just used to it. Out in the hills you get knocked down all the time. Yaks, mules, rock slides . . ."

"*No.* I'm telling you, she went rolling through *shit*. Totally ruined her clothes. No reaction at all."

"The curry's probably ready." I didn't want to argue with Coal about enlightenment; that would entail pretending I knew what the word meant. The exercise didn't appeal to me. The truth was, I was getting sauced.

"Mark my words. You will exhaust many masters, my friend, but you will never find a more useful definition of the 'awakened state.'" Coal rose beatifically to his feet, stability in action, and stepped on Yogini, who howled. I coughed Bushmills down the front of my shirt.

"Let it go, Yogini." Coal tossed me a sponge and found two bowls. "Just let it pass." He was stirring the curry, wearing a quilted mitt in the shape of a salmon, when the dogs began yelping. The front door opened and Clarice appeared, bending to tousle the hounds. Her face lit up when she saw us.

"Hello there." She sniffed the air. "Smells fantastic. Oh, thank God for Saraswati. I have to say, the food at the baby shower was abominable. Inedible. Lots of little fried-up things with mystery meat inside. And deviled eggs. Ugh." She came into the kitchen and pecked Coal on the cheek. "Is there enough?"

"I'm eating downtown," I said. "Just give me a taste."

Clarice walked over and kissed me as well. Coal's wife wasn't glamorously beautiful—she could sometimes look clerkish—but her laugh came so easily, and she smiled with such warmth, that I found her irresistible. "How fares our foreign correspondent?"

"Very well. It looks like things may finally be reaching the flash point around here."

"Don't hold your breath." Clarice, who counted a handful of well-to-do Nepalis among her yoga regulars, was a cynic. "There will be a few big strikes, a few noisy demonstrations, and just when it seems something might happen, the palace will rattle its saber. And everyone will go running home with their tails between their legs. Isn't that right, Khumbu?" The white also flew to her ankles, quivering with fealty.

Coal served the curry, and we sat at the cane table that filled half of the tiny kitchen. "I think you're wrong," I said. "The equation has changed.

The king is making the people feel inferior—to the Filipinos, the Romanians, even the Indians. The Nepali people can put up with a lot of abuse, and a load of inconvenience, but they can't stand being humiliated. Something's gonna snap."

"I agree," Coal volunteered. "I'm sure that if you study it closely, the entire history of conflict, every revolution and crusade, was ultimately motivated by humiliation, or the fear of it. Humans are such a sensitive lot. Deny them fresh broccoli, take away their penicillin, but don't laugh at their haircuts."

"What a brilliant analysis." Clarice rolled her eyes. "In my opinion, it's all about testosterone . . ."

"Exactly the same thing."

". . . and when it comes to a dick-measuring contest, why, the king's got to have the biggest one of all, doesn't he?"

"That's what the press releases say."

"Ceaucescu," said Coal, "had a big dick, too. As did Marcos. And Mussolini. And Louis XVI, no doubt. One might suggest," he mused, "that the road to freedom is paved with big dicks."

"No wonder the footing is so difficult." Clarice stood up and collected the dishes. "I've got a class," she said. "Beginning and intermediate. Jeff, are you coming? It would do you a world of good, you know."

"Not today, sorry. I'm heading downtown."

"Will we see you at Pashupati, then? On Shivaratri?"

"I'll be there," I said. "But you know what a mob scene that is."

"I plan to spend the day at home," announced Coal, "practicing yoga and counting my money." He sighed with satisfaction. "The perfect blend of East and West."

6

Make Me Laugh

AMERICAN EXPRESS WASN'T the most convenient mail stop in town—they kept sporadic hours—but using their service allowed me to avoid the slow-motion feeding frenzy at the downtown Poste Restante, where one could grow old and die waiting for the hash-addled backpacker at the front of the line to flip, envelope by envelope, through the endless expanse of G's.

The clerk at AmEx clients' mail, a sharp-looking engineering student with a pressed blue shirt, recognized me. "At least two items," he said, pleased to convey good news. "Actually three. One arrived just today."

He handed me the letters. There was a packet of recent clippings from my old college roommate, now a sportswriter for a Fairbanks newspaper. There was a postcard from Rachel, a filmmaker friend who hoped to visit California in the spring. And there was a letter from my younger brother, Jordan.

It was his first communication to me in more than six months, and its appearance produced a slack sensation in my stomach. My brow furrowed as I pondered my brother's narrow handwriting on the envelope. The letters slanted awkwardly to the right, as if rushing ahead of themselves.

During my early visits to Nepal I'd corresponded with Jordan frequently. Our letters were entertaining, but they weren't much of a dialogue. I wrote about life in Kathmandu, heavy on the festivals and filth; he wrote back describing his discoveries in ancient Greek grammar, interjecting the occasional snippet from Thomas Mann or Friedrich Hölderlin. Between his titanic vocabulary and shameless use of foreign phrases, it took a shelf of reference books to get through each paragraph.

But it had been communication, even if between different worlds. And beneath it all, we'd understood each other. We were like far-flung space-ships that, inhabiting different orbits, respond to the same signals.

Recently, though, our bond had decayed. It had been a gradual pro-cess. During the past seven years, Jordan had spiraled into a depression. A mysterious malaise had warped his personality, crippling his spirit and eroding our long camaraderie. Last summer, during his visit to California, a confrontation divided us. We hadn't spoken since.

I slipped the letters into my daypack and walked up Durbar Marg, past curio sellers and travel agencies, to the Nanglo Café. There were still some good seats on the rooftop patio.

As I scanned the menu, a Nepali family took a nearby table. The paunchy husband, about my age, was attired in a sports jacket and knock-off Ray-Ban Wayfarers. His frizzy-haired wife was wrapped in a yellow sari; their little girl sported pigtails and a neat pink blouse. The son, about ten, wore a Batman T-shirt.

The boy grinned at me, the sort of open smile that American children are warned never to bestow upon strangers, and as I smiled back it occurred to me that Westerners, as tourists and expats, were uniquely familiar strang-ers. For as long as this kid had been alive, he'd seen pale-skinned foreigners in all the popular restaurants. He'd watched us hailing cabs, riding rented bikes down the narrow streets, focusing elaborate cameras on the temples and rickshaws and cows. He'd seen us everywhere; we were part of the landscape.

The parents ordered *dal bhat*: the traditional dish of stewed lentils, rice, and vegetables. It was what the family ate, more than likely, almost every day of the year. The boy tacked on an order of fries.

There was no visible tension among them. They seemed at ease with each other. The marriage, likely arranged by hopeful parents, had succeeded. The couple laughed together; the girl hand-fed her mother french fries. The boy was clownish and assertive, but kept an arm around his sister's waist. It was probable they lived in one or two rooms, in a multifamily building with a shared bath and toilet. Somehow, it had not driven them berserk.

But I'd visited Nepal too many times to see their apparent contentment as part of the Shangri-la myth. This kingdom, even if one ignored the political crisis, was no paradise. There were bad families here, too, saddled by alcoholism, abuse, and poverty. But if healthy families were not the rule, neither were they the exception. The very concept of *family*, in Hindu culture, carries more weight than it does in the West. Blood is thick in Asia. Children stay close to home. Roles are often oppressive, but they're well defined.

I picked up the dull knife at my place setting and sliced open Jordan's envelope.

Dear Jeff,

Forgive the long silence. I can no longer pretend to blame you for reclaiming your space spring last, even if it came at the cost of some hardship to me. Cohabitation with the likes of myself, mired in such a sorely oppressed state, must have confounded even the most well-meaning host. Please accept my apology.

After my return to New York, it needed but a day for me to comprehend the difference between San Francisco and our northeastern cities. This difference, I submit, consists not so much in "accidents" such as the humidity of Philadelphia in August, or the filth, noise and congestion of Manhattan, or the hostility and degradation of our urban blacks. It consists rather in this: that in the northeast there is a terrible sadness in the air. I think it is the sadness of a dying world.

I perceive this sadness, or at least an emptiness that makes one sad the moment one reflects, in the haggard faces, the slack step, the pointless frenzy of the streets; I perceive it in the billboards, in the movie marquees, in the headlines of the tabloids; I perceive it in the eyes of the stationer with the rounded shoulders, who cheated me out of a quarter; in the cashier at the grocery store who did not respond when I wished her well; and in the short laughter of the desiccated middle-aged women who, bent over pulp romances, share my bus-stop bench.

Supremely important to me these days is the lustrous surface of the Pacific and the motion of its waters, the light of foggy mornings, the parkland meadows that on weekday afternoons, unpopulated, resemble English gardens, and on weekends could be so many scenes from Watteau.

Be that as it may, earlier this week I spent a wretched hour on my bed in that disturbing state of half-sleep when familiar thoughts visit one with new, sometimes terrifying force. In particular I reflected that, at 32, I have accomplished precisely nothing, and— this was the crux of the horror—by electing to return hither, have in effect declined an opportunity to make my own way in the world, favoring instead a prolonged adolescence. Indeed, as I later walked across campus I seemed to myself as hideous as the superannuated reveler whom Aschenbach spies on a quay in Death in Venice.

Why, in the end, did I return to university? Perhaps because I surmised that only under the stress of academic obligations am I likely to produce any of the theoretical or belletristic works that I have long nursed.

And yet, as I sit in this rather comfortable room of mine, the air cool this evening, before me the prospect of a tolerable living in return for mere study—as I sit here, I say, I feel quite certain that I erred. On the one hand, I suspect that, had I stayed in San Francisco, I could have made my fortune. Too (and this I saw too late, while gazing over the city, over Golden Gate Park and the land on either side as far as the ocean, from a third-story apartment halfway up Ashbury Street), San Francisco offers a thousand possibilities in point of love. The life of a graduate student promises little in that regard.

It occurs to me that my happiness here turns upon whether I can enroll in the Classics program. Interest in theoretical problems of linguistics beyond my own theory, that is, of the genesis and operation of language, I have none. Indeed, I undertook graduate

*study initially because I wished to internalize the particular
timbre and rhythm, as well as the rhetorical devices and general
sensibility, of the Greek and Latin tongues. I derive immeasurably
more pleasure from reading the ancients than ever I shall from
linguistics.*

*Wishing you every success on your Eastern odyssey I close
thus, with the promise of further reflections as they offer.*
Yours faithfully,
Jordan

I folded the letter away.

THERE IS A scene in Thomas Harris's *The Silence of the Lambs* where Clarice
Starling asks Hannibal Lecter if he ever wonders what "happened" to him.
"Nothing happened to me," Lecter replies. "*I happened.*" The line reflects a
scary truth. America, with its power, narcissism, and chaotic freedoms, is a
petri dish. Social tumors grow uncontrolled. Things "happen" in the United
States that do not happen elsewhere. Charles Manson happens. Disneyland
happens. Moonwalks happen. Thomas Jefferson, Lizzie Borden, Dr. Seuss,
and the Grateful Dead happen. Inspiration, depression, and mania, nurtured
by mixed genes and infinite choices, weaned on junk food and the Interstate
Highway System, drive people into lives unimaginable in Himalayan valleys
ringed by golden-tiered temples and ash-painted holy men.

Could Jordan, I wondered, have happened in Nepal? Or did it require a
place like America, with its double-edged affluence and fragmented families,
to create a person as brilliant and tortured as my little brother?

WE WERE CHILDREN of the '50s: that strange, suspended period between
Korea and Vietnam, bee-bop and the Beatles, highballs and Thai stick. Me
first, in 1954; Jordan, three years and three months later (our sister, Debra,
would follow in 1963). My earliest memories are of a warm, small apartment on Ryer Avenue, in the Bronx, a year before my brother was born. We
lived near my mom's parents: Bella, originally from Baltimore, and Sam, a
Russian immigrant and kosher butcher. We were never short of meat.

Our dad had grown up in Hell's Kitchen and told stories about how the kids in his neighborhood doused cats with gasoline, set them on fire, and swung them around their heads like shrieking censers. Wise guys were stuffed headfirst down the curbside sewers. This practice became a childhood myth, invoked by our father when a bully chased one of us home from school: *Where I grew up, we stuffed kids like that down the sewer.* I wondered, then and now, if this was really true, or if it was my father himself—born by accident in 1930, the runt of the litter—who fell victim to these thugs.

We left New York and moved north to Arlington, a quiet Boston suburb. Dad went to night school on the GI Bill, paying the rent with a series of odd jobs. He smoked heavily; his other addiction was music. In 1963 we left Arlington and bought one of the tract homes springing up among the potato fields of Plainview, Long Island. One evening Dad brought home our first record player: a box-shaped object with a white plastic handle and single three-inch speaker. He'd also bought three LPs: Edvard Grieg's *Peer Gynt*; *The Divine Miss V.*, by Sarah Vaughan; and *Sheer Ecstasy*, by the Cesana Strings. *Sheer Ecstasy*'s cover featured the naked Diane Webber, lounging on a cane recliner: an image that would inspire countless pubescent fantasies.

For a while he worked as a salesman at Pergament, a household and hardware store. When Jord and I dropped in, he'd run the paint mixer for us. Dad was amazed that human civilization had created a machine for the express purpose of mixing paint, and he mused about the scores of designers and engineers involved in the project: the foundries and molding machines and assembly lines called into action for this monumental effort. We didn't share his awe, having grown up in an era when machines, like meat, simply appeared on the shelves.

My father had a red crew cut, marsupial eyes, and a huge nose that became, with his soulful profile and self-effacing jokes, an asset. He was charming, and enormously popular. Mom was equally attractive, a sparkling and articulate art teacher with an hourglass figure. They found plenty of time for their friends. At least two nights a week, the Plainview split-level was filled with loud laughter, jazz, and the comingled smells of scotch and cigarette smoke. Jordan and I lay in our beds in an upstairs room, listening to our father's jokes, our mother's laughter, the loud voices of their friends. I was ten; my brother, seven. Our baby sister slept in a separate room.

As soon as the guests left the kitchen and moved downstairs to the recreation room, Jordan and I would dare each other to perform "impossible" tasks.

"Good evening, Mr. Greenwald. Your mission, should you decide to accept it, is to sneak out of our bedroom and into the living room, returning with a handful of M&Ms, Raisinettes, or pretzels. If you are caught or killed, I will disavow any knowledge of your actions."

I could never resist these dares. I'd slither out of bed, open the door, and move catlike down the hall. A short flight of uncreaking steps led almost directly into the living room, with its silent carpet. Crystal bowls blossomed with candies; lacquer trays overflowed with chips and dip. Poised amid this cornucopia, a super-spy in pajamas, my life was thrilling.

JORDAN FELL ASLEEP long before I did. Reading in bed was not an option; the room had a single overhead lamp, two 75-watt bulbs beneath a glassine shade decorated with hand-painted rodeo cowboys. Burrowing under the covers with a flashlight made me claustrophobic. I tossed and turned, full of reckless energy.

I was able to distract my brother with inane word games. My favorite of these was "Make Me Laugh," a bedtime ritual with a game show format and its own theme song:

> *Make Me Laugh*
> *Make Me Laugh*
> *Make . . . Me . . . Laugh*

The challenge was simple: Jordan and I took turns telling jokes, or mouthing absurdities. The first one to make the other laugh was the winner.

"Who goes first?"

"I will." Jordan shifted in bed. "Okay. Ready? Knock knock."

"Who's there?"

"Penis."

I thrust my face into my pillow until I recovered. "Penis who?"

"If you don't know penis, I feel sorry for you."

This was ingenious, but I was out of the danger zone. "Okay," I countered, "why can't witches' husbands give them babies?"

"I give up."

"Because they have *holloweenies*."

"Knock knock."

"Who's there?"

"Ash."

"Ash who?"

"*Gesundheit.*"

I leaned on my elbow. "Did you just make that up?"

"Yes."

"Okay. Here's a good one." I smacked my lips, preparing for the delivery. "Two deaf men meet on the street. The first one says, 'Are you going fishing?' The second one says, 'No . . . I'm going fishing!' To which the first one replies: 'That's too bad—*I thought you were going fishing!*'"

I waited, but there was no hint of laughter.

"You forgot to say their names," Jordan declared.

"What?"

"The deaf men. Don't you know their names?"

"What difference does it make?"

"It's a part of the joke."

"It is not."

"It is."

"Not."

"You think that because you don't know."

"You're crazy," I said.

Jordan sighed. "I'm going to sleep." Silence.

"Okay," I conceded. "What are their names?"

"Who?"

"The deaf men!"

"What difference does it make?"

"You said it was part of the joke!"

"I lied." He yawned. "No. Actually, one of them had the same first name and last name."

"What are you talking about?"

"The first deaf guy. He was Chinese. He had the same first name and last name."

"What name?"

"Hee."

"Hee Hee?"

"You laughed. Good night."

ONE SUMMER MORNING I woke up and saw that my brother was gone. He wasn't in the bathroom, the living room, or the kitchen. His sheets were askew; it was as if he had fled the bed and vanished. I found our mother, who searched the house frantically. The neighbors were alerted. Twenty minutes later, as Mom picked up the phone to call the police, I heard a muted cough from upstairs. We ran back into the bedroom. Another cough. My mother dropped to her knees. Jordan was beneath his bed, curled into a fetal position. He was sleeping peacefully and sucking his thumb. Mom put her forehead on the carpet and began weeping softly.

I wondered, even then, what her reaction would have been if it had been me who'd gone missing, whether she would have searched at all. Because Jordan and I were not loved equally. While I was loud and resilient, a hyperactive comic who rarely shut up, there was a quiet translucence about my brother. Like an ancient Egyptian vase, he seemed both fragile and immortal.

Our parents captured a few scenes from our childhood with an eight-millimeter movie camera. I'd watched these films as an adult. He is the beautiful one, with the curly hair of Dionysus, his dark eyes wide as an owl's. And there I am, a snaggletoothed clown, prancing and posturing. We were an odd pair—but during those early years, at least, I was the difficult one.

DAD BEGAN SENDING out résumés, and was hired by General Electric. He rose through the ranks of their data processing division. I have a snapshot of him in his office, lounging in an executive chair, laughing into a phone.

His legs are outstretched, crossed on his mahogany desk. He'd made it: left the sewers and the flaming cats behind.

His career provided us with a level of security that made the years of paint mixing and door-to-door sales seem like a brief aberration. We were riding the new wave of middle-class affluence. Jordan and I collected Spider-Man comics, played soccer, and eviscerated dead birds with the stainless steel dissecting kits we'd bought, eons ago, at Pergament.

Dad traveled a lot on business. Postcards arrived from any number of exotic destinations: Chicago, Houston, the Los Angeles International Airport. These jaunts didn't satisfy his well-concealed wanderlust. He was one of those guys who'd married too soon and rushed into parenthood, at the cost of an inner longing he'd been too young to define. He did define it, eventually. He wanted to see the world, sleep with Swedish girls, smoke weed with his hip, young nieces. Resentment simmered inside him, never reaching a boil. One afternoon when I was a teenager, we were driving through New Jersey—my dad and I—on a two-lane blacktop bordered by fields and farmhouses. A dirt road snaked off toward the south, leading God knew where. Dad craned his neck.

"I was in the Army, in Texas, when your mother was pregnant," he said. "I drove out to see her. It was about an hour, from the base into San Antonio. I was listening to the radio. Texas was all open country, just tumbleweeds and snakes. Along the way, I saw a little dirt road. No idea where it went. I stopped at the junction. And I said to myself: 'Bob, you can drive on into San Antonio—or you can take that turnoff, and live your life as you please.' To this day, I wonder what might have happened, where I'd be today, if I'd made that turn."

Take it, Dad, I wanted to say. *Take it with me. Let's have an adventure.* But that wasn't the kind of adventure he wanted.

In Massachusetts, Mom had made pocket money teaching art classes on the porch of our duplex: macaroni collages and block printing with sponges. When we bought the house in Plainview, she did a remarkable thing. Our plastic lunch plates were decorated with an Oriental design of a flowering plum tree. Mom transferred this motif to an entire wall of our kitchen.

She copied the drawing exactly: every color, every branch, the shape of each blossom. Completed, it dominated the room. It was a daring and self-confident act, executed with a level of skill that even a ten-year-old could recognize.

But for many of those years she was essentially a single mother—and despite her many talents, she couldn't cope with Dad's absences. I now understand that she suffered from monophobia: an acute fear of being alone. To a child, though, her panic attacks were inexplicable and terrifying. She shouted at us unpredictably, often in front of our friends. She sobbed, alone, in the bedroom. She was subject to fits of rage. On one occasion she threw a pair of scissors at the kitchen wall; they stuck, scarring her master-piece. When my father returned from his trips she'd yell at him, too, behind the closed doors of their bedroom. We listened, our hearts pounding, as she damned the trap her life had become.

But the tempest always passed. Life settled back to normal. Our parents resumed their whirlwind social schedule, entertaining during the week and going out every Friday and Saturday night, returning long after midnight. Alone in the house, Jordan and I staged "cowboy" fights, emulating bar-room brawls. We'd use folding bridge tables and picnic chairs as props, throwing ourselves over the furniture in stuntman fashion. We taught our-selves how to roll down short flights of steps, as if we'd been shot. We made planks out of balsa wood and broke them over each other's heads.

When I entered high school Dad partitioned the downstairs recreation room, walling off an eight- by ten-foot space adjoining a half bathroom. This tiny suite became my domain. I filled my shelves with science fiction and travelogues, Estes rockets, and an amateurish rock collection with spec-imens chosen more for their sex appeal than their rarity. The very fact that I thought rocks had sex appeal speaks volumes about the geek I'd become by fifteen.

The lower floor of our split-level was sunken, and my new bedroom's windows were level with the backyard lawn. During the summer, water from our oscillating sprinkler drummed against the glass. The warm evenings were spent in my room, burning incense and listening to Ravi Shankar, the Supremes, and the soundtracks from Z, 2001, and Lawrence of Arabia.

Our house had a crawl space: A dim and dusty storage area reached through a tiny door, hidden in a corner of the recreation room. The floor was packed dirt, with a three-foot-high clearance of wooden beams, protruding nails, and spiderwebs. No one ventured into that creepy cave, no one but me. I transformed a corner of the dreary recess into my secret den. Sheets of aluminum foil, suspended with thumbtacks, formed a partition. Though crude, the sanctuary was private: a place to meditate in silence, and smoke pot with friends as my mother's tirades thumped through the floorboards.

It all seems so emblematic of the age: the bong smoke, my space-age fascinations, my symbolic hideout from the draft board. I imagined myself a cipher, but this was a vain conceit. I was exquisitely typical.

Not Jordan. He behaved more like an alien exchange student: a member of a highly advanced species who, late for class, had been forced to accept Earth as the subject for his anthropological studies. Like me, Jordan was deeply inspired by *Star Trek*'s Mr. Spock: the unflappable Vulcan who reluctantly suffered the crew of the starship *Enterprise*. But while my parents could at least react to my rebellion, they were bewildered and intimidated by Jordan. His self-containment gave them no purchase. Retreating into a cerebral solitude, he shielded himself from an emotional connection with either of them.

"A boss drives his secretary to a woodsy place and begins to fondle her," my father declared in a rare show of dinnertime levity. "'What are you doing?' she asks, obviously upset. 'I thought you were taking me to Florida!' 'Not at all,' her boss says. 'I just said I was going to *Tampa* with you.'"

"His poor locution proved an asset," Jordan observed. "Please pass the *schmaltz*."

My brother was not above goading our parents for his own amusement. Swearing, for example, was forbidden in our household. Jordan would arrive at table, protrude his upper jaw, and cross his eyes, like Mickey Rooney in *Breakfast at Tiffany's*.

"*Who says I have fuck teeth?*" he'd ask, turning to me. "*What's wrong with fuck teeth?*"

Dad would set down his fork, red as a caged bull: "*What did you say?*" My brother would glance at me, his crossed eyes squinting with glee. "*The fuck stops here.*"

Jordan quietly despised our father: not just for being a weak and clumsy parent, but for suppressing his passions and venting his frustrations on the rest of us. The two rarely spoke. When they did, their exchanges were monosyllabic. There was no violence, no yelling, nothing to shatter the tension between them, just an icy détente.

I spent as much time as possible outdoors. Trees fascinated me. I carved a walking stick out of an elm branch and took the air like an English lord, trekking to the public library. There was no need of a cane on the groomed sidewalks of Plainview, but I liked the feel of wood in my hand and the tapping of the tip on the pavement. The walking stick had a hook on the end, a natural nub that fit perfectly over my thumb. If anyone attacked me, a mugger or a mad dog, I would grapple a tree branch and hoist myself out of danger.

Jordan and Debra were too young to flee the house. I didn't consider their fate during my sojourns around the neighborhood or my frequent flights to the library. As a teen, I sought only my own pleasure: sitting cross-legged on the floor between the high metal stacks, devouring novels by Ray Bradbury, Isaac Asimov, and Arthur C. Clarke.

My brother found diversions of his own, immersing himself in an alternate world that kept him away from home as much as possible. An adolescent Renaissance man, he showed high aptitude in all the classic disciplines: athletics, music and especially language. He became president of the Junior High German Club, qualified for track and soccer, and played trumpet in the band. He was brilliant, but the only light our parents saw was the thin crack of illumination that escaped from beneath his bedroom door.

My grades were awful. I had little talent for music and none for sports. I dreamed only of travel, preferably by spaceship, to some faraway corner of the galaxy—or to the equally alien mesas in my *Navajo Wildlands* book. Toward my brother I felt increasing ambivalence. On the one hand, he amazed me. I was envious and admiring of his intellect and independence. But there was an unmet hope that simmered into resentment. With no parental role models, nor any reliable compass to orient myself toward maturity, I needed Jordan. I needed him to be like the younger brothers I'd seen on TV: someone who would seek advice, and honor me with a mantle of responsibility. At the very least I needed him on my side, as an ally in our increasingly tense household.

But as my hair got longer and my reading list angled toward Jack Kerouac and Ken Kesey, Hunter Thompson and Hermann Hesse, Jordan began to shun me as well. He installed himself on a pedestal of classics and athletics; I climbed onto a magic mushroom. I wondered if I'd ever win his respect, or share again the pranks and banter that had kept us awake as kids.

"Excuse me, sir?" The Nanglo patio, with its underage waiters, reclaimed its place in my sensory sphere.

"*Hajur?*" I replied instinctively.

"You are having something?"

"Fresh lemon soda, please. And one chili chicken, boneless." I slipped Jordan's letter into my daypack. My Nepali neighbors were scooping up their dal bhat with appreciation, enjoying the luxury of a prepared meal, as their kids doused french fries in spicy green ketchup. I wondered where their lives would take them.

7

Otherwise Engaged

G RACE HAD SAID "after four." Not wanting to seem overeager, but unable to help myself, I called at 5:10. A chill was penetrating the air, as the sun descended toward a premature eclipse behind the spine of Nagarjun Hill. She was editing, immersed, and there wasn't as much wisecracking as we'd allowed at the strike. She asked distractedly if I'd written my story, and I wondered if she was having second thoughts about getting together. But when I asked her to suggest a dinner date, she replied eagerly: She was free tomorrow, Thursday, after six.

We met at Ras Rang, a dimly lit new Chinese restaurant near the Shankar Hotel. I pulled a couple of cushions next to the fire pit, and we spent the better part of three hours drinking Star beers out of thick brown bottles, eating *mu shu* chicken, and telling our stories. She was skittish, but adorable: bright, animated, and very quick. Testy, but I liked that too.

Grace Modena was twenty-eight; she'd grown up in Rolla, Missouri, where her dad taught physics and astronomy at the university. Her mother, the daughter of an Argentinean diplomat, had moved to Washington DC at the age of fourteen. Her parents met in high school. According to Grace, they still passed notes to each other at concerts and lectures.

"Sounds like a storybook," I said.

"Not really. Mom loved Buenos Aires. She was very popular, as a teenager. It killed her to leave. We went back every year when I was growing up, but it was never the same. I don't think she ever got over it."

Grace dipped a pot sticker in hot sauce. "Meaning, she had some issues with alcohol." There was one sibling: an older sister who'd relocated to California after high school, and taught English to migrant farmworkers in Watsonville.

Grace had been the kind of kid who'd spent hours in the attic, swimming through back issues of *National Geographic* so old they had ads for wringer washers. She'd always wanted to take pictures, but had followed her father into hands-on science. Her field was neurobiology, but after two years in grad school—"cutting up rat brains"—she had a meltdown during a routine lab session. It was traumatic enough to retool her life. Two months later she was in Paris, renting a cold-water flat and stringing for the AP.

"You dropped out?"

"Yep. Just like that."

"Wow. What did your dad say?"

"I'm sure he was disappointed."

"You didn't talk about it?"

"Not so much. Why?"

"I'm just curious," I said. "What happened in the lab? I mean, after two years I'd think you'd have seen everything. Did a rat rise from the dead?" I curled my fingers and leered, Nosferatu-style.

She looked downward. A shadow of pure vulnerability crossed her face. "There was an accident. I dropped something."

"A vial of Ebola?"

"No."

"A beaker of . . ."

"I'd rather not talk about it."

"Okay. Sorry." I felt a flash of insecurity and wondered if I'd already blown it. But she refilled our glasses.

"So, you moved to Paris . . ."

"I just shot lots of pictures. Then I got into photo-essays. When my stuff on the neofascists was picked up by *Figaro*, I put all the money into new gear. And a one-way ticket to Asia." She grinned in triumph, holding a single green pea in her chopsticks. "Then New Delhi, then here."

"How did you meet Coal and Clarice?"

"It was literally the day after I arrived. Do you remember the bar that used to be across from the American Embassy?"

"Flo's?"

"Coal was in there, talking to some Marine sergeant about how the CIA used to supply arms to the Khampas during the Cultural Revolution. Even earlier, maybe. Anyway, he seemed pretty interesting. Very down-to-earth. We hung out a few times, and he hired me to shoot some ads for his business, then I ended up modeling for him. They're fun, I love them. Clarice is a riot. Do you know she originally went to school to be a vet?"

"I had no idea."

Grace tucked her legs in, topped my glass, and leaned forward. "Okay, enough. Tell me about you."

What about me? I gave her the general rundown: a younger brother, an even younger sister. My own bizarre, vaguely interesting arc from sculpture to writing. And then, because he was on my mind, I launched into an anecdote about Jordan: his academic brilliance, his gift for languages, and his sharp eye for art and photography.

"After my first long trip to Europe and Asia, eleven years ago, I was showing my brother my slides. There were about 140 images, a full Kodak carousel, mainly of smiling Greek kids, fish hanging on clotheslines, monkeys on temples . . . you know."

"I have the same ones."

"When I finished, I asked Jord if he could guess my favorite picture. 'Not only can I guess it,' he said, 'I'd like a print for my wall.'"

Grace raised her eyebrows. "Was it the same one you liked?"

"Well, this is typical of my brother. He refused to tell me, or to let me tell him, which one I meant. He wrote a one-line description of it on a scrap of paper and sealed it in an envelope. 'We shall break the seal on delivery,' he announced." I paused to sip my tea.

"And?"

"I came back to New York again that December with an eleven-by-fourteen print in a mailing tube. Before he opened it, Jord fished the envelope out of his sock drawer. I opened it. The note said 'Amsterdam. Snow-covered bicycle, leaning against a pole.' Then he opened the tube and unrolled the print. It was the bicycle, of course."

"Sounds like he knows you pretty well."

"We're usually pretty close. But he's been through some tough times lately. Not much fun to be around. To tell you the truth, I've been out of touch with him for a while. "

"For how long?"

"Until today, actually. He wrote me a letter. Using words like *thus,* and *belletristic.*"

I was quiet for a minute.

"He sounds strange," Grace said. "But I think I'd like him."

The intimation that what we were starting here might extend into the future, as far as an encounter with my brother, made me momentarily dizzy. "So. I have a question for you," she said. "Are you seeing anyone back home?"

I wasn't prepared for this, although I'd suspected it might come up. There was someone. Her name was Carlita, and we'd been dating for several years. The relationship was already on shaky ground when I'd left the United States last fall. In spite of that, or because of it, our parting at the airport had been sentimental and painful. There were tears and promises. But five months of separation, punctuated by sporadic and increasingly confrontational letters, had reminded us of what we'd known when I bought my ticket: We were looking for different futures. It was hard, almost impossible, to imagine myself sinking back into that dynamic.

On the other hand, I didn't feel like starting off with a lie.

"When I left the States I was involved with a woman in San Francisco. Carlita. My extended absence is not going over well, but it's probably telling us both something we already knew."

"Do you hear from her much?"

"Not lately. She was furious when I wrote to say I might extend my stay here. Which of course I have."

She nodded. "Well. Thanks for being honest. I hope you figure out where that's going." I looked for a sign of retreat, but saw nothing of the sort. She tipped a Star toward my glass, but the bottle was empty. "So how long *will* you stay?"

I shrugged. "To be honest, I'm not sure."

"Fair enough, I guess none of us are. I'll put it this way: Why would you leave?"

It was an interesting question. The waiter materialized. "One second." I ordered two more beers and a plate of spring rolls. "I never thought of it in those terms. It's been more like, 'Why would I go home?' But I'd leave if I felt useless in Nepal. If it starts to look like the movement will never get anywhere. I mean, I love it here, but there are only so many stories I can write about what might eventually happen."

"That's true—if the only stories you can sell are about the revolution. But there's always so much going on . . . I don't know, right now I can't even imagine being anyplace else."

"You're right," I said. "But while all this *is* going on, it makes writing about other stuff—festivals, whatever—seem clueless."

"Like going to South Africa and writing restaurant reviews."

"Exactly. That's another wild place right now . . . and didn't they just release Mandela from prison?"

"On the eleventh. It's amazing." Grace linked her fingers and stretched her arms above her head. Her small breasts rose, taking my pulse with them. "It's almost enough to make you believe the world is changing."

"Do you think it is?"

"I do. I feel like I'm on the edge of a gigantic wave—with this crazy idea that I have some kind of control. I think that's what attracted me to photography. It's not about possessing things, or capturing them; it's about control. This illusion that if I focus on the changes, literally focus on them, I can keep my balance. And be a part of what's changing."

It took a minute for this to sink in. Once it had, I realized I felt exactly the same way. "Listen," I said. "I like you."

"That's good," she said. "Because I like you, too."

"Okay, then, it's your turn. Are you otherwise engaged?"

"I'm not. Right now. I was, back home. For a while. Not actually engaged, but living with someone. But it didn't work out. I might as well tell you." She drew a breath. "Guys get spooked around me. And not just guys. I have this weird thing . . . I'm sort of accident-prone."

"Really?" It seemed hard to imagine.

"Really. Actually I have a reputation as a walking disaster zone. I'm not kidding. It scares people."

"That's ridiculous. It can't be that bad."

"No? You think? Okay. This is just the past *year*."

Grace began what sounded, to my ears, like a practiced soliloquy. During ten months in Asia she'd been robbed four times: passport, travelers' checks, everything. She'd spent two weeks in a Thai hospital, being treated for a violent allergy to a mysterious substance that turned out to be tamarind. Her weekend bicycling partner had run into a sacred cow, and was shipped home with a broken pelvis. On a trek to the Annapurna Sanctuary, Grace had stopped to shake a stone out of her boot; fifty yards up the trail, the rest of her group was hit by a landslide (no fatalities, but a lot of sprains and bruises). On various other occasions she had stumbled into a wasps' nest, fallen through the boards of a Nepali outhouse, and watched an India-bound night coach careen off the road and into a rice paddy. On a recent river trip, the inflatable raft in front of hers had somehow burst into flames.

I listened with amazement, unsure whether to laugh out loud or console her. It wasn't at all clear what kind of response she was after.

"At least you've come through in one piece," I offered.

She snorted. "More or less."

"No? What happened?"

She started to say something, but stopped. Her eyes, green in the candlelight, studied her plate. I wondered again about the lab accident she'd mentioned. After an uncertain moment, she shook her head. "I'm fine," she concluded. "Anyway, it's pretty weird. It's hard, sometimes, not to take it personally. Like it's some weird karma thing."

"Your luck might change," I said. She looked at me thoughtfully, and I reached past the soy sauce for her hand. "I'm not scared of you."

"That's sweet." She let her hand be held. "I hope you're right."

I was being reckless. Her tales did concern me, but months of involuntary celibacy also had their say. We took a cab back to my flat and listened
to Babar Maal for a while. There was chemistry between us, but a wavering as well, as if the smallest first step would commit us to a high-wire
act. Finally, in the kitchen, I sort of cornered her near the refrigerator and
stroked her hair away from her cheeks. She leaned back against the pale
green metal. I slid my hands down to her shoulders and behind the base
of her neck, beneath her collar. My fingers crossed the gristle of a scar.
She flinched, but held my eyes. We kissed, lightly, and then deeply. Despite
the Chinese food, she tasted delicious, but as my hands moved toward her
breasts, she slid away.

"Slow down," she whispered.

She didn't seem angry; just protective. We kissed a few minutes more,
but the potential turning point of the evening had passed. When she collected her jacket, I wondered if we'd even see each other again.

"I'll walk you to a cab."

The street was dark and shuttered, but a taxi had pulled up into a pile
of gravel near the corner. I opened the door for her.

"Are you doing anything special this weekend?" I said obliquely.

"Shivaratri's on Saturday," she reminded me. "Are you busy
tomorrow?"

I hid my surprise. "What do you have in mind?"

"Let's walk through Asan. To Indrachowk. You can buy me a necklace."

8

Nag Pokhari

EBRUARY MORNINGS IN Kathmandu are bone-chilling but beautiful, draped in a milk-white fog. Women emerge from the mist, wrapped in woolen shawls, carrying brass pots and puja trays toward the neighborhood shrines. Cows bend over rubbish piles, nosing through damp paper and broken straw for wilting lettuce or rotten apples. Muted bicycle bells betray, with fading Doppler chimes, the vectors of hidden riders. From Nag Pokhari itself comes a steadier, more persistent ring: the monotonous clanging of the heavy brass bells flanking the stone Ganesh statue by the entrance.

It was Saturday, Laxmi's day off. She'd be off regardless; today was Shivaratri, one of Nepal's most important festivals. My didi would already be at the sprawling Pashupati complex on the banks of the Bagmati River, standing in line with thousands of other pilgrims for the opportunity to pay her respects to Shiva, the great creator/destroyer of the Hindu pantheon. I had never been inside the actual temple at Pashupati; entrance is forbidden to non-Hindus. But I'd glanced through the main gate, catching a glimpse of the gigantic golden Nandi that faces the central shrine. Nandi, Shiva's mount, is a powerful bull; from outside the entrance one can see his anatomically correct hindquarters, with huge golden testicles gleaming like Super Bowl trophies.

Grace had gone home late. But I'd awakened early, and walked through Naxal to Snake Lake. Rarely did I enter the shrine. I'd just stand near the low fence surrounding the complex, watching the neighborhood kids on their way to school. They trotted by in packs, chattering in singsong voices, toting textbooks tied with twine.

Today, of course, there was almost no one about. The few people I saw were walking briskly north, toward Pashupati, offerings in their hands. From Naxal, it was a thirty-minute walk to the temple grounds. Grace would meet me here, arriving from the opposite direction.

Nag Pokhari—the "lake" itself—is a rectangular water tank, fed by aquifers and surrounded by a brick wall. Rising from the center is a tall column, crowned with a sculpted cobra's head. At each corner of the pool, a fountainhead in the shape of a serpent faces the *pokhari*. The brass snakes are meant to spew fans of water in elegant jets, but fail to fulfill their purpose. This particular morning, three of the spouts weren't working at all. The fourth issued a lame trickle, which drooled over its gold-plated jaw and into the water.

Overlooking the site is a row of dilapidated apartments. I wondered how old they actually were. Perhaps they'd been built when the sacred site was discovered, to accommodate devotees. When a new shrine reveals itself in a Hindu kingdom, things happened fast. I'd actually seen such a phenomenon in action. In 1983, two snakes had popped their heads out of a muddy little pond on the outskirts of town. Within a week the place was surrounded by refreshment stands and ringed with a continual procession of naga worshippers. The devotees arrived in the morning, poured their offerings of milk into the water, and waited until dusk, hoping to catch a glimpse of the serpents that had been seen to rise, like a Hindu caduceus, from the murky waters. When, after a month, someone provided lighting—a single incandescent bulb, suspended over the water—the place became a day-and-night attraction.

This Nag Pokhari may have gotten its start the same way: as a local phenomenon, like an image of the Virgin emerging in the moss of a Mexican grotto.

An old man, or so he appeared, walked around the perimeter of the tank with a long-stemmed net, pulling leaves and insects from the water. This was Ramana, the shrine's attendant. He lifted his hand in greeting.

"How's the fishing?" The fog muted all sound.

"*Tik chha!*" Ramana called back. "Very good. Yesterday I found a thong." He flapped it in the air. "I'm looking for the twin."

"I have some old shoes, but I don't think they'll fit you."

"Bring them! I'll put newspaper inside."

Ramana returned to his scooping. I puffed on a bidi. "*Tapai Pashupati janee?*" I called out.

He straightened, and flexed his shoulders. "My wife is there, with my daughters. Me, I don't like it. Too many people. Are you going?"

"In a few minutes. I'm waiting for a friend." Meaning, of course, Grace.

"*Haus.*" The groundskeeper took my statement in stride. But already, the word *friend* tasted funny. I realized that, pretty soon, I might have to start calling her something else.

YESTERDAY—FRIDAY AFTERNOON—we'd taken a cab down Kantipath to the junction of Kamalachi: the long, diagonal road leading through Kathmandu's urban bazaar. The sun had slanted out of the narrow lane, and the air was cooling. A steady human tide, flowing up and down the street, took off the chill.

Grace held my arm as we strolled past the microdistricts that lined the street, moving toward Asan. It was a path that led us slowly back in time. Here, near the throat of the market, one could shop for shiny new Chinese bicycles, ready-made snow jackets, India-made transformers and fans. As we moved along, the imports gave way to local wares. Handwoven carpets and runners hung from the latticed windows of traditional Newari homes. Just below, popcorn and toy vendors pushed their carts past shops selling wooden lime squeezers and plastic pails.

We emerged into the frenetic confluence of Asan. The open *tole* was the hub of old Kathmandu. Six lanes, from all corners of the downtown district, converged here. The winter market was a mosaic of colors: red radishes, green onions in tight bundles, carrots so hilariously orange they might have been yanked from a Bugs Bunny cartoon. It appeared riotous, but everyone had their place: Saffron and chili sellers dovetailed against carts crammed with Indian shampoos and vermilion *bindhi* powder. Apple sellers shouted into the crowd, and bikes tilted between the hounds and cows that nosed through the castoffs. Asan was an ever-changing labyrinth, with a thousand possible centers.

"It's *medieval*," I said, not knowing where that idea had come from— and realizing, to my embarrassment, that the nearest thing I'd seen to this joyful chaos was the Renaissance Pleasure Faire in California.

Nepali women sat cross-legged around blankets and plastic tarpaulins, selling homegrown ginger and cilantro. Rickety wooden tables tilted under displays of river fish. The smells were gorgeous and rank, changing every time we turned our heads.

Grace was already at work, focusing her lens on the flickering butter lamps outside the ancient, gold-roofed temple honoring Annapurna, the goddess of abundance. Every person who entered Asan, whatever their origin, gravitated toward the temple, orbiting clockwise around the shrine before spinning off toward their next destination.

I left her alone to take pictures and wandered into the Annapurna Cassette Emporium, emerging ten minutes later with a new Sonny Rollins tape. Grace was squatting next to the low, ornate temple doorway, snapping pictures of devotees as they offered rupees and rice to the image of the goddess inside. She stood as I approached. Her knees popped.

"Let's go," she said. "I want to get to the Bead Market while there's still some good light."

We left Asan and walked down Jan Bahal toward Indrachowk. This was one of my favorite parts of town. Everything for sale along this lane held a strong association with Nepal: cream-colored pashmina shawls, block-printed tablecloths, woven rope, formal black topis arrayed in flat, glass-covered display cases. I especially loved the brass shops, their gleaming water pots and *dekshis* and copper plates spilling out onto the street like the booty from Ali Baba's cave. I could spend an hour in any one of those shops, searching behind the newly minted wares for the occasional treasure: an old *sukunda* or temple bell green with neglect, forgotten for thirty years. Such objects were customarily sold by weight; an antique brass bowl, hammered by the artisans of Chainpur, might cost no more than a mass-produced dish trucked up from the Indian border.

Just before we arrived at the broad, low temple in Indrachowk, we ducked left into a narrow lane. It was as if we'd spelunked into the barrel of a kaleidoscope. The creaky wooden shops selling rice paper and coils of hemp rope disappeared. We were suddenly in a labyrinth of cubicles, surrounded by a million strands of glass beads in a thousand shimmering colors. They dangled in bunches from hooks and hangers, like the seedpods of hallucinatory plants. Each string held hundreds of the tiny beads (which reportedly came from, of all places, the Czech Republic). They could be combined and consumed in infinite combinations, like jelly beans. Muslim merchants in white skullcaps sat in stalls no bigger than phone booths, cross-legged on white cushions. Incandescent lightbulbs hung suspended above their heads.

Grace walked up to a stall and ran her hands through a curtain of beads. "C'mere. Listen." I put my ear close. The sound was a sun shower on jungle foliage, or a distant rain stick.

The fashion possibilities were intimidating. It was seductive to believe that somehow, with the right combination of strands and colors, the perfect necklace could be designed. I'd tried designing necklaces for ex-girlfriends a few times. The end result was that I inevitably left the Bead Market with at least a dozen, each of which had seemed like a masterpiece during its creation, but none of which anyone had actually ever worn.

Fortunately Grace knew precisely what she wanted, and where to find it. A studious-looking bead *wallah* with a wispy black beard and mismatched glass eye nodded as she approached. She sat on a pad of the grass matting inside his stall, while I remained standing.

"Three of the ivory white," she said, reaching up to run a strand through her hand, "and three of the blue." The merchant reached for a hook. "No, not those. The dark ones. Midnight blue. Those." She pointed with her lips. "The shiny, dark ones."

Each strand held six thin strings of beads, so the final necklace would be ropelike: thirty-six strings thick. Grace held the strands together, then twisted them into a cream-and-lapis spiral.

"That's beautiful," I said. "How about light green and purple? Or licorice and lime green?" Gumdrops, lollipops, it was impossible to think of anything but candy. And like sweets, the beads provoked a childlike reaction: You wanted them all, immediately, if only to put them all side by side and show everyone what you had.

She shook her head. "Not my colors." The merchant offered a wood-framed mirror, and Grace held the strands to her throat. "But this looks even better than I hoped it would. The trick is, you have to know what you're going to wear it with first. Otherwise you end up buying a million necklaces, and none of them are right."

"But how do you know how this will look with your outfit?"

Grace squeezed my hand, delighted by my stupidity. "I'm wearing it," she said.

She picked up a matching blue bead bracelet, which looked about right for a child. "That won't fit," I said. But it rolled easily onto her wrist.

"From the time I was a girl, I wanted to play the piano. But my hands were too small." She held her wrist out, self-approvingly. "Can I have this, too?"

"Of course." I paid the price without bargaining. The merchant tilted his head, motioning us around a bend to where three *patwaris* sat. Grace selected her clasp of choice: a simple gold ball and loop. Using gold thread and a spindle, with hand motions too quick to follow, a necklace-spinner wrapped the ends of the strands together in a perfectly formed coil, the clasps affixed to each end.

Grace opened her vest and leaned toward me. "Care to do the honors?"

I reached behind her neck, lifted her hair, and pushed the small ball through the loop. The necklace lay on her throat, a little longer than a choker. It looked dazzling with her saffron blouse. Before I pulled my hands away she reached up, held my wrists, and kissed me.

"Taboo behavior," she sighed. "It's such a turn-on."

Behind her, the patwaris averted their eyes. I was culturally sensitive enough (or self-conscious enough) to feel slightly uncomfortable. But I breathed her light perfume and wondered if I'd get to take the necklace off, later.

Which I did—along with her earrings and cream-colored sweater. Though she didn't spend the night, we frolicked by candlelight until nearly midnight. She seemed to have come to a decision; any apprehensions about her personal history were being ignored. As was my ambiguous situation with Carlita. Before she left she'd suggested we meet this morning, and ride together to Pashupatinath.

Three dates in a row would make us suddenly significant. That was all right by me. I was becoming infatuated with her smart humor and edgy relationship with Nepal. And I found her gorgeous, physically, with cool, responsive skin and a delicious mouth. I'd loved touching her, and being touched, in a way I hadn't felt for years.

RAMANA CLEARED HIS throat, waited a beat, and spat a ball of mucus the size of a walnut. A bicycle rickshaw circled in the nearby square. Usually, the area around the towering pipal tree was clogged with vehicles; this morning the *chowk* was nearly empty. All the shops were closed. The rickshaw boy, perched on the seat of his rickshaw, began peddling backward as fast as he could. A black dog jumped up from the curb and barked maniacally at his feet. Within seconds, an avalanche of yelping cascaded through the neighborhood. The melee was so inspiring that even Ramana's mongrel, snoozing on the cold walkway along the pool's edge, rose on his arthritic haunches, bent his tired neck, and croaked into the fray.

The fog was thinning. The cobra on the capital in Nag Pokhari gleamed in the mist, sacred and lonesome. Few people ever entered the shrine; most were content to leave their offerings by the Ganesh statue in front. But the truth was that even Ganesh got scant attention. There was an older, more revered statue of the elephant-headed god a short walk away, in Tangal. Devotees mobbed that shrine every Tuesday and Saturday, their puja trays heavy with fruit and flowers.

The problem, I realized, was that Nag Pokhari had never been user-friendly. Not in my memory, at least. During my first visit to Kathmandu it was a stagnant trench, more a mud hole than a sacred site. A film of green algae had covered its surface like a moldy tarpaulin. The central column stood at a precarious angle, and the old stone walls surrounding the pool were collapsing into the soup. An effort was made to restore the place, but they'd overdone it. Nag Pokhari now seemed cheaply, self-consciously modern. The bricks were too pink. The framed pictures of "Panch and Rani" (the king and queen) were ostentatious, and the ritual bell in the Ganesh temple—cast from cheap new brass—tinny and shrill. The purpose of temple bells is to alert the god who is being petitioned, but this one sounded like a cheap telephone. When a passing devotee rang it, I half expected to hear Ganesh's answering machine click on from some celestial alcove.

The mists shifted above the water, and the cobra's tongue flickered. The truth was, I barely knew anything about this place. Had a naga been seen here long ago, like the ones that created a sensation at that muddy pond near Boudha in 1983? Or had some well-connected *nagaraja*, a serpent king displaced from his throne during construction of the nearby palace, been forcibly relocated to this down-market neighborhood?

It was ironic. I'd studied many of the Kathmandu Valley's major religious sites, discussed them with locals, and described their legends in my books. But Nag Pokhari, so close to home, remained a mystery.

"Namasté. Been waiting long?" Grace walked up and kissed me, flaunting Nepali mores. The pockets of her photographer's vest bulged with gear.

"No, no. Just chatting with my *saathi* over there." I nodded toward the shrine-keeper.

"Hey, did you hear what happened to Dr. Mishra?"

"No." I felt my face flush. What had I missed?

"Larry Prince called. After Wednesday's demonstration, he and some other doctors headed over to Singha Durbar with a list of demands for the prime minister. They made the delivery, but were arrested as they left."

"Shit." Prince was the *Asia Week* correspondent: a brilliant, loud-mouthed photojournalist who'd lived in Nepal for more than twenty years and seemed to know everything two beats before anyone else. "I guess I'd better phone the *Examiner*."

Grace shook her head. "No need. It was just for show; they let them all go after an hour." She glanced at me impishly. "You sleep okay last night?"

"I slept alright. A bit of an ache."

"Really? Where?"

"You know where. What about you?"

"I was up awhile." She leaned forward and kissed me again. "We'd better go," she said. "This light's not going to last much longer." She peered at me with narrowed eyes. "Did you remember your film?"

"Yes."

"Show me."

9

Shivaratri

T HE ENTIRE POPULATION of Kathmandu seemed to be funneling into a single purposeful stream and flowing down the narrow, brick-sur-faced road that dipped, past ramshackle brick houses and screech-ing chickens, toward the temples along the Bagmati River. Pilgrims arrived from Kathmandu city apartments, Helambu's rhododendron-covered hills, and the dry villages scattered across the Terai lowlands.

This late February morning had the sweet sharpness of early spring. An unexpected rain had polished the sky. Tin can buses spun their wheels on soggy soccer fields, gave up, and disgorged their passengers onto the flat-tened grass. A thousand bicycles navigated the mucky streets, spraying thin fins of mud; taxis honked their way into the surging crowds, only to find themselves mired in a stew of humanity. Their fares abandoned ship and walked, carrying garlands of marigolds.

Shivaratri, the Night of Lord Shiva, begins before dawn on the new moon of the month of Falguna and continues for twenty-four hours: through the whole day and night. It is an uninhibited celebration of Pashupati, the protector of animals; Mahadev, the supreme lord; Nataraj, lord of the dance; and Shankar, the sound-source of all existence. These are just four of the 1,008 names of Shiva, the all-powerful creator/destroyer who wields the double-headed drum of creation in his right hand and the flames of annihilation in his left. His scalp is the source of the Ganges; live cobras nest in his hair.

In all of Kathmandu, the city of ten thousand gods, no deity is more feared or revered. Shiva is the consummate ascetic, smeared head to toe with the ashes of cremated corpses, meditating in the jaws of a live volcano. He is the spouse of Parvati, a goddess so gorgeous that a single glimpse of her naked body will make a mortal man self-immolate with desire. Only Shiva, an incomparable lover whose divine phallus is the flaming lingam, can fulfill her. In his wrathful form he is so terrifying that the Earth itself shudders and the moon skips across the sky like a skittish deer. In his female aspect—as Durga or Kali, with her necklace of severed human heads and limbs—Shiva is distilled into pure *shakti*: the liqueur of universal energy, whose source resides beneath the ribs and between the legs of all women.

GRACE AND I purchased boats, made of folded banana leaves and filled with flowers and incense, from a little girl squatting behind a blanket just outside the temple grounds. After rising toward a masonry bridge, wide stone steps brought us down to the edge of the Bagmati. The water was shallow, but quick. We placed our leaf boats in the current, intoning private prayers. They sailed away, spinning and tipping. From the cremation ghats across the water, bodies burned. The smell, a pungent barbecue, drifted toward us.

It was a short walk to a terraced hillside, where a row of benches overlooked the river. We bought three tangerines from a fruit seller and sat down to enjoy the sweeping, smoky vista over the balconies and gilded rooftops of the Pashupati complex. From here, we could see into the area forbidden to non-Hindus. The grounds swarmed with activity. Thousands of men and women, each carrying a heaped offering tray, formed a snaking queue toward the inner sanctum of the main temple. Other worshippers stood knee-deep in the Bagmati, faces raised to heaven, tossing water into the air.

A brown rhesus, one of hundreds that lived on the grounds, leaped onto the back of our bench and snatched Grace's tangerine right out of her hand. She yelped with fury, and moved to grab it back. The primate bared its teeth. Grace picked up a rock and brought her arm back. The animal scampered off, peeling the fruit as it ran.

"Fucking monkeys . . ."

"It's amazing, isn't it?" I stuffed my tangerine peel into my jacket pocket and offered Grace a wedge. "They'll imitate everything you do, except for that. Something in their brains stops short of learning how to throw rocks."

"Thank God. Can you imagine where we'd be if they could?" She tossed the stone down. "On second thought, maybe that's exactly where we are."

We ate the third tangerine and set off to explore the hill. Shivaratri is a sacred circus, a carnival of ecstatic devotion. *Babas* and sadhus arrive in Kathmandu from all over the subcontinent, some journeying hundreds of miles by foot. Devotees evoke Shiva's transcendent consciousness with alcohol, or by smoking enormous balls of hashish. Nepalis and foreigners alike flock to the temple grounds, surrounding troupes of musicians as they beat tambourines, pump harmoniums, and chant *bhajans* to their Lord. Curious crowds mass around red-eyed sadhus meditating on tiger skins, their ash-smeared bodies surrounded by human skulls.

Some ascetics go to even greater extremes. Over the river from the main temple is an open-air hostel, a *dharamsala* where visiting sadhus eat and rest during the festival. Here one finds the real fanatics: men compelled to prove their love for God through divine self-mortification. One sadhu has held his right arm in the air for fourteen years; his bones and muscles have rusted, Tin Man–style, into place. Other sadhus sleep standing up, perch for days on one leg, or fill endless composition books with the divine name of Shiva. Rumors circulate about a sadhu who, every year at Shivaratri, cuts off one more inch of his arm.

Most popular of all, though, is the celebrated Penis Sadhu, who's become sort of a cult figure among these career cultists. "I saw him last year, right here, at Shivaratri," I said, stopping on a patch of flattened grass just a few steps from the paved pathway.

"Let's steal his spot." Grace spread out her shawl and sat down.

I flopped down next to her. "It was a scene. Hundreds of locals were massed around his little tent. When he finally came out, I was underwhelmed. He was just your average middle-aged sadhu, with sad eyes and gray dreadlocks. He kind of gazed at the crowd and lifted his loincloth, revealing a long, completely flaccid cock. Then he tied something around his balls—a kind of collar with two metal rings—and slid a bamboo pole through the rings. And he started turning the bar around and around, winding it up like one of those rubber band airplane propellers."

"Ouch."

"Tighter and tighter. Until—you can guess—he arched back and let go of the pole. I half expected him to take off."

"It couldn't have spun *that* long."

"Just a couple of seconds, but it definitely got everyone's attention. And that wasn't even the main act. One of his assistants put together a stack of bricks. It must have weighed at least fifty pounds. He wrapped the bricks in a burlap sack and tied it with leather straps. Then the sadhu slid out the bamboo pole, and pulled the straps through the rings. He crouched down, tightened up the straps, stretched out his arms, and began to stand up. Very, very slowly. The stack of bricks shifted slightly, and rose off the ground. Like, a foot."

"All of you guys must have been howling."

"The crowd went wild. And at that exact second, with everyone pushing forward, I felt a hand slip into my pocket. In and out. When I checked for my wallet, it was gone. I tried to turn around and see who'd done it, but it was hopeless. Everyone was pressed together. Everyone was staring straight ahead. You couldn't even see where anyone's hands were."

"No one looked suspicious?"

"*Everyone* looked suspicious. Luckily I hadn't lost much—a few hundred rupees, and my press pass."

"Wow. The pickpockets must love that guy. He's the ultimate distraction."

"I think there's more to it than that."

"What do you mean?"

"My theory is that the pickpockets are actually working *for* the Penis Sadhu: like Fagin with his band of Artful Dodgers."

"Of course," Grace nodded. "We're like sitting ducks, with our bulging wallets and both hands on our cameras."

"Still," I shrugged, "It's hard to hold a grudge against the guy. Whatever he makes, it's not enough."

I scanned the area. There was no sign of the famous fakir. A few solitary sadhus sat on blankets, smoking clay chillums or reading from religious texts. Rather than celebration, there was an odd air of weariness.

Grace, too, had expected more. "Is this the wrong day?"

"No." I looked at my watch. It was 8:30 in the morning; the area should have been covered with sadhus, and clouded with the mingled aromas of incense and ganja. There wasn't much music, either; a few babas stood together under a tree, clapping to the accompaniment of a tabla and harmonium. The muzzle of a film crew's microphone poked into their midst.

"No, it's definitely today. You saw: There are a million people down at the temple. It's just up here that it's empty. Let's check inside the dharamsala. It was pretty cold last night; maybe the sadhus are hanging out in there."

But the shelter was also a disappointment. Traditionally, the place was filled with red-eyed pilgrims from the far corners of Nepal and India. This morning, there were no more than twenty mendicants. They sat cross-legged on woolen blankets and mouthed prayers from holy texts, pausing only to polish their spectacles or reach automatically for the hot tea beside them. One of them was applying red toenail polish; another held up a small, round mirror, fixing the bindhi on his forehead. A young man in a white shirt circulated among them, refreshing their cups from a huge aluminum kettle. He approached us with a smile.

"Namasté. Are you having tea?"

I looked at Grace, who nodded. "Sure."

The man set down his kettle and skipped away, returning with two ribbed glasses. He poured a caramel cord of chiya into each, serving us with a flourish. We sipped slowly as he watched. "Good?"

"*Mito chha*," Grace agreed. "*Danyabat*."

"Oooh, you speak Nepali! Very good, very good!" He turned to me. "I am in love with your wife," he announced. "Together you are looking too beautiful."

"Thank you," I said. "She's lovely indeed."

The man bowed and departed. "Your wife," Grace said. "I'm sure."
But she gave me a glance that I felt in my pants.

At the edge of the dharamsala stood a statue of Hanuman, the heroic
monkey-god who steals the show in the *Ramayana* epic. His figure, painted
from ankle to crown with vermilion paste, gleamed day-glow orange. As I
approached the statue, a Westerner emerged from behind the pedestal. He
was dressed in black leather, and held a helmet under his arm. I recognized
Lou Tanner, one of Kathmandu's longest-enduring expatriates.

Louis was four parts fixture, three parts legend. He'd lived in Nepal
since the late 1960s, enjoying the then-plentiful hashish and enriching himself by smuggling gold, in Snickers-sized ingots that fit neatly up his ass,
from Hong Kong to Kathmandu. Friendships with high officials, sweetened
through a regular schedule of gifts and bribes, kept his visa afloat. Three
years ago, though, Lou had run aground; the popular immigration officer
he had cultivated was uprooted and imprisoned, and a purge of nonofficial
residents brought him within inches of exile. Lou avoided exposure, but
the payoffs had cost 50 percent of his savings and 90 percent of his nerve.
He'd mothballed his false-bottomed briefcases and spent the remainder of
his fortune importing Macintosh computers into the kingdom. As information became the new addiction, Lou prospered. The former outlaw was now
CEO of Nepal's top IT consulting firm.

"Hey," I greeted him. "Small world."

"How ya doing?" Lou slapped my palm and gave Grace a hug. "Can
you believe how fuckin' lame this is? There are more people here on
Valentine's Day." Neither financial solvency, nor twenty years on foreign
soil, had sweetened his Brooklyn mouth. "It's unbelievable. The royal palace has its head up its ass." His eyes darted around as if he was looking for
someone he could hit.

"Give me a break," I said. "You can't blame the king for a slow
Shivaratri."

"*Hello?*" He looked at me wearily. "It's His Majesty's government, man.
All the way. Motherfuckers. They're terrified by this democracy shit. They
think India's behind the whole movement—which could be true! Anyway,
about a week ago some highly placed asshole decided that Shivaratri would

be the perfect chance for India to smuggle antimonarchy instigators into Nepal. Cleverly disguised as sadhus. Brilliant, huh? So the border police have been stopping the pilgrim buses and sending them back to where they came from. Thousands of pilgrims, shit out of luck. There've been riots at the border. It's a fucking mess."

"You're kidding," Grace said. "How come no one's protesting here?"

"Oh, they will." Lou nodded over across the river, toward the rows of shops and tea stalls lining the entrance to Pashupati. "First of all, tomorrow's a huge strike. Nepal *bandh*. You know that, right?"

I nodded; Grace shook her head.

"Black Day," I explained. "Everyone's supposed to close up shop and wear black armbands."

Grace kicked my foot. "Thanks. I just didn't know there was one *tomorrow*."

"From what I hear, a bunch of students from TU are coming here to pass out democracy flyers," Lou said. "Around nine, by the side entrance. Keep your eyes open. Should be a real party."

I looked at my watch: It was quarter past nine. I could see the general area near the gate. People were milling about, but there was no unusual activity.

Grace studied the scene with me. "Anything going on?"

"I doubt it. They'll be late, if they show up at all. This is Nepal."

I pointed my chin at Lou's motorcycle helmet. "Where's your bike?"

"On the Ring Road, half a mile from here. Tried to ride it down the hill, but forget it, no way." He squinted across the river. "Hey, we're having our annual rally and picnic out at Godavari this afternoon. Fifteenth anniversary. I'm amazed that any of us are left, but we got sixteen guys together. How about that?" Lou raised his eyebrows at Grace, who registered cluelessness. He unzipped his jacket, revealing a faded blue T-shirt emblazoned with an image of Shiva astride a black Harley. His consort reclined on the gas tank, buck naked, her legs wrapped around his waist.

"Shiva's Slaves," Lou declared. "Kathmandu's original bikers' club." He shrugged. "It's a long story."

Grace nodded dubiously. "Neat."

"Anyway." Lou snapped the waistband button on his jacket. "Good seeing you guys." He nodded at Grace and looked at me. "If you ever need to fax a story, you can do it from my office." He spoke in a stage whisper. "Save you a trip to Dillibazar prison, if you catch my meaning."

"Thanks, Lou. Let me get your work number." I tapped my pocket for a pen and was fishing out my notebook when Lou grabbed my arm.

"Fuck, you guys. Look!"

On the far side of the Bagmati, in the plaza near Pashupati's south entrance, a demonstration had begun. A dozen young men had started shouting slogans and throwing handfuls of pink paper slips into the air. While some onlookers were fleeing, an equal number of people were rushing toward the students, forming a crowd.

Grace twisted her hips in a sharp, practiced motion that swung her camera around her body and into her hands. She pushed a switch with her right thumb, engaging the motor drive. "I'm outa here," she announced, her voice thickened by adrenaline. She darted from the sadhus' encampment, taking the steps to the river two at a time. We saw her run across the stone bridge a moment later, both hands cradling her Canon A-1.

"She's crazy," Lou observed. "She'd get better shots from right here."

"No." I shrugged off my daypack and pulled out my own camera, slinging it around my neck and arm. "She's right. I'm going down, too."

"You're both crazy motherfuckers. Be careful."

I ran across the bridge, bumping tourists and Nepalis aside. Rhythmic chanting rose all around me as the crowd joined in. "*Demo . . . cracy! Demo . . . cracy!*" Just as I reached the plaza, a flatbed truck swerved into view. Soldiers in full riot gear—helmets, *lathi* clubs, and woven cane shields— leaped onto the pavement. The crowd surged back in a panic, retreating blindly, seeking the safety of the temple grounds.

I was in their way.

A heavy woman ran directly into me, and I fell backward, landing on my ass and elbows. I rolled quickly onto my belly and struggled to my knees. Someone stepped on my ankle; a knee slammed me between the shoulder blades, knocking the wind out of me and driving me down again. My camera was on the ground, next to my hip. As I tried to maneuver it into the safety of my armpit someone stepped into the lasso of the strap. The leather snapped, and I watched helplessly as the camera was kicked out of reach. Then there were only feet: In the small of my back, on my neck and shoulders, in the cleft of my ass, kicking into my ribs. I shut my eyes and folded my arms over the back of my head as my nose and cheek were mashed into the ground.

Funny, the things that go through your head as you're being trampled. The dirt beneath my nose smelled like my high school baseball glove. The leaflets littering the ground were hot pink, an odd choice for political flyers. I even felt a pulse of gratitude that this was happening in Nepal, where people are small and everyone wears flip-flops. And I wondered, with real concern, what had become of Grace.

AT SOME POINT, I came to. But before that blow that knocked me out (a kick to the head, guessing from the bump above my right ear), I'd had a powerful image of stampeding sheep—and a brief memory of my brother, who specialized in imitating them. It was a skill he'd learned in school, at Deep Springs. One evening we were in Macy's together, buying Mom a gift. We'd gotten lost, and found ourselves in the lingerie department. Jordan chose that moment to pause. He raised a finger. "Here is the cry," he announced, "of a young male sheep being castrated." With that he cleared his throat and produced an incredible sound: "Mmmmnnnnbbhaaaaaaaannnggghhhh." It was ear-splitting and heart-wrenching, a ventriloquist's yodel that might have come from anywhere. Every woman within earshot stiffened, seeking the sheep in her midst. My brother affected similar confusion, glancing every which way. He then turned back to me. "But we were looking for sweaters," he said. "Perhaps something in wool?"

Lou and Grace helped me up. My face was striped with dirt. There was blood under my nose, and my legs were bruised, but nothing seemed to be broken. I staggered to my feet. A crowd of Nepalis, including sadhus and policemen, stood around us. The demonstration was over, and I was the new attraction.

"You're all right," Lou said. "You look like hell, but you're okay. Which is more than I can say for those protesters."

"Someone's getting a cab." Grace had her arm around me, but her eyes still wandered in search of pictures. "I'll take you home. Unless you want to get some X-rays."

I breathed deeply, flexed my fingers, and tested my teeth with my tongue. "No, I'm okay. Jesus. How long was I out?"

"Less than five minutes. They beat the shit out of those kids and hauled them away. Everyone else scattered."

"What about our bikes?"

"Don't worry." Grace wet a lens cloth with her water bottle and dabbed around my eyes. "We'll get them later."

A red Toyota with a yellow roof pulled into the square. Grace helped me into the backseat and climbed in beside me. "Nag Pokhari," she announced. "*Chitto janus*. And by the meter."

The driver looked for Grace in his rearview mirror, ready for an argument, but got an eyeful of me instead. He dropped the flag and took off, his custom horn blasting the opening bars from "Flight of the Bumblebee."

10

On the Ghats

B Y SEVEN I'D showered, washed the gravel and cow shit out of my hair, eaten a grilled cheese sandwich, and napped. I felt almost human again. My worst injury was the bump on my head, which continued to rise like the membrane of a Jiffy Pop pan. My legs and back looked like fields of pansies, blooming in a breathtaking array of reds, blues, and purples.

Grace phoned. "Our bikes are still at Pashupati," she said. "Might be a good idea to reclaim them."

"It's hard to think of going back . . ."

"I know. Anyway," she said, "they're locked up. They should be fine until tomorrow."

"But tonight's the big night, isn't it? They could get swiped."

"Maybe. But it's a weird year. I doubt it'll be much more crowded than it was this morning."

"Hmmm." I stretched my legs; they'd carry me. "What the heck, let's go. It might be fun. Oh, *fuck!*"

"What's wrong?"

"My Nikon. It got kicked away from me. Shit, now I won't . . ."

"Relax. Lou picked it up. People were too freaked out to steal it, if you can believe that. I have to tell you, though, the wide angle lens is cracked. The filter, at least. But the body's fine. I have it here. You want me to bring it with me tonight?"

"No. Thanks." I breathed a sigh of relief. "I'll pick it up later."

"Fine. So how should we do this?"

"I'll come to you."

"Good. Meet me at nine, at the overgrown temple in Hadigaon. We'll grab a cab from there."

DESPITE THE NEW moon, Pashupatinath wasn't as dark as I'd hoped. In years past the temple would have been lit with palm-sized butter lamps; these days, amber streetlights illuminated the stone bridge and riverside steps with a dull alien gleam, like sunset on an outer planet.

We found our bicycles and climbed to a forested hillside. Singing and chanting filtered from the woods, seeming to emanate from the trees themselves. Cords of incense wove through the breeze. It was just cold enough for our breath to fog.

I preferred Shivaratri on this diminished scale. Bands of sadhus sat by bonfires, heating water in aluminum dekshis and warming their hands. In the midst of the forest was a complex of centuries-old wooden temples, beautifully carved stone lingam shrines, and shuttered rest houses where the oldest devotees lived year-round. Outside the door of the women's kitchen, venerable *anis* and *aamas* squatted around crackling pyres, the wrinkles in their cheeks writhing in the firelight. They ignored us, muttering mantras into the night. We passed by quietly, dropping a few coins at their feet.

"We can get to the river this way." Grace took my arm, leading me away from the nun's hostel and down a narrow trail that fed back into the woods. "We'll come out by the smaller cremation ghats on the north side of the temple. Away from the lights. It might be pretty spooky . . ."

The path led among moss-laced trees, ending at the top of a stone stairway that led steeply down to the Bagmati. A few of the steps, and most of the masonry retaining wall, had been dislodged by roots and rains, creating a dangerous descent. It was very dark; neither of us had brought a flashlight. We negotiated the steps one by one, gripping each other's hands, elbows bent. I limped slightly. As we came within sight of the river I saw an orange glow rippling on the water, and I swallowed hard. Bodies were burning.

A moment later we emerged onto an ancient cornice. The crowded temple itself was about two hundred yards downstream, around a bend in the Bagmat, hidden by trees. The downriver sky glowed with an ambient halo, laced with smoke.

At the river's edge stood two round, flat cremation ghats, a dozen paces apart. One of them was empty and appeared freshly swept. Upon the other lay a shrouded human body, engulfed in flames. We watched in silence, reaching again for each other's hands.

"It's weird that no one's around," I whispered. "Isn't someone supposed to *attend* these things?"

Grace shook her head. "Usually. Maybe it's different tonight. Maybe, on Shivaratri, no one wants to get anywhere near a cremation; they just light the fire and run. I don't know. It's Shiva's night: Shiva *ratri*. Isn't he supposed to hang out near cremation ghats?"

"I think so. So what are *we* doing here?"

"Don't you want to meet him?"

It was a recently lit fire. The upper layer of straw had just been consumed, revealing the charring corpse of what might have been a man. But the body's hair had burned away and the skin was roasted and crackling, making it hard to guess his age. One leg was twisted away from the center of the pyre and protruded toward us, out of the flames. We couldn't see the face.

"A sight you won't see in Missouri," I remarked.

Grace smirked. "Not these days." As she walked closer to the ghat, the wind shifted, blowing the scent of burning flesh our way. "Ugh."

"You don't want to get too close. I've watched these things before. At some point the skull will burst, and you might get scalded."

"Scalded?"

"With blood. It can shoot out in a stream."

She backed off and stood very still. "It's very beautiful." She trembled slightly. "The whole body, turning back into energy and ash. I think it's much more poetic than burying people. Not to mention the *finality* of it."

"That's true. When you're cremated, you're really gone. The whole idea of zombies and vampires, the 'undead,' wouldn't work here."

"Instead you come back. Fresh. As something completely new."

I looked over at her. "Do you believe in reincarnation?"

"I do." She was silent for a moment. "Do you?"

"I want to. Very badly." I remembered Chokyi Nyima's talk, and his insistence that the elements of Buddhist doctrine should be tested, and well checked, before they were trusted. Though the idea of rebirth would be a great comfort, I couldn't accept it on faith, much less find a way to test it. This, it seemed to me, was a fundamental problem with this whole karma business.

I told Grace about something else that happened at the teaching: A Dutch student had insisted that reincarnation is a fantasy.

"'Fine,' the Rinpoche told him. 'You can believe, or not believe. Up to you! But if you believe or not, makes no difference. Reincarnation is a *fact*.'"

Grace smirked. "So much for lively debate."

I shrugged. "Maybe it *is* blind faith, or maybe Chokyi Nyima has witnessed it firsthand. I'm sure there's some pretty robust evidence out there. I hope so. Because, at the end of the day, I'd like to believe that our life-essence sticks around—and that no one we love is ever really gone."

The body on the ghat burned steadily. The errant leg had burned clean and now hung across the logs at a ghoulish angle. The man's face was clearly visible, a blackened and expressionless mask, the eyes and nose gone.

Grace walked upriver and sat on the edge of the second, clean-swept ghat. Her face glowed, illuminated by the fire. I stayed where I was, arms folded across my chest, awed by this direct experience of the human body's *stuff*-ness.

"Come here," Grace said, brushing a twig from the spot beside her.

I left the heat of the pyre and joined her. We sat together, watching the flames, our fingers intertwined. Neither of us spoke. There was the snap crackle popping of muscle and wood and fat, temple bells ringing from the distant Pashupati shrines, and an occasional scream from the forest of monkeys. Otherwise, the night was still.

Grace turned toward me. "Make love to me," she said. "Here."

It was breathlessly strange. We must have looked like the lovers in those Tibetan paintings: Grace on my lap, her strong legs around my back, our open mouths pressed lightly together. She moaned in a beautiful erotic cadence, her hips moving as if on a swing, her eyes open and wild.

As we came I heard a muted crack, like two cupped hands clapped fiercely together. Beyond Grace's shoulder, a few yards away, a wine-red fountain rose from the corpse.

11

Meet the Artist

N EW ROAD IS one of Kathmandu's oldest paved roads, built after the great earthquake of 1934. At the time it might have been a humble homage to the Champs-Élysées, filled with trendy shops and visited by royalty. Six decades on, it was a pastiche of sweet shops and tailors, opticians and dentists, goldsmiths and electronics stores selling gray-market TVs, speakers, and cassette decks. A hundred yards beyond the entrance gate—with its painted bas-reliefs of Shiva and Ganesh—was an ancient pipal tree, shading a small square that served as the city's main newsstand and intellectual gathering spot. Dozens of newspapers and broadsides, from the royalist *Gorkhapatra* to Mahesh Regmi's upstart *Nepal Press Digest*, lay in the dappled shade, or folded open in the hands of middle-aged men in topis, Tribhuvan University students, and local merchants.

But my rare visit to New Road had nothing to do with newsprint. Once in a while I got a craving for *gundpak*, a local snack as seductive as catnip for Nepalis. I didn't know all the ingredients, but it was basically a loose, gritty fudge of sugar, boiled milk, salt, and flour, with a handful of broken cashews, chestnuts, coconuts, or raisins thrown in. The locals were crazy for it; five tiny shops were clustered in a one-block area. Gundpak Vendor, on a corner just inside the New Road Gate, was the oldest of the lot, though my attempts to learn its true age produced wildly varied results.

At eleven in the morning the stall was mobbed. I pressed in with the crowd, a 20-rupee bill waving from my hand. People of all ages strained forward with ragged notes to buy their daily fix of the thick, brown mass. It was one of the reliably wonderful things in the valley.

Gundpak had long been a staple for locals, but few tourists—or expats—were aware of its existence. When friends came to town, I brought them here right away. They were always reluctant to taste the brown goop, taking a tiny sample on their pinkies. Like Kathmandu itself, it was a bizarre, over-rich concoction that somehow worked. No one, once they'd overcome their initial aversion, could resist it.

EXCEPT, OF COURSE, for Jordan. He would be able to resist it—as he currently resisted everything that existed outside his small, rigorous sphere of approval.

I tried to remember when he'd changed. When had everything to do with sensory pleasure and the physical world become repulsive to him? Thinking back, it happened when I was in my midteens. Sometime in junior high, Jordan began to despise food: food, at least, as I understood it. Suddenly, apparently on a whim, he would eat nothing containing sugar or salt. He prepared his own Spartan meals in a corner of the kitchen as our mother dished up lasagna, veal cutlets, roast chicken, blintzes, and pound cake.

Despite my mom's excellent cooking, dinners were an ordeal. There was little conversation, and we sat in silence to the awkward rhythms of mastication. Jordan mastered the art of racetrack dining. "Time me," he'd demand, dropping into his seat. He could polish off a serving of brown rice, kale, and steamed broccoli in three minutes. The instant he finished, he shot to his feet and quit the table with a preemptive "excuse me." A moment later, his door would bang shut.

He kept the red burlap curtains closed, which gave his bedroom the odd glow of a darkroom. When I dared to enter (after his barked command that I identify myself), I'd find him bent over his desk, the high-intensity corona of a gooseneck lamp illuminating the texts of German or Greek literature arrayed on his desk.

"What are you reading?"

"Heine," he declared nasally.

"Is this a bad time?"

"You'd fare better interrupting me whilst I devoured a succulent peach, or pleasured a fulsome maiden "

His eyes were eaglelike, with a focus that was almost frightening. This was the quality that best defined my brother: the ability to narrow his attention unflinchingly, with a raptor's precision, on whatever prize he was after. Once, when he took a break from a survey of lyric verse, I leaned over his desk and examined the text, half expecting to see scorch marks.

Jordan's aptitude with German blossomed into a love of all languages. Their study dominated his thoughts, and was one of few things that animated him. While I lusted for open spaces, dreaming of journeys to Monument Valley or Damascus, Jordan withdrew into the world of Hölderlin, Cicero, and Aristophanes. Their ethics became his ethics; their perfected language, his precise method of speaking.

Like the classical cultures, he placed a high value on fitness. Early each morning, before jogging to the high school track to run his daily miles, he'd descend to the kitchen and boil water. I watched him remove the Sanka jar from the cupboard above the sink, unscrew the lid, and extract a few grains of freeze-dried coffee between his thumb and index finger. He would drop these crystals into a cup, pour in hot water, and sip with contentment. I regarded his pale brew with disdain.

"It needs a strong cup of coffee," he remarked earnestly. "A *bold* cup of coffee, to see a man through a winter's morn."

I snorted. "You can't even taste the goddamned coffee."

"A robust drink," he continued, savoring the anemic bouquet, "against the cold morning. It's all a man really needs."

He would follow his beverage with a bowl of oats and a slice of whole-grain toast spread with a layer, one molecule thick, of margarine. After rinsing the dishes, he disappeared into the dawn.

His resolve and self-confidence shamed me. I faced the unsavory fact that my weird little brother—unlike my cool, rebellious friends—was the true nonconformist. I'd given up any hope of winning his admiration. But he possessed powers of discrimination that I lacked, and I sought his respect to vindicate my own sketchy behavior. This was not a prize given lightly. Thinking back on those days, I recall Primo Levi's description of his friend

Sandro in *The Periodic Table*: "He had the nature of a cat with whom one can live for decades, without ever being permitted to penetrate its sacred pelt."

When Jordan was fourteen, our father confronted him. He opened the door of my brother's bedroom, cigarette in hand, and demanded to know what his son planned to do with his life.

"I plan," Jordan replied curtly, "to be a philosopher."

"And how will you make a living?" Dad asked sarcastically. "Open a philosophy store?"

Jordan smiled thinly, inclined his head, and closed his door. Years later, he would name that incident as the end of their relationship. I believe this is true, and our sister, Debra, concurs. As far as we know, it was the last time our brother and father ever spoke.

"Hajur! Linus na!"

The rupee note was snatched from my fingers and a small parcel of gundpak—wrapped in a page from the *Gorkhapatra*—pressed into my hand. I was starting to feel like Billy Pilgrim, the hero of Kurt Vonnegut's *Slaughterhouse-Five*, migrating from one timescape to another.

The memory of my father and brother seemed harsh—but that kind of alienation was practically a tradition in Nepal. The history of the ruling class in the Kathmandu Valley was a bloody saga of brother against brother, father against son. As I carried my gundpak down New Road, I glanced with amusement at a display of plastic gift plates in a shop window. There were two designs, featuring images of King Birendra and Queen Aiswarya. I wondered when there would be a portrait plate featuring Dipendra, the eighteen-year-old crown prince, whose exploits with drugs and alcohol—often in company of his wild cousin, Paras—were the subject of disgusted gossip and apprehension among Nepal's upper and middle classes. It was hard to imagine what the prince's relationship with his parents must be. I doubted there was much mutual respect, or a lot of lively dinner conversation.

My scruffy reflection in a jewelry store window reminded me that I needed a shave. There'd been a place on Kicha Pokhari, across from the old American Cultural Center—the Ramu Saloon. And here it was still: a bright, large shop painted mint green, with gold-trimmed lettering on the window.

Inside, five wood-and-leather chairs faced a mirrored wall. There was no waiting. The moment I walked in, I was steered to a chair. A fresh blue towel was tossed over my chest and tucked into my collar. My head was coaxed back.

"Shave only?"

"*Haus.*"

The barber squeezed an inch of white paste onto my chin and dipped a brush into a small silver bowl of water.

"New blade, please."

He wagged his head, unwrapped an India-made stainless steel blade, and slid it into a bright orange straight razor holder.

There's no sound quite like the rasp of a straight razor against your skin. The barber worked in quick, short strokes, briskly wiping the accumulated cream off the razor and onto the flat of his hand. When the first pass was finished, he lathered me up again and began the fine tuning: around my Adam's apple and in front of my ears. He pinched my nose up and flicked the blade down my philtrum, an intimate and tensifying gesture that reminded me of *Chinatown*.

The sight of my reflection, chin lifted high, looking down at myself as if from a height, turned my thoughts back to my brother. At a certain point, I realized, he had made a deliberate decision to be an outsider. I thought again of *Star Trek*'s Spock and his irrepressible aura of superiority. But even that comparison was inadequate. The iconic Vulcan was smart, alright; but he lacked my brother's gift for performance.

Jordan was one of a handful of students to receive perfect scores on his SATs, a feat that won him a small mention in the *Long Island Press*. He had his pick of schools, but accepted a scholarship to Deep Springs: a small, exclusive college and working cattle ranch near Bishop, in California's high desert. The place was a good match for him. It was geographically isolated, barely accessible. During the two years he attended I rarely saw him—despite the fact that I'd moved to California myself and was completing my own studies at UC Santa Cruz.

Our separation, paradoxically, brought us closer. We began exchanging letters. His were salted with German verses, Greek idioms, quotations from Cicero, and words that, plain English though they were, had me groping for the dictionary: *lycanthropy, ungulate, susurrus*. He was wrestling, he told me, with a project that had obsessed him since the age of thirteen: a "calculus of language" that would make it possible to define once and for all abstract concepts like Truth and Beauty.

My brother's academic efforts were admirable, but baffling. More accessible to me were his gutsy episodes as a prankster, an agent provocateur who continually courted disaster.

He had described his motivation (and the pranks themselves) on various occasions. Social intercourse, for Jordan, was a kind of mad experiment, and the human race supplied him with an ever-changing pool of subjects. He took insane chances with people: challenging them, mimicking them, deliberately confusing them in the hopes of drawing out spontaneous and revealing responses.

A favorite among his stunts was "Going Up," which he performed three or four times during a summer job with a New York publisher. Jordan would enter an office lobby—the RCA building had the right kind of elevators—and wait gamely, pretending to sort through his documents. When a car had filled up with passengers and the doors began to close, he ran toward the lift: "Please! *Hold that door!*" The occupants usually complied, grinning with Samaritan satisfaction as Jordan squeezed in. He then nodded in acknowledgment and turned to face the control panel.

As soon as the doors hissed shut, Jordan immediately depressed his own button—for the highest floor possible. He then proceeded, with utter nonchalance, to *pull out every other pushed button*. The elevator thus rose unhindered, stopping at no one's floor but his own.

Startled, electric murmurs boiled through the compartment as people watched their floors tick by. Jordan's gaunt body blocked access to the panel. Elsewhere, he might have been murdered for such impunity, but his well-heeled benefactors were too stunned to move a muscle. Imagining my brother, rising toward the Rainbow Room in a sealed compartment of seething New Yorkers, I realize what he was: a kind of behaviorist Houdini. He viewed America as an arena of conditioned responses, and saw his pranks as a form of guerrilla theater.

He specialized in mimicry. He'd spy an individual with a peculiar gait (neither the elderly nor the disabled were spared his attentions) and move beside them, imitating their every nuance. A heavyset man in a fedora, with bowed legs and a penguinlike stride, would glance to his left—and for a moment, the annoyance of having his space invaded would cloud his recognition. Then the man experienced a vertiginous confusion, as if he'd caught a glimpse of himself, unexpectedly, in a mirror. As his disorientation passed, an incredulous anger would descend.

Jordan was invincible in these situations. What made him so—whether mimicking a petite Chinese woman or a drunken longshoreman—was his self-possession. He never broke character. He conducted his experiments with total conviction, neither scorn nor amusement crossing his face. Sometimes, though, when he mimicked the lame or elderly, his eyes would wince, as if he were experiencing their pain.

He *wanted* to experience it, I think. He knew little of human suffering, save the idealized behavior he had read about in classical literature. (He did not count our parents in this category, as he believed they suffered by *choice*.) Underlying his mimicry was an obsessive humanism: a desire to literally inhabit the skin of the people he studied on the streets, to feel what they felt. There was no one he respected more than the rare person who would invite him more genuinely into their world. One afternoon, a shuffling and overweight woman—laden with bags from Gristedes—saw Jordan huffing along beside her. She shook her head and handed him her bags. He carried them back to her apartment—not just that day, but once every week for two months afterward. This was the flip side of his social bargain: Any request for help, or charity, was answered. All one had to do was ask. Jordan did not shy from an outstretched hand, or from inviting a homeless person up to his apartment for a hot shower or cup of sugarless tea.

BY THE AGE of twenty, my brother was conversant in a dozen languages. Nothing delighted him more than visiting one of New York's great museums and attaching himself to a vacationing couple from France or Germany, Spain or Israel. He would shadow the visitors as they roamed the galleries. After ten or fifteen minutes he had focused his attention upon either the man or the woman—mastering that person's accent, syntax, and inflections. At that point, the hapless tourists became unwitting participants in whatever odd theater my brother might devise.

One June afternoon, in New York together for a cousin's wedding, Jordan and I made a visit to the Museum of Modern Art. This was a major concession. Contemporary painting and sculpture were my thing, not his.

Shortly after we entered, Jordan spied a well-dressed French couple. We tailed them through Cubism, watched them puff at Alexander Calder's mobile, and hovered nearby as they navigated the chairs and lampshades of the Design Gallery. But they were fleet of foot and never gave Jordan an opening. He finally gave up, abandoning the couple as they loitered over Gitanes in the Sculpture Garden.

Before we left the MoMA, I suggested a brief stop in the temporary galleries. The exhibition on view was appalling, but our visit gave me an opportunity to witness my brother's "art" firsthand.

Jordan entered the room, read the artist's biography, and surveyed the work with contempt. A sculpture was mounted to the wall right before us. The piece consisted of a skunk pelt, bound with raw twine to a nest of leaves and sticks. Who had decreed this was art? Art, for Jordan, was the sinewy muscle of Michelangelo's *David*, the chiaroscuro of Eugène Delacroix, the Poseidon of Artemision. Aside from some early Picassos and a few Expressionists, everything created since the 1860s was, in his estimable view, trash.

"If you don't mind," he muttered, "I'll take my leave of this mortuary. And when I say *mortuary*," he added, "I speak not only of this unfortunate weasel, but of Art. Art itself is buried here, in body and spirit; and here it rots, festering with worms while lauded by the masses as living. And not just as *living*," he added pointedly, "as *vibrantly alive*."

But luck was on Jordan's side. As we turned to go, the French couple entered the gallery. They gravitated immediately to the collage of twigs and fur beside which my brother and I still stood.

"*C'est fantastique*," the woman said, continuing in French: "Can you tell . . . it is a real animal?"

"It is real," her partner returned. "Real fur. *Incroyable.* I love the combination, the interplay of animal and vegetable. And the bound-up sticks, the leaves; it's magnificent. We are bound to the cycle of mortality."

"Ritual," she declared. "Ritual and renewal. Like the building of this nest. The suggestion that dead things can somehow provide a home for the living. *C'est profond.*"

"*C'est merde.*"

Jordan had crept up behind the couple and now spoke, in fluent Parisian French, to the backs of their necks. "It is an abomination. How one longs for true art, honest visions of life; for the living, breathing passion of Man!" He spoke as if addressing the sculpture itself. "What we see here is a representation not of ritual, or of renewal, but of narcissism and self-delusion. The individual responsible for this monstrosity should be managing a parking garage, or stuffing sausages. Both better-suited vocations," he concluded, "than roping dead rodents to a panel and proclaiming it 'Art'!"

The man pivoted on his heels. "Who is this fool?" he barked. "Who do you think you are?" His companion turned as well, regarding the gaunt young man with the beaklike nose, black eyes, and patchy stubble on his arrogant chin.

"*Je suis l'artist!*" Jordan cried. "And the only thing I loathe more than the smell of dead rodents is the stink of intellectual pretension. Now get out of my gallery, and embarrass me no more with your pompous clichés!"

The couple fled the room. Jordan did not watch them go. Instead he moved closer to the work in question, studying it with fresh interest.

"Now that they've explained it," he confided, "it's not half bad."

IN 1979, WHILE I vagabonded through Europe and Asia and made my way to Nepal, Jordan was enrolled as a linguistics major at the State University of New York. He soon established his brilliance, uncovering in some hoary text a Greek verb form that had eluded scholars for centuries.

He was also dating, but with mixed results. The problem wasn't an inability to meet women; it was the way he perceived courtship. The tango of the sexes was, in Jordan's eye, yet another opportunity for satire and confrontation. Inanely, he expected the women he met to indulge his acid observations.

"As we sat upon a bench, upon a grassy promenade," he wrote in one letter, "I placed my arm around Cynthia's shoulder; and, in doing so, felt her delicate clavicle beneath my fingers. Her ribs felt the same: fragile as a bird-cage. Touching her this way, I was stunned by the direct experience of the classic gulf between men and women: specifically in upper-body strength. It was at this point that I remarked to Cynthia, 'Your bones seem so fragile, it seems I could crush your ribcage with a firm embrace.'

"My remarks distressed her far out of proportion to their intent. She fled quickly, and I admit to you with some embarrassment that I've not heard from her since."

Over time, Jordan acquired a better grip of dating etiquette. He even became something of a ladies' man. But he never stopped treating his girl-friends as abstractions: reflections of the impossible, "ideal" woman.

His real problems began a few years later, during an active and optimis-tic period in my own life. This was in June 1983. I'd received a Journalism Fellowship from the Rotary Foundation and was preparing to leave California for a year in Kathmandu. I decided to reach Nepal via Europe and stopped in Plainview for a family farewell.

Jordan had sublet his Binghamton apartment and was home for the summer. Everyone was at home. Debra, who'd just turned twenty, was working nights at a biker bar in Farmingdale. Mom had completed a degree in Early Childhood Education, and was directing preschool programs at the Mid-Island "Y."

Dad wasn't faring so well. After seventeen years, he had been laid off by GE. There was no future, the corporation had decided, in fax machines or personal computers, and they'd scrapped their entire data processing divi-sion. Dad sent out a barrage of résumés, but data was a young man's field. I returned from California to find him rooted in front of the television, wait-ing for the phone to ring. His eyes seemed dull, and his copper-colored hair had gone white.

Jordan was in crisis as well. The move back into his childhood room, at
the age of twenty-five, was an indignity, challenging his notions of self-reliance. He worked on his texts behind closed doors, Virgil Fox's *Heavy Organ*
surging through his room. As we sat on his bed—the same bed beneath
which he had disappeared as a child—I was shocked by how morose he'd
become.

His mood was not the result of his financial straits. There was a more
serious cause, he admitted quietly, for his gloom. Something had happened
to him: something *physical*. During sexual intercourse—he used the clinical
term—he'd felt a short, sharp pain at the base of his penis. It was as if a
switch had been thrown. At that moment, all pleasurable sensation ceased.

"And this happened *while* you were having sex," I repeated.

"Yes. A sudden pain, as if something had snapped."

It was more than a loss of sensation. It was as though his very will, his
life energy, had fled. He was still able to have sex, after a fashion. But there
was little sensation connected with it, and no enjoyment.

As he spoke I sensed how disheartened he'd become: not just about sex,
but about his life in general.

"Depression itself might be the cause of your problem," I offered. "One
of the symp—"

"My state is rooted in my sexual dysfunction," he interrupted, "which
I absolutely believe to be corporeal in nature. It's as if part of my hormonal
system has shut down."

"Have you even considered visiting a psychologist?"

"It is a physical problem," he repeated. "I don't believe in Ouija boards
or faith healers."

I wondered, vaguely, if coming to Nepal with me might not be a solution. At that point I'd been to Asia only once, but the trip had forever altered
my sense of the world. Maybe all that Jordan needed was perspective: the
realization that there *was* a world out there, bigger than the one behind his
eyes.

Bringing Jordan to Asia might have inspired him. Or it might have
repulsed him, driving us farther apart. It was impossible to predict whether

he would view my beloved Hindu kingdom—with its living goddesses and towering Buddhist shrines—as a center of spiritual power, or a backwater of superstitious mumbo-jumbo.

"BHAYO." THE BARBER folded the razor. He lifted a spray bottle and spritzed my face with a fine mist. I closed my lips tightly, wary of the water. Once he'd toweled me dry, he launched into a brief head massage, punctuated by percussive claps against my skull. A few skillful, chiropractic twists cracked my neck back into—or out of—alignment. And that was that.

"How much?" I asked.

"Pay as you like."

Above the mirrors hung a framed print of Laxmi, bestower of wealth. Fresh incense burned beneath the goddess, whose hands dripped gold coins. The hint wasn't subtle, but Nepal was an easy place to be generous.

12

New Diamond Intermezzo

To: Foreign Desk, *San Francisco Examiner*
From: Jeff Greenwald, Kathmandu, Nepal

Unrest Escalates in Nepal

KATHMANDU, 25 FEB 1990: Over 900 pro-democracy activists, including the Mayor of Kathmandu, were arrested this afternoon during city-wide sweeps by riot police. Hundreds of other arrests occurred in districts throughout this Himalayan kingdom, and several towns were placed under 24-hour curfew.

Police in the capital effectively crushed "Black Flag Day," during which demonstrators planned a march in honor of their colleagues killed during the past week. Official figures put the death toll at 11, but witnesses claim that more than 30 people have died, with many more wounded. An estimated 4,500 Nepalis have been arrested since the National Liberation Front launched its campaign for free elections on February 18th.

There were few vehicles on the streets of Kathmandu this morning, and downtown shops were closed and shuttered. Asan Tole, the normally bustling marketplace in the center of town, was abandoned. Instead of the usual fruit and vegetable sellers, helmeted police stood among the ancient Hindu and Buddhist shrines.

Early this afternoon, bands of police wielding canes and bamboo shields combed Kathmandu's neighborhoods in search of potential demonstrators. Dozens of young men were pulled from their homes and shops, herded onto trucks, and driven away to undisclosed locations.

At 4 P.M., Haribol Bhattarai—the Mayor of Kathmandu, suspended from office because of his ties with the pro-democracy Nepal Congress Party—appeared on a downtown street. He was accompanied by two supporters. The men chanted anti-government slogans and waved black flags. They were immediately arrested, and dragged off to prison.

Moments later Mahesh Dixit, a 55-year-old journalist, emerged from his hiding place one block away. A solitary figure, the renowned writer waved a black flag as scores of Nepalis shouted encouragement from windows up and down the street. Dixit was surrounded by police, beaten across the legs with bamboo canes, and taken away.

Other demonstrations are planned for the remainder of this week. A nationwide bandh, or general strike, will occur on Friday.

—END—

I PUNCHED THE "save" button and ejected the diskette from my laptop.

"You better grab some of these." Grace pointed to the plate on the night table. Stale french fries lay in a murk of ketchup. The hotel bed was cluttered with camera bodies, empty film canisters, wadded-up lens tissue, peanut packets, and batteries. "The Reuters guy said they're closing the kitchen at six. Did you order anything?"

"No. You think they have a printer downstairs?"

"No printer, no fax. The hotels are under orders not to fax stuff for foreign journalists. You'll have to use Coal's if you want to send that story tonight."

Taking a room at the New Diamond had been Grace's idea. It was a stroke of genius. Along with a desk, telephone, and functioning toilet,

the hotel provided a bird's-eye view of the city center. Through Grace's
aggressive charm, our room had become an informal gathering point for
the foreign press corps. Tonight there'd be a rumpus. There was something
sophomoric about the scene; I was reminded of my college days, and the
nightly high jinks in the dorms.

And while the reporters were drinking Johnnie Walker, where would
the local teens be? Packed into a flooded dungeon below Singha Durbar,
knee-deep in cold water. Blood on their shirts. My bone-dry article recorded,
as dispassionately as possible, the events I'd witnessed earlier in the day. If
I hadn't conveyed the horror, I'd tasted it. Racing down Sukhrapath alongside the riot police, I'd felt like a squirrel running with wolves. I kept up
with the pack, always a few steps back, trying to remain invisible, waiting
in the street as they flooded through narrow doorways and raided private
homes. It was always the same scene: a wife's or mother's voice, screaming
from within, the sounds of a scuffle, and the huddle of troops squeezing
back outside, a young man with a bloody nose or split lip pressed between
them, staggering on tiptoe as they held him up by his hair.

Similar scenes, and worse, were being played out across the kingdom.
Kids were being beaten up, imprisoned, shot. Right in front of us. The press,
of course, enjoyed total immunity. It was an accepted convention that we
belonged in the center of the action, that we had permission to tag along,
snapping pictures and jotting down notes as teenagers got caned in the
teeth.

I wanted to rewrite my whole fucking article. But there wasn't time, and
it wouldn't run if I did.

"When does curfew start?"

Grace looked at her watch. ' One hour. It's six now. You can hurry up
and come back, or just go home if you want. I don't think anything's going
to happen tonight. I'm staying, in any case."

"Should be cozy. Is the gal from Agence France-Presse here tonight,
too?" I stood up and stretched; my spine made a sound like popping bubble
wrap.

"She managed to get her own room, so we could have this one to
ourselves."

I picked up a french fry, dragged it over the edge of the plate to scrape off the ketchup, and threw it into my mouth. "What about the BBC guy?"

"Across the hall."

I walked to the window. Kathmandu lies at the same latitude as Daytona Beach, and though this was February it was still bright outside. The intersection of New Road, Dharmapath, and Sukhapath, visible from our seventh-floor window, was virtually empty. Half a dozen riot police slouched on the pedestal of the Jung Bahadur Rana statue. The monument to the nineteenth-century despot, whose reign had been marked by assassinations and political chaos, seemed an appropriate perch for the goons.

I turned around. Grace had finished off the fries. "I'm on my way."

"Better call first," she suggested. "They might not be home."

"Where else would they be?" But I reached for the phone. It rang three times. I braced myself for the machine, but Coal picked up.

"Hey, Coal, it's me. I'm down at the Diamond. The hotels won't transmit anything, and curfew starts at seven. Can I come over and fax from your place?"

"This might not be the best time, old chap."

"What's going on?"

"Perhaps you'd better ask Clarice. Let me get her, she's right underneath me . . . Clarice, sweetheart, are we . . . oooooh . . . are we too busy to talk?"

"Give me a break," I snorted. "Do you always answer the phone during sex?"

"Of course. One never knows who might be calling. This morning it was the British Consulate. Just after lunch it was my Hong Kong silk supplier. But this time, alas, it is only you."

Who knew when to take him seriously? It was quite likely Clarice was beside him in bed, naked and giggling; it was equally possible she was outside feeding the dogs, while Coal sipped tea in the living room.

I realized, with a start, that Coal reminded me of my brother. Like Jordan, he was a social prankster: always testing, always teasing, always eager to shock.

I vividly recalled a weekend, nearly fifteen years ago, when I was a senior at UC Santa Cruz. Jordan had taken the Greyhound from Bishop to spend a few days with me. I wasn't sure when he was arriving. At three o'clock on Friday afternoon, the phone rang.

"*Meet me at the bus stop.*" Jordan whispered, all but inaudibly, into the receiver.

Deep Springs was an unusual school. Along with his academic load, Jordan was learning how to brand cattle, shear sheep, and butcher his own meat. My own extracurricular experiences were quite different. During my first semester at Santa Cruz I'd attended an all-night Woody Allen festival, learned how to repair a two-stroke Yamaha, and dropped acid for the first time. During the trip I'd gotten hungry and tried to fry myself an egg—but the yolk had a blood spot, and I freaked out. My brother, meanwhile, was castrating calves.

I arrived at the bus station and saw Jordan at once. He wore a jean jacket and was gesticulating in an odd manner at a man feeding a pay phone. The man dug into his pocket, pulled out a few coins, and handed them to my brother with an irritated expression.

"Jordan! *Jord!*" I waved both arms as he pocketed the change. He gave no sign of hearing me. When I approached, he smiled broadly but said nothing.

"How the hell are ya?" I hadn't seen him in two years.

He continued grinning but nodded blankly, placing a hand on my shoulder and guiding me toward the bus.

"It's 50 cents. Do you have enough change?"

He nodded emphatically and boarded first, paying both our fares. As we moved toward the rear of the bus, we walked past my psycholinguistics teacher. I introduced my brother. Jordan nodded and shook the man's hand, but offered no verbal greeting. I covered the awkward lapse and fell into a seat near the broad rear window.

"What's wrong? Have you got laryngitis?"

Jordan shook his head briskly and reached into his shirt pocket. He handed me a faded, yellow card printed with blue ink. It bore this message:

Hello!

I am a deaf person

I am selling this

Deaf Education System

card to make my living.

WILL YOU KINDLY BUY ONE?

Pay any price you wish!

Thank you!

On the back was a series of drawings illustrating the "American Single-Hand Manual Alphabet for the Deaf": twenty-six hand gestures, each symbolizing a different letter.

I regarded him with confusion. "What are you doing with this?"

He tapped the card with his finger and launched into a spasm of hand movements, too rapid for me to follow. Then he patted the pocket of his coat. It was the Ghost of Christmas Past: a hearty, sustained jingle.

I pieced things together gradually. Arriving in town hours ago, he had been accosted by a deaf-mute soliciting donations. Jordan bought the card for a quarter. He mastered the simple language immediately. From noon until three he had canvassed Pacific Avenue, raking in contributions. He'd already reclaimed the cost of his bus fare from Bishop to Santa Cruz, and was working toward the goal of a round-trip air ticket to Tel Aviv. He did not doubt he could achieve this—but doing so would require total immersion in his role.

This meant, in short, that there would be no speaking at all: neither in public nor in private. Not to my friends, and not to me. "We can at least exchange written notes," I pleaded, facing him directly to facilitate lip reading. "Will you accept that?"

He nodded, jotted something on the back of his bus transfer, and handed it to me. *If you'd like to spend tomorrow working together,* he'd written, *I'll find you a white cane.*

He didn't speak a word for the next three days. The situation was initially tiresome, but the rhythm of writing notes soon appealed to me. I enjoyed the prevailing silence around my brother and, as always, the arcane tone of his prose. It was like having a live-in pen pal.

I had decided, years ago, that I would always back up my brother during his daredevil pranks. Such petty ruses now came naturally to me. My dorm mates quickly adapted to my brother's deafness; in fact, it gave me a bit of panache. When they asked why I hadn't mentioned his condition earlier, I shrugged; I hadn't wanted them to harbor any preconceptions.

Jordan, meanwhile, nurtured his role with unwavering fortitude. He spent his first afternoon in the university library, poring through Amslan manuals. During his second day in Santa Cruz, I was astonished to run into him after my fencing class. He was sitting behind a spinach salad at a campus coffee shop, engaged in lively conversation with the half-dozen members of the campus deaf-mute society. Not one of them, he later assured me, suspected his infirmity was a sham.

Before returning to Deep Springs, my brother did some soul searching. He wondered, reasonably, if it made sense for him to go back to school at all. I understood his dilemma; in two days, he had cleared $513.44 in charitable donations.

Jordan was capable of that kind of thing. Coal had a narrower range, and he wasn't fond of taking risks—not on that level. But the dry wit, the sarcasm, the deadpan delivery: there were similarities.

I WALKED TO the hotel room window, telephone still in hand, anchoring myself in time and space. The riot police still stood in the intersection below, as carefully spaced as synchronized swimmers.

"Listen," I said. "I called for a reason . . ."

"Do you remember what it was? I certainly don't."

"Can I come by and fax my story?"

"Of course. Come by. Bring the lovely Miss Modena. We've rented a video. You can crash on the couch if you like. Better still, I'll ask Clarice if she's keen for a foursome. Not for your benefit, mind you."

"Of course not. I'm sure Clarice will thank you for it."

He barked, "You're quick for a Yank. I was about to suggest that Grace may enjoy a change."

This was a surprise; I hadn't told Coal that Grace and I were lovers. She must have spoken to him herself.

"Not yet. I hope. Anyhow, Grace is staying here at the hotel, and I need to get back too. It'll be a short visit."

"Ah, well. I suppose we'll just have to nurse the Bushmills by ourselves."

"Save me a shot. I'll need it."

I hung up the phone and grabbed a motorcycle helmet from the dresser top. "See you later."

Grace put her hands on either side of my face. "Wow. So smooth." She rubbed her lips against my cheeks, then kissed me on the lips. "Try to come back in one piece."

A tight spiral of steps descended to the lobby. I'd mothballed my Hero bicycle and rented a sporty Honda CG125 in its place. It was parked half a block away. I walked with my helmet under my arm, nodding to the riot troops. They regarded me in silence. There was a veldtlike feel to the scene: The hapless herbivore moves across the plain, observed by a pack of hyenas. A single shouted command, possible at any moment, could ruin my whole day.

The bike started instantly. I began to put my helmet on, but on second thought strapped it to the frame. Kathmandu had a helmet law—but on this occasion I opted for recognition over safety. These troops had grown up around foreigners. In these conditions, I gambled, they'd grant me an extra margin of respect.

It was a lonely, exhilarating ride. The sun was setting behind Nagarjun, and the air had a gunmetal sheen. Fruit bats filled the sky. There was no traffic at all. Flatbed trucks were parked at all the major intersections, filled with card-playing soldiers. The troops scrambled to their feet as I approached, then waved me on with greetings and catcalls.

"*Pheri auncchu!*" I called out. "I'm coming back!" They laughed and shouted back: "*Pheri bertola!*" See you later!

Fools. Mahesh Dixit, the journalist they'd tossed in prison, was far less a threat to the venal regime that they served. But the color of my skin gave me right of passage. For the first time in my travels, I was glad to be an outsider.

13

In Person

I'VE LONG BEEN intrigued by the concept of parallel universes: the theory that at this very moment, in other dimensions, alternate realities are unfolding. I stand at the kitchen counter, drinking a glass of orange juice. Meanwhile, in a few of those infinite parallel dimensions, other versions of me are ironing a shirt, walking my six-year-old daughter to school, or preparing an optics experiment on the space shuttle.

In Nepal, parallel universes are not theory. They exist in plain sight, for all to see. As riot troops patrolled the streets and thousands of citizens languished in prison, the spiritual life of the Kathmandu Valley continued unimpeded, as it had done through centuries of upheaval, assassinations, and overturned regimes.

The sense of multiple realities felt especially sharp that February. Thanks to the vagaries of the lunar calendar, two major festivals—one Hindu, one Buddhist—followed on each other's heels. The madness of Shivaratri had barely ended; now Lhosar, the three-day Tibetan New Year festival, was about to begin.

Grace had decided to stay another day and night at the New Diamond. She was in her element among the other reporters (some of whom could use her images with their stories). For me, the cultural aspect of Kathmandu was as compelling as the political. It was, after all, what had bonded me to Nepal in the first place. I also felt a budding inner tension between my role

as a journalist and my opportunity to get closer to Buddhism. The goal was
to do both, if possible, in something more than a half-assed fashion.

THOUGH LHOSAR'S CLIMACTIC celebration was still two days away, the
Boudha kora was already jammed with devotees. I walked clockwise over
the cobblestones, navigating among dogs, goats, and scattered fecal haz-
ards. Scores of mendicants had already claimed their spots on the circular
path that surrounds the enormous stupa. Kindly souls filled their begging
bowls with boiled potatoes, cooked rice, and coins. I stopped at a shop and
changed a few bills into paisa. These I distributed liberally, following the
kora until I reached the path leading toward the Ka-Nying Shedrup Ling
Monastery.

A significant number of shoes lay outside the entrance to Chokyi
Nyima's assembly room. I removed my sneakers, feeling a familiar mix
of thrill and dread. This time, I was prepared; there was a kata scarf in
my hand, and a small gift for the lama. Parting the heavy cloth curtain, I
stepped into the room.

The Rinpoche sat cross-legged on a carpet-covered couch. A dozen
students occupied the floor around him. They stirred to view me as I
approached.

A tall, pale, and very thin woman knelt by the lama's side. She was
slitting envelopes open and handing him the day's mail. When he spied me
the Rinpoche placed his hands together and extended his lips in a comical
pout.

"Oooooh! Mr. Giraffe! Isn't it? Come on, come on; hurry!" He signaled me forward with a rapid hand-flutter. I approached, knelt, and placed
the silk kata across his outstretched hands.

"Very good! Learn fast!" The Rinpoche leaned forward and draped
the scarf around my neck. He then reached into a cloth bag and extracted
a few tiny, turdlike pellets, which he sprinkled into the palm of my right
hand. "Eat," he commanded. I popped them unquestioningly into my
mouth. They tasted bitter, almost acrid. "*Men-drub*," he explained with
satisfaction.

I chewed, wincing. "Rinpoche . . . what is this?"

He nodded. "Means two things. *Men* is herbs. Natural herbs. *Drub* means, we do a ten-day puja And we mix these herbs with many holy things: ground bone and relics of past buddhas."

"Bones . . . okay . . . what else?"

"Not necessary to know!" Chokyi Nyima declared. "If a doctor gives you a pill and says it will cure headache, you accept; it's more easy than asking what's inside!"

"Well, then, can you at least tell me the purpose of the medicine?"

"The purpose is to make the mind clean and clear. We call this *nyong drol*: 'eating liberation.'" I raised my eyebrows. "I'm not joking! Liberation through eating. Meaning, it makes a karmic connection. So even if we cannot be liberated in this lifetime eating such holy things will sooner or later connect us with a holy teacher or teachings."

Years of travel through Asia, and the osmosis that occurs when one blunders into enough Buddhist temples, had made me familiar with the concept of karma: the Buddhist view of cause and effect, in which every deed that we perform ripens, over a period of lifetimes, into a positive or negative result. On a global scale, this chain of deeds and consequences is what keeps the wheel of samsara—life on Earth—turning. And it's not just our deeds that carry weight; the intentions behind them are even more important. Only a deed that is free of impure thoughts, a deed not rooted up in greed, anger, or self-interest, is without karmic impact.

"I have something for you, too." I handed the Rinpoche a small parcel, wrapped in rice paper.

"Oh! A present! Very nice!" He removed the paper and looked at the gift with a baffled expression. "What's this?"

"Jazz," I explained. "Music. I think you'll like it." I'd found the Miles Davis tape a few days earlier, at the Annapurna Cassette Emporium: *In Person, Friday Night at the Blackhawk*. It was one of my favorites, and the Rinpoche already had enough tangerines.

"Very good, very good." He placed it on the couch beside him. "We listen later. Okay? Now, business. You are working here?"

"Yes, Rinpoche." I wondered what aspect of my life could possibly be of interest to a liberated lama. "I'm a journalist. I write for an American newspaper. I'm reporting on Nepal's democracy movement, and waiting to see if there's going to be a revolution." It sounded so lame, pronounced out loud.

"Yes, I know. Dr. Dan told me this. So, what do you think? Revolution coming or not?"

I shrugged, uncomfortable on my knees. "It's hard to say. Many people feel angry towards the king and the government. Personally, though, I don't think the revolution will come very soon. There's too much fear. A few people have already been shot, and thousands of people are in prison. There are reports of torture and other human rights abuses. Have you heard about any of this?"

"Little hear. Sometime on radio we hear. Mostly not hearing. Newspaper never say anything." He turned to his assistant. "Rebecca? You hear?" She shook her head rapidly, as though an admission of political awareness would cast doubt upon her single-minded devotion to the dharma. "No one hear," Chokyi Nyima concluded. "No one see. Difficult to see. For big view, far view, what need? Hmm? What need?" I said nothing. "Long neck! So! Must be giraffe!" He returned his attention to his mail.

I stepped back, finding a place among the other students. Despite his offhanded dismissal of the kingdom's political turmoil, I understood the Rinpoche's concern. Tibet, Nepal's northern neighbor, had been occupied by the Chinese since the 1950s. Thousands of Tibetan refugees were living in Nepal, with more arriving each month. They were permitted to live, work, and practice their religion in Nepal. But what if Nepal's government changed? A new regime might seek closer ties with China. Such a relationship might bode ill for the Tibetan community, from carpet merchants to incarnate lamas.

The Rinpoche had received about a dozen letters, mainly from Europe. A few were picture postcards: Earthrise over the moon, a sea otter, a Georgia O'Keeffe flower. Others were friendly letters, containing gifts of money. Some were requests for blessings. But many were litanies of woe, from students in distress.

"*Dear Rinpoche . . . Meditation practice is not going well . . . I feel much fear . . . I cannot stop blaming myself for my faults . . .*" Chokyi

Nyima nodded gravely as each of these letters was read aloud, promising to answer the most dire cases as soon as his Lhosar obligations had ended.

Listening to the plaintive letters, I thought of Jordan. Despite my earlier misgivings, I suddenly wished he were here. My own travels in Asia had taught me, first and foremost, how vast and complex the world was. I'd seen true suffering and learned to put my own trials in perspective. Most important, my travels gave me a visceral sense of belonging to the Earth; of sharing a spiritual bond, and maybe even a spiritual destiny, with every creature on the planet. The idea of a wrathful, Judeo-Christian God had been replaced with a more objective truth: that we are all interdependent, yet individually responsible for our own liberation.

The core of Jordan's problem, I realized, was that he had no *community*. He had no anchorage. There was nothing in the universe larger than himself. Intellectual and romantic adventures sustained his existence; to fail them was to fail at life. With those supports cracking, his world was falling apart.

I wasn't naïve enough to think that simply visiting Asia, or sitting with Chokyi Nyima, would be a cure-all. My brother might well end up like one of the Rinpoche's fretful pen pals, wrestling with the demons of inadequacy and discontent. But at least he would have a foundation. He would be on an effective path, a proven escape route from the labyrinth of self-involvement. And if he stuck with it, took his spiritual growth half as seriously as he took his translations of Cicero, who knew what he might attain?

Chokyi Nyima put away his letters and whispered to Rebecca. She rose silently and left the room. The Rinpoche turned toward us.

"So. Last time we talk about basic conditions: suffering, impermanence, emptiness, egolessness. Everybody check? Everybody test? Hmmm?"

It was a joke, and there was laughter, as if a week of superficial introspection could relieve us—the generation of Reagan and Thatcher, Disney and Madonna—of the burdens of dualistic existence.

"It takes time," the Rinpoche acknowledged. "But have no doubt. If you study carefully, meditate well, all true." He glanced at his watch. "Today, though, we have only small time. So. Some questions?"

A stocky Japanese man, whose tight jeans prevented him from crossing his legs, spoke up. "You often talk about meditation," he said. "But you never tell us how to do it."

"Meditation, in Tibetan, means *gom*," the Rinpoche replied. "Direct translation is 'mental work.' Meditation is really a set of techniques: 'gross' techniques and 'subtle' techniques."

The man frowned. "How can there be a 'gross' technique in meditation?"

"Sounds, funny, yes?" Chokyi Nyima surveyed the room. "*Gross*. Like, big. Or maybe ugly. But true! It's because, for beginners, all ways of perceiving the world are dualistic. They come from the habit of holding objects in our mind. Therefore, one kind of meditation is to keep an object in our mind. A simple object, like a pebble or flower. Or our breath. Because when we focus our mind on one thing, it isn't occupied by anything else. We are not planning future, worrying about past, feeling angry, wanting love, getting jealous. So by meditating on just one thing, very simple, very small, it is possible for a feeling of peace and relaxation to take place.

"This is what's meant by 'gross' techniques. This is one form of meditation. But it is not the ultimate meditation. That's because as long as we focus on some other object—even breath!—we have two ideas: the one who focuses, and the object of focus. The real meditation is without *any* object. This is the 'subtle' technique of meditation. But to reach that stage, we first need to use 'gross' concepts."

"It sounds like a lot of effort," the student remarked, "for a state of peace."

The Rinpoche stared at him mischievously. "Maybe. The very best method, of course, is effortlessness. But effortlessness cannot be taught! So, at first, we have no choice but to use our bad habits to help us. We have to use effort, in order to arrive at effortlessness."

The student shook his head. "This technique you're describing . . . it's so *intellectual*."

Chokyi Nyima nodded. "Right now, this is difficult to understand. But as we get more teachings, our minds become more subtle. Here's one example . . ."

"Stop!" The Japanese man slapped his hand sharply on the floor. "I don't want words! I want to know how to meditate! I want to know this *now*."

There was a startled silence in the room. "Of course," Chokyi Nyima replied calmly. "Nobody likes to cook. But everyone wants the best food. *Immediately*. None of us want to study; we want to be liberated. But what we need to experience for liberation is very subtle. And for anything so subtle, we need to study. We need to *listen*. Sometimes it takes time. It all depends on the person. For you? You want to meditate, but you have no time to study. You want liberation, but you have no time to listen. That way will not work. What you want to experience, you first need to study."

"Just tell me what to *do*."

"Eat and shit!" declared the Rinpoche, slapping his own hand down.

A beat followed, and then the student's timid reply: "While thinking of food and shit as illusions?"

Chokyi Nyima laughed. There was a collective exhalation, and the tension drained from the room. "Seriously, though. There is one thing to do: *relax*. Even Buddha did not say more than this: 'Rest calmly.' But, one problem. We don't know *how* to relax.

"Right now, even if we think we are relaxing, we're not. We're *thinking*." Chokyi Nyima closed his eyes and assumed a strict lotus posture, wagging his head in mock rapture. "*I want to relax. Now I am relaxing. Oohhh. So relaxed.*" He opened his eyes.

"This is the ego, the 'I' speaking. From very beginning this is a dualistic idea. Second problem: *I am relaxing*. Can this be true?" He looked around the room. "No! It is impossible. Because complete relaxation is not dualistic. There is no object, no subject, no 'I.' When there is no ego, only then are we 100 percent relaxed."

A moment passed as this deceptively complex teaching was absorbed.

"Okay? So when you practice, please remember: Meditation is the *opposite* of the ordinary state of mind. It is the opposite of the state of mind that thinks, *I am here, and the world is out there*."

Rebecca returned from her assigned errand, carrying a small paper bag. The lama nodded at her, placed the bag inside the fold of his robe, and scanned the room for fresh queries. I raised my hand. The Rinpoche nodded.

"What," I asked, "is enlightenment?"

A few people chuckled, but I wasn't offended. I suspected this was a query most of them had raised themselves in private, if not at the open teachings.

"Hmmm." Chokyi Nyima elongated his lower lip. "Many people, all the time, say, 'Enlightenment, enlightenment.' But who knows what enlightenment is? Hmm?" He gestured to me. "What do you think?"

"Me?" I fumbled for words. "Well . . . On the one hand, I think it's just a state of mind: the ability to see the world as it is, without preconceptions." The Rinpoche nodded. "On the other hand, it seems like a kind of mental field goal . . ."

"A what?"

". . . a prize. An explosion of light, and a dozen buddhas swooping out of the sky on flaming rainbows to shake your hand and buy you lunch."

Chokyi Nyima nodded. He shifted his legs beneath him, rocking slightly from side to side. "Okay. Let's make it simple. The Tibetan word for enlightenment is *sang gye*. *Sang* means 'purified.' All disturbing emotions and ignorance are purified. Then, *gye*. *Gye* means that all the qualities associated with enlightenment—wisdom and compassion—are perfected. So *enlightened* means 'fully purified and perfected.' Do you understand?"

I mumbled my consent, and the Rinpoche continued.

"Disturbing emotions, and ignorance: These are bad. Wisdom is good. So our main job, in this precious human lifetime, is to purify all our negative emotions, and fully develop wisdom. When this happens—when one is fully purified, fully perfected—one becomes a buddha.

"That is the meaning of enlightenment. Simple meaning!" The Rinpoche grinned. "Complicated meaning I have, also. But not right now." He craned his neck and surveyed the other students. "Okay? Other question?"

No one responded, so I decided to make a nuisance of myself.

"Listening to your letters," I said, "made me uncomfortable. You clearly have a lot of students who are trying to meditate and purify their emotions. But they're miserable! All they want is to be happy, or relaxed. But something's holding them back. What is it? What's keeping them from becoming happy?"

"That's a very good question. No?" Chokyi Nyima peered at Rebecca, who nodded eagerly. "The main obstacles to awakening," he said, "are hope and fear. These arise directly from the ego: from the illusion that 'I' exists." He held one hand palm-down over the coffee table, and pointed at the resulting shadow. "The hand is like the ego. This, the shadow, is hope and fear. Without the hand, no shadow. Without ego, no hope or fear. Understand?" I nodded. "Good! So. Hope and fear are big problems. The *biggest* problems. But they are not the enemy!" He paused. "Who? Who is our real enemy?"

Five people answered in unison. "Ego!" They looked so pleased with themselves that I had to laugh.

"Ego," Chokyi Nyima affirmed. "The one who *really* disturbs us is our ego. And that is within ourselves.

"If you have an ego, you cling to *me*. Then, automatically, some kind of *you* is created. And *you* is not *me*! That duality creates a subtle fear—and a subtle anger arises, as well. Because the very idea of *me* creates a kind of selfishness. This is the cause of many types of negative emotion: anger, envy, greed. It can create extreme problems. So the root is right there, in *me*. It is not a small root!

"Buddha showed the truth: the cause of samsara, of rebirth and suffering, is ego. The cause of nirvana, of liberation, is wisdom, or egolessness. Wisdom is within us; ego is also within us. We are good; we are bad. We are demons; we are buddhas. We contain the cause of samsara; we contain the cause of nirvana. Both are within ourselves! Isn't it?" He surveyed the group with raised eyebrows.

"Now enough. Time finished. Go enjoy yourself. Practice well, and don't get drunk!" He grinned broadly, like a cartoon egg. "Lhosar comes, everyone drinks *chang*, falls down steps. Okay?" The students rose, favoring their knees.

The Rinpoche turned to me. "You! Stay one minute. The rest can go." He waved them out. "Happy Lhosar!"

As THE ROOM emptied, Chokyi Nyima picked up the bag that Rebecca had brought and removed a small stack of greeting cards. He flipped through them, finally finding the one he was looking for.

"Okay!" The lama beamed with satisfaction. "You give a gift, I also give. This is for you." He held the card out with both hands, ceremoniously.

I reddened. "Rinpoche, it's really not necessary . . ."

"Take, take!" He pushed it into my hands and closed my fingers around it. "You keep in your room. Make frame, put on wall. Very beautiful!"

I looked at the card. It was a view of the African savanna. In the foreground, a giraffe nibbled at the high branches of a tree.

"If ever forget what you look like, look at this. Okay? Okay? *Ha ha ha ha ha!*"

I accepted the gift with thanks. Life was very strange. Who could have predicted that my initiation into Tibetan Buddhism would include this kind of mockery? I had no idea why the Rinpoche was lavishing his attention on me, or why it was taking this particular form. Still, I wasn't going to discourage him. After only two meetings, we had developed a relationship. It delighted me. Shouldering a nickname (of a rather elegant and attractive animal, if the truth be told) was a small price to pay.

I stood up. Chokyi Nyima rose as well, taking his mobile phone from the couch. "Now lunch," he informed me, adjusting his robes. "Then puja. Lhosar time, so many pujas! Giraffe . . . You come next Saturday, also. A little early, so we can talk. Maybe 9:30. Yes?"

"Yes." I took his hand, affection welling through me. "Thank you, Rinpoche. Have a wonderful New Year."

He smiled. "If you come to Boudha on Lhosar, after three days, please visit. Just to say hello. I give special blessing. Many people are coming. We'll drink *chang*!" The Rinpoche released my hand and left for his quarters, closing the door behind him.

14

Swayambhunath

WHEN THE TEACHING ended I jumped onto my motorcycle, hoping to reach the American Express office before it closed for lunch.

My ride from Boudha to downtown Kathmandu passed in a giddy adrenaline rush. Cars wove between oncoming traffic; the lines in the road might as well have been painted by Jackson Pollock. Piles of garbage punctuated the intersections, grazed at by bulls and cows who could, at any instant, lumber into my path. Driving required the concentration of a complex pinball game, but a single mistake might spell death. I zipped along in a state of sublime awareness, eyes gazing straight ahead, my peripheral vision twitching: meditation at gunpoint.

The door to American Express was open. A single envelope awaited, addressed in a familiar hand. The arrival of a second communication from Jordan within one week spooked me; I hadn't even responded to the first.

Normally, I'd trot over to the Nanglo and read the letter right away. This time, it seemed best to wait I needed some spiritual protection, a layer of insulation to blunt my anxiety about Jordan's condition and help me fashion a response. On an impulse I decided to drive up to Swayambhunath: the famous "Monkey Temple" on the northwest edge of town.

I TOOK THE crosstown route, circling the bandstand at Chhetrapati. The usually vibrant neighborhood was quiet. A teacher's strike was in progress;

people were lying low. I crossed the Vishnumati on a wooden bridge, climbed past the Vajra Hotel, and continued along a narrow, tree-lined road that led to the foot of the ancient temple's stairway. The northern fields of the valley lay to my right, vivid green, ending abruptly at the foothills of the Himalaya. Swayambhunath loomed ahead: a high, wooded hill, crowned by the white snowball of the temple's dome.

Two street urchins skipped toward me as I parked beside the temple's arched gate. Their palms were out, demanding protection money. We agreed on 5 rupees: 2 in advance, and 3 when I reclaimed my bike, with tires and mirrors intact.

The final approach to the temple is a climb of more than three hundred steep stone steps, worn into deep grooves by the feet of countless pilgrims. After eleven years I was intimate with the route and gratified by the unchanging procession of Buddha statues, *mani* stones, and shrines that lined the way. Seeing them reminded me of my first visit to Nepal, and the overwhelming mystery embodied by these sacred stones and their hand-painted eyes. I'd shot hundreds of photos in an effort to possess the place, somehow imagining that it could escape, or that I could somehow lose it.

Monkeys leaped through the trees, dropping down to pilfer discarded mango skins, pick lice from their coats, and generally terrorize each other. If these were Hanuman's cousins, something in the gene pool had gone horribly awry. Despite their nasty, aggressive nature, the primates were usually harmless—as long as you didn't try to sneak past them with a sack of bananas.

The final section pitched steeply upward, more a ladder than a stairway. Statues of the five divine vehicles—a bird-woman, peacock, horse, elephant, and lion—watched impassively as I clung to the metal handrail, pulling myself upward.

Reaching the summit, I paused to catch my breath, staggered a few steps forward, and touched my forehead to an enormous bronze *vajra*: a highly stylized thunderbolt that, symbolizing the indestructible clarity of the awakened mind, rested on a circular pedestal at the crest of the stairs. The vajra's base was surrounded by a group of Nepali teenagers wearing designer jeans and smoking Yak cigarettes. Behind and above them, the great white dome of Swayambhunath's stupa rose into the sky. Deep inside are the sacred relics of revered lamas, and perhaps cremation bones from the Buddha himself. No one knows for sure. The stupa is inviolable; there is no access to its innermost chamber.

Swayambhu (the *nath* adds "place of worship") truncates in a broad, flat plaza, dominated by the gigantic white stupa: the oldest relic of the valley's creation. After Manjushri had raised his sword and drained the primordial lake (the surface of which had been graced, you will recall, by a flaming lotus), the flower's root system condensed to form a hill. Atop the hill sat Swayambhu: the flower's inner flame, now crystallized into a radiant gem. The Newars who settled the valley became the jewel's custodians. One of their first gestures was to cover it with a white stupa, sometime around the fourth century. The point was to protect the gem from a predicted "Age of Confusion"—an era that, I strongly suspect, is currently in progress.

Swayambhu's dome isn't as big as Boudha's. But its location, commanding a view of the entire valley, is stunning. On clear days the Langtang and Ganesh Himalaya tower above the northern foothills, blinding white against the shimmering sky.

To the left of the big bronze vajra is a flagstone courtyard. Pilgrims and visitors can relax in the plaza, eat peanuts, and take in the view. Today there was something new: a local entrepreneur had set up a small telescope and was charging 5 rupees for a look through the lens. I paid the fee and swung the scope away from the mountaintops. After a minute I located Nag Pokhari, a few arc-seconds beyond the palace. My neighborhood shrine seemed inconsequential at this distance: a tiny square of gray-green felt, with a spark of gold teetering in its center. A slight nudge upward was my house, all but hidden behind quivering trees. Familiar blips of color hung on the clothesline.

And there was Grace's flat. Or was hers the one with two water tanks on the roof?

A pair of Indian honeymooners waited behind me; the groom cleared his throat. I readjusted the scope and stepped off the viewing platform. Jordan's letter crinkled in my pocket, feeling like something alive.

Swayambhu is covered with a maze of buildings, temples, and shrines. I began my circumambulation, walking clockwise around the stupa. Burnished prayer wheels snaked around the perimeter of the dome, punctuated by small niches containing figures of buddhas and various saints. I spun the heavy drums—creaking copper cylinders as plump and warm as Thanksgiving turkeys—and tossed coins into the laps of the gods.

HALFWAY AROUND THE dome is a compact, two-story temple built in typical Nepali style, with gilt pagoda rooftops and carved wooden lintels. The little Hariti temple is usually packed; despite its small size, it's the most popular temple on the hill.

Hariti was an ogress who lived during Buddha's time. She had five hundred children, and in an effort to feed them, she routinely kidnapped other children and added them to her menu. The population appealed to Buddha, who agreed to help. One day, while Hariti was out hunting, Buddha turned the table: He abducted the ogress's youngest baby and hid him in a begging bowl.

Hariti returned home to find her baby gone. Mad with anguish, she searched the world for him . . . but in vain. Finally she, too, appeared on Buddha's doorstep. Buddha returned her child, but pointed out that the parents of Hariti's victims had suffered the very same way. The abashed Hariti pledged to reform.

Within the week, though, Hariti ran out of food. The ogress again accosted Buddha, demanding he find her an alternate source of provisions—or else. Buddha solved the problem by placing Hariti at the head of his retinue, giving her the pick of the abundant offerings passed his way.

Today, Hariti is known as Ajima: great-grandmother of the world. She is revered as the goddess of pediatrics and the protector of all children. And—after twenty-five hundred years—she still gets first dibs on Buddha's bounty. Before any offering is made at Swayambhunath, a portion must be left with Grandma Ajima.

All myths are parables, and I unraveled this one for a while. Despite the colorful touches, its main point seemed to be the importance of empathy: the shared experience of sadness and suffering, even when it's not our own. The insight made me draw a deep breath. Jordan had tried, often through bizarre means, to arouse his own sense of empathy. I liked to think it came to me naturally. But I'd fallen short when my own comfort zone had been threatened.

LAST MARCH, JORDAN had decided to abandon the East Coast and spend the spring in California. He'd been enrolled in Cornell's Department of Classics—a long-awaited return to his formal studies—but conflicts with the administration had forced him to leave the program. He needed to clear his head in a nonacademic setting. I invited him to stay with me at my Oakland apartment. He agreed.

My flat was spacious and bright, and I relished the prospect of sharing it with my brother. I'd introduce him to the marvels of the modern world: Zakir Hussain concerts, Italo Calvino novels, Pedro Almodóvar films. We'd talk politics over Vietnamese coffee; we'd rent mountain bikes and ride down the Bear Valley Trail at Point Reyes. Maybe we'd even double-date, escorting our girlfriends to virtuoso gigs at Yoshi's legendary jazz club.

Hell, yes! We'd be buddies! We'd borrow each other's shirts! We'd drink pale ale and drive to Lake Tahoe at two in the morning!

The truth was, I knew little about him. When I'd returned to America in 1984, after sixteen months in Nepal and Southeast Asia, I moved directly to the Bay Area. My contact with Jordan was limited to brief phone calls and the occasional visit home. His life during those past five years was a mystery to me. We'd been separated, as we were now, by great distances. There were letters and phone calls, but Jord was hard to read this way. The virtuoso missives and clipped conversations seemed more like caricatures than genuine engagement. It took face-to-face contact, and a real commitment, to get under his skin.

What I had learned, from my annual visits to the East Coast, was that his physical crisis had begun to overwhelm him. His interest in books, music, even language had flagged. He consulted urologists and neurologists, spending a small fortune in an effort to pinpoint his affliction. But these specialists found nothing wrong with him.

Jord's westward move struck me as an unconscious stroke of genius, an intuitive gravitation toward a cure. Even if he was suspicious of psychotherapy, the translucent air of the Bay Area would fix whatever ailed him. And if good fun and sea breezes weren't enough, I knew plenty of alternative healers who could poke, massage, or needle Jordan's chi back into shape.

At first, Jord's visit put me in high spirits. I bounced around the flat with ionic excitement, working under the assumption that a noisy, lively environment would act as a tonic. Friends dropped in constantly; popcorn exploded on the stove; bebop and Indian ragas spun through the air.

Jordan tolerated these activities, but he rarely joined in. He pined for the comfortable and familiar: a monastic cell in which to continue his studies. He was adrift in California, held captive by his manic brother. He'd snatch up his texts and retreat into my bedroom, mumbling with annoyance when the phone rang. The door slammed shut at the sound of my music.

My attempts to interest him in my literary world, the books I loved, hit a wall. He would not touch Kurt Vonnegut, Salman Rushdie, or Gabriel García Márquez. On one occasion I handed my brother a copy of *Wedding Song*, by Naguib Mahfouz. "You might enjoy this," I said. "This guy's an Egyptian. He just won the Nobel Prize for . . ."

"*Please.*" Jordan held up his hand in an arresting gesture. "There is no such thing as a *translation.*"

My notions of brotherly camaraderie had been absurd. Jordan had no interest in my life and made no effort to include me in his. He was mired in self-pity. A pall of ill-will infected our shared space. Worse, it was contagious. Was my existence as vacant as his behavior suggested? I began to suspect my own life. Maybe Cheerios *were* unhealthy, my towels too plush, my love for Alfred Hitchcock pedestrian.

One weekend morning, while cooking breakfast, I put John Coltrane on the stereo. *A Love Supreme*: an incredible album, the essence of reverence and invention. Jordan walked in from the living room and stood by the doorway of the kitchen. He inclined his head with curiosity. "Is this what your people call 'music'?"

I looked at him carefully. Was he joking? "I'm not clear what you mean by *my people*," I said, beating eggs with a fork, "but if you define the term as those of us who love jazz in general, and John Coltrane in particular, the answer would be yes. Yes. *My people* call this music. It *is* music." I poured the beaten eggs into a hot pan. "*Great* music."

"It's noise," Jordan replied. "A great deal of noise. I'll be taking my leave after breakfast. Might I prevail upon you to play some Bach or Albinoni—something with the hint of a tune—until then?"

I replaced the CD with a Vivaldi concerto and returned to my eggs, tight-lipped. After wolfing down a slice of wheat toast and dispatching the dishes, Jordan left for a run. There were no trails in my neighborhood; he jogged on the pathways of a nearby cemetery.

When he was gone I paced the apartment, feeling despondent. After all these years, I still yearned for his respect. Yet all my attempts to reach him, to share myself with him, were repelled. But how could I give up? We were still brothers, with a shared history. We'd shared a bedroom, played a thousand games of Ping-Pong, gone to the same schools. As kids we'd peed side by side into the same beige bowl. No matter how rough things got, could I really tell him to leave?

The doctors Jordan had visited on the East Coast found nothing wrong with him, and counseling—in his view—was out of the question. He decided to make one more attempt to find a physical cause for the extinction of his libido. After many calls, he was able to schedule an appointment with a neurologist in Berkeley. If this specialist could not divine his problem, Jordan said, he would succumb to despair.

"I can state without exaggeration," he declared, "that I have become the most wretched creature you have ever seen. No man, no beast, no creature of the sea is as wretched as I."

"Stop bragging," I said. "You sound ridiculous. And you're breathing new life into your problem with every word. Are you quite sure that a part of you doesn't thrive on the anguish, the poetic suffering?"

"It does not. And I add this: If there is no relief to this disability, I cannot abide another year. To love not is to live not. I shan't have one without the other."

Jordan's life, it struck me again, had been an experiment in disconnection: a deliberate distancing from humanity. But that had been by choice. Now he was being *forced* into isolation, and the prospect was terrifying. He was like a man who, in love with the solitude of the Scottish coast, suddenly found himself shipwrecked on a North Sea island.

"I respect your point of view," I nodded. "But you've barely begun to look for answers. Even if it takes years to work out, it's worth it. Whatever's going on with you can be fixed. I know it."

"I wish I shared your confidence," he snorted. "But when you're up to your *arse* in alligators, it's hard to remember . . ."

". . . that your main objective was to drain the swamp."

We laughed together, for the first time in weeks.

The results of his office visit were negative. The neurologist recommended psychotherapy. Jordan sank back into his morass, more embittered than ever. Once again I became an unwelcome guest in my own flat, self-conscious about my music, ashamed of my snacks, embarrassed by my love life. This could not go on.

On a damp April morning, I steeled myself and, as gently as possible, asked my brother to move. "Two weeks," I said. "I'd like you to find another place within two weeks." I knew he wouldn't be homeless. A classmate from Deep Springs lived in San Francisco's Richmond district and had invited Jordan to share his apartment.

"As you wish." He made no other response.

That afternoon I took a bike ride up into the Berkeley hills. When I returned, Jordan was gone. The sheets had been folded and shelved, his futon rolled up, the floor beneath his sleeping area swept clean. His oatmeal, bread, and Sanka were gone. Every trace of his presence had vanished.

He'd left no note. The next morning, though, I found the crumpled draft of a letter in the trash bin beneath my desk.

"The West Coast is lovely," Jordan had written. "The light is of Grecian intensity and the air, unlike the over-breathed miasma of New York, arrives refreshed by the sea. Rest assured, my decision to repair here carries with it no regrets.

"I have been boarding thus far with a relative. But I shall soon relocate to San Francisco, and stay with a friend."

A relative. As if our entire connection were based on nothing more than an accident of genetics. Jordan must have known that I would ferret through the trash, seeking a clue about his premature departure. His barb was well chosen. No schoolyard taunt, or reckless insult at the end of love, had ever wounded me more than those words.

NORTH OF THE Swayambhu kora stands a forest of small white shrines. I wandered between their neat rows. Just beyond them was Shantipur, one of the most enigmatic, inaccessible temples in Nepal.

The thick-walled white building now boasts a corrugated tin roof. Tiny windows are cut into each side, set well above the ground. A latticed wooden gate, secured with an ornate padlock, forbids entrance. Two men sat outside, playing checkers on a stone ledge. A brightly painted Buddha watched over them.

Pressing my face to the gate, I peered into the musty interior. Directly across the chamber was a soot-blackened altar. Two massive black doors—each painted with a wide-open eye—lay behind. On either side of the doors were murals illustrating the mythology of the valley—its origin as a lake, and the kingdom of the snake gods. Two massive brass locks of ancient manufacture sealed the door. It was the sort of barrier that Indiana Jones might encounter.

Shantipur was a well of tantric mysteries: secrets I'd never be privileged to share. But there was a direct relationship between this bolted temple and the murky pond near my home. They both concerned nagas, working their magic again.

The Shantipur myth unfolds eons ago, when a crippling drought parched Kathmandu Valley. In a bid to bring the monsoon rains, the nine great nagas were rounded up by a disciple of a saint named Shantikar. It took more than coaxing; Karkot Nagaraja, the serpent king, had to be kidnapped and brought to Kathmandu by force. Eventually, of course, the nagas complied, and rain filled the reservoirs. For this they were rewarded, with a teaching by the great saint himself. When the audience ended, these noble nagas paid homage to Shantikar. As a parting gift, they each drew portraits of themselves—using their own blood as ink. The paintings would serve as a kind of proxy, to be used at desperate times. When the images were worshipped, the snake gods claimed, the crucial rains would fall.

The snake blood paintings are sealed in a chamber, deep below the Shantipur doors. Six rooms must be crossed to reach them. Each is guarded by hungry spirits, hooded cobras, ogres, beasts, and other deadly obstacles. Once every few centuries—when drought threatens to parch the land—the king of Nepal purifies himself and unlocks the bolted doors of Shantipur. Armed with purity of intention, he makes his way into the temple's depths and recites the mantras on the ancient scrolls.

"No matter what's going on in your life," I'd written in *Shopping for Buddhas*, "if you walk down the streets of Kathmandu you'll run smack into a metaphor for it." The Hariti myth, which baldly reflected my shortfall with Jordan, seemed like an obvious prod. What Shantipur portended, I had no clue.

I RETURNED TO the kora. A Tibetan monastery stood on my left. I ducked in a doorway, climbed three flights of narrow steps, and emerged onto the roof: one of the highest perches on Swayambhu Hill. Red chrysanthemums stood in clay pots along a waist-high cement wall, and blue plastic pails were stacked in a corner. A dozen vivid yellow shirts—the monks' laundry—dripped from a line.

Thirty feet away, at eye level, the epiphany of the temple's dome—a square golden *harmika*, painted on each side with the half-lidded eyes of the Buddha—seemed close enough to touch. Above the golden cube was a majestic finial, as high again as the dome itself, composed of thirteen rings. Pigeons nested between these golden bands, which formed a high-rise aviary. At the tip of the cone, crowning the entire structure, an ornate gold parasol symbolized the Buddha's ultimate victory. From beneath this spire, cords of colorful prayer flags radiated downward in every direction. I pulled my brother's letter out of my jacket pocket.

> *Dear Jeff,*
> *Last month, vexed by dark thoughts, I complained to a friend that, while the gods had granted me profound knowledge on this earth, it happened to be sadness they had granted me knowledge of; to others it was given to know joy, or passion, or love; to me, sadness.*

I say to you now, brother, that the gods heard my complaint and have given me also to know love; but oh deep and bitter pity, as of a boon come long too late!

Last night this woman, her name is Lindsay, left for Maine; her parents live there, and the whole family is to gather for a week. While Lindsay awaited her departure at the airport, I, at home, pondered the emotion that lay upon my heart—not such an emotion as to prostrate me and make me wish to smother consciousness with sleep, but enough to baffle for an evening other thoughts and efforts; so that, as a geologist in his laboratory assays a new sample, I assayed my emotion. And I found it compounded, familiarly, of love and jealousy, but also of fear: not, this time, that I lose Lindsay, but that I win her—only to bring to grief one who so unquestioningly deserves to be happy. I knew that this dread argued my love genuine. And I knew also that, to the extent it reflected an actual difficulty—my unrelenting dysfunction—it argued my life pointless.

For I can no longer conceal from myself, not by pages read or miles run or hours spent in picture galleries, the fact that I am in decline. I have called the years of my affliction los años muertos, "the dead years." They have been exactly that; and this show of life has been but a danse macabre.

Lindsay indeed represents a chance at life, but I no longer believe it will "take" in my leached earth. I pound life into my lungs, my legs, ram it into my ears and eyes in the hope that if this dear woman entrusts herself to me, I have something in lungs and legs and mind to give her; for a certain thing I may never be able to give, at least as she and I could wish.

Adieu.

J.

I read the letter twice before folding it away. The birds and sunlight, the flags and stupa, returned to my consciousness in a sudden wave.

The urgency of my brother's crisis no longer seemed like an abstraction. I recalled a scene from the film *2001: A Space Odyssey*, in which one of the astronauts is knocked off a spaceship. He flails desperately, spinning into the blackness of space, as his companion mounts a grim rescue effort. Jordan was in an equally dire predicament. I had to reach out to him, whatever the risk or cost.

Then and there I made a decision. I would not extend my ticket. I would fly back to America in one week, on March 5: the date on my original round-trip ticket.

The choice was agonizing, but necessary. If the revolution seemed imminent, my reaction might have been different. But the Nepalis were clearly cowed by the recent crackdowns. It could be months, years even, before they worked up the courage to openly defy the king. Meanwhile, my brother was taking a beating. This latest letter was a naked plea for help.

I left the roof the way I'd come, at peace with my decision. I'd been in Kathmandu for five months. That was enough for now. If things reached a head politically, I would hurry back.

On the ground floor of the monastery, inside the altar room, rests a towering statue of Shakyamuni, the historical Buddha, who left his family and kingdom in 534 BC to win the "deathless state." I've always liked that statue; there's something in its eyes, a sort of omniscient grin, that appeals to me. Shakyamuni is awakened, but he doesn't beat you over the head with it. "Give it a try," he seems to be saying. The statue reminds me of the irresistible premise underlying all of Buddhist philosophy: that anyone, even a Bronx-born journalist, is a candidate for enlightenment.

In front of the statue is a broad wooden table, covered with small butter lamps. I lit the end of a long Q-tip-like wand and lit three of the candles: one for myself and the long journey ahead; one for Grace, whom I was starting to care about more than I dared admit; and a third for Jordan.

A strong draft gusted through the front door of the monastery, threatening my flames. I moved them to a sheltered corner of the table.

"Stay lit," I demanded, but they flickered precariously. The Gioconda Buddha watched from above, offering an ambiguous smile.

15

Nighttime in Hadigaon

A SWITCH, A SERIES of blinking flickers, the familiar fluorescent glare of a light table. There was just one stool in Grace's office nook, so I stood. The room was typical of the profession: cluttered with magazines, plastic photo sleeves, scraps of notepaper, cassette tapes, and used ceramic mugs with desiccated tea bags stuck to their insides.

Slide processing—by the one lab in town that wouldn't destroy your film with scratches and dust—took a few days. Grace had gotten her pictures back from Shivaratri and invited me to her Hadigaon flat. She arranged herself on the stool, shifting from side to side, and picked up an Agfa loupe.

"Why do people do this?" she asked, leaning over the first image in the box. "I mean, no other animal stares this way into an artificial light source. It can't be good for you."

"Moths."

She shrugged. "Is it good for them?"

But we knew why she did it. The pretense of doubt was a game, a way she teased herself. All her life, from the bio lab to the light table, she had liked to look at things closely. They had always been small things, lit from behind by a clinical glow.

It was late, already past nine. Grace had biked home half an hour ago from an event at the Annapurna Hotel; one of those *pakka* functions where you show your face, drink with the right people, and express keen interest in their well-meaning development schemes, hoping that your earnest attention will lead to a well-paying gig.

Tonight it had been a UNESCO banquet, surgically scheduled to slip between the major Hindu and Buddhist holidays. She'd worked for the organization before, shooting a paper-making project near Pokhara. Now they were talking about a sexier job: documenting vocational schools in Nepal's economically depressed northwest. An assignment like that would pay real money, maybe even lead to a show in DC.

"My one mistake," she said, "was eating the appetizer. I broke the prime directive: *Never eat shellfish in a landlocked country*. But I was longing for seafood."

"It was the UN," I said. "They've got refrigerated planes, probably. I'm sure it was okay."

"Yeah. More likely they were left to sit at the airport for three days before clearing customs."

"So why'd you eat them?"

"They were shrimp. Anyway, we'll see. Hopefully I won't find out until tomorrow." Grace leaned closer to the light table, steadying a slide with her thumb. Her walnut hair, falling straight down on either side of her face, created a kind of photographer's blind. I wondered if she'd grown it long that way on purpose.

The telephone on her desk—an old black rotary—began to ring. "Who could that be?" Grace picked up the handset and wedged it between her ear and shoulder. "Hello?" She glanced at me. "Rhoda," she mouthed.

Grace had mentioned this person. She was a former literary agent, living in Kathmandu in what amounted to exile; she'd lost a fortune shepherding a score of "New Beat" writers into obscurity under a dubious imprint called Elysium Editions. Rhoda had married a journalism student she'd seen at Hunter College: This was Kunda Mainali, the *Shaligram* reporter I'd met at the doctors' strike. They'd lived awhile in Brooklyn and moved to Nepal three years ago. Now Rhoda was four months pregnant, teaching English to privileged teenagers, and bored out of her skull. She hated Kathmandu: the soot, the noise, the chaos. She'd hated those things about Manhattan, too, but at least you could find fresh rye bread.

"On my bike," Grace said in response to something. "Not so bad tonight. There must be a ban on harassing Western women. The 'suck my dick' guy wasn't around. Oh, one kid yelled that he wanted to marry me. Very charming."

There was a long silence as Rhoda spoke. "That's probably normal. What did Dr. Dan say?" Grace nodded, and gave me the talky-hand gesture. "Listen, Rhoda . . . I know . . . Rhoda, I have company. Jeff's here."

"Tell her to say 'hi' to Kunda for me."

"He says 'hi' to Kunda. Mmmm." She cupped the receiver. "He's working late." Back to Rhoda. "Well, I'm not surprised. We all are. Yes. So I'll see you soon. Yes. Good night. Love you." She hung up the phone. "They want us to come over for dinner."

"When?"

"Soon. After Lhosar." She positioned the loupe over a slide. "Here, look at this one."

The photo showed a Nepali teenager with curly, close-cropped hair—a Tribhuvan University student, probably—holding a fistful of pink flyers. He was shouting something to (or at) someone past the camera. The depth of field was shallow. The protestors behind him were indistinct, like figures in the background of an impressionist painting. There was something iconic about the youth's rage; he could have modeled for Auguste Rodin.

"That's very good."

"Thanks. And this one. Look."

It was the same student, this time in close-up. Now he wore an expression of glee, anticipation. Looking at his face, it was easy to imagine that the point of these democracy protests was less political commitment than an opportunity for breathless juvenile delinquency.

Grace appraised a few more slides without comment, tossing three of them into the trash bin beneath the table. "Here's another one." A view of the soldiers from the bridge across the river, watched by a pair of monkeys in the foreground. The sentiment was obvious: Will the real apes please stand up?

She peered back into the loupe, then slid it toward me. "Wow. Here's my favorite so far."

The image showed an ash-smeared sadhu, positioned near the entrance of the temple complex. The holy man sat cross-legged on a small mat spread out on the pavement. Heavy dreadlocks hung to his thin knees. He gripped a trident—the emblem of Lord Shiva—in his right hand. The mendicant's ganja-reddened eyes stared dead ahead, as wide as headlights. But what made the shot was the line of riot police, out of focus but clear, assembled behind him.

"It's a great picture," I said. "I hope this isn't insulting, but I saw a postcard that was similar, taken in Sri Lanka. Army troops marching in front of a big Buddha statue. I mean it wasn't the same at all, really, but the contrast . . ."

"I know." Grace slid another slide under the loupe. "There are only, like, ten great compositions you can come up with during a revolution. People tearing down a statue, mothers screaming over their fallen husbands, lines of soldiers with hippies putting flowers in their guns; it's like anything. There's a formula that sells.

"The problem is, I'm not a news photographer. I'm not even that interested in politics. But while I'm here, the People's Movement changes everything. It guarantees, more or less, that almost anything a photographer does in Nepal right now is marketable. Careers are made at times like this. You just need to be in the right place at the right time. All it takes is good timing and dumb luck."

Walking through Asan, Grace had told me of her real passions. She wanted to document Kathmandu's sacred cows, and the secret plan to relocate them in the parched Terai. She wanted to shoot long time-exposures, in the early evening, showing how everyone—coming from every direction—circled the Annapurna temple on the way home from work. She wanted to photograph the hand-painted bicycle rickshaws, the umbrella repairmen and disposable lighter refillers, the ragtag kids thrashing like Labradors in the funky public pool across from Nag Pokhari.

"But every time I walk out the door there's another demonstration, and I can't afford to ignore it. I mean, Shivaratri was a perfect example. I'd hoped to get some shots for a series about cremations, and we ended up in the middle of a riot."

A moment after she took the shot with the sadhu, the soldiers had charged. Grace had gotten that on film, too: the flurry of loose flyers, the wide-eyed terror of the student, his bashed head and bloodstained shirt.

"I'll tell you something. I really wondered what the hell I was doing. I should have yelled at the army guy, or even yanked him off that kid. My God, they were the same age!"

"But what could you have done, without getting clubbed yourself? The instant we get involved, we're a fair target."

"I don't know. Something Anything. I've always found it bizarre, the idea that photojournalists don't get involved. That we don't even *think* about getting involved."

"I agree," I said. "But it's the old argument. Our job is to witness events, record them, provide images. How else will anyone know what's going on here? Or anywhere?"

"I know. I'm just telling you how I feel. The fact is I *didn't* do anything. And I wish I had." She studied a new slide. "Oh, my God." She laughed nervously. "Okay. I hope *this* isn't insulting. Actually, I hope you don't hate me for it. You might." I looked at her quizzically. "You have to see it, though. Come on."

I squinted into the loupe. It took a few seconds for me to understand what I was seeing. At first all I saw was a slightly blurry mob, caught in the moment of stampede, the brick walls of the Pashupati shrines behind them. Then I made out the dark figure, curled in fetal position beneath their feet.

"No."

"I swear, I didn't know it was you. The second I realized, I ran over. Lou also. Actually I sort of panicked. You'd been kicked in the head, but you were only out for maybe a few seconds. Seriously, though," she said. "Ignoring the fact that it's kind of tasteless. It's a pretty priceless souvenir of Nepal."

"A souvenir of an outing with Grace, apparently."

This had not been an especially sensitive thing to say, though I felt within my rights saying it. But Grace stood up, left the slide table, and walked into her bedroom, instantly in tears. They were automatic tears: the kind that come when a button is pushed and a pain center lights up.

I hesitated a minute then followed her in, a bit flabbergasted. "I'm sorry," I said.

"You should be." She was sitting on the bed. "Come here." I sat next to her, put my arm around her waist. The glare of a sodium streetlamp shone directly through the bedroom window. "Did you ever feel," she asked, "like one of those characters in a movie who just gets, like, *used*? Like, whenever they need something absurd or tragic to happen, it happens to that character. Except, it's never me. It's whoever's standing *next* to me."

"Listen," I said. "No one died. And it was my own choice, to be in the middle of that scene."

Grace stood up and went into the kitchen. I heard a pop. She came back a minute later with two glass tumblers and a bottle of Jekel wine.

"Wow." Good wine was as rare as good cheese, or good chocolate, in this frill-challenged country. "You found this at Bhat-Bhateni?"

"Are you kidding? I brought it here. A year and a half ago."

"Really?" I was floored. "Well, thank you."

"Thank me later," she said. "I have to tell you something." She filled my glass, and hers. "To the Jana Andolan," she said.

"Within our lifetimes." We clinked. There was a brief silence.

"My lab accident," she said. "We talked about it at the Ras Rang."

"Actually we didn't talk about it."

"That's because there wasn't one." Grace took a long drink. "It was something else. And by the time we finish this bottle, you'll be the only person I've told. Ever, anywhere. Promise me you'll keep it that way."

I set down my glass, took her hands, and promised. She squeezed mine, released them, and told me.

It was during Grace's senior year in high school, shortly after her mother entered the alcohol treatment center, that her career plans shifted. Stability suddenly became very important. Grace considered psychology, but it seemed too sketchy. She preferred definite answers. Her father suggested neurology. He'd showed her around the university bio labs, and made neuroscience sound like an adventure: a field where—like astronomy—known facts were still scarcer than mystery.

Grace had always been mishap-prone, attracting random calamities. As far back as eighth grade—when a stolen butane lighter had exploded in her locker, immolating her books, purse, and boyfriend's letter jacket—her classmates had joked about the Modena Curse.

She'd taken possession of it. She'd turned it into a pet. And it really was funny how, when you nourished a character sketch of yourself, everything conspired to prove it true; how every disaster, large and small, found in her its inevitable cause. The pyramid of marinara sauce jars that fell from the supermarket shelf as her cart rumbled by; the skunk that turned up at Betina's baby shower; the time she'd been at Maxim's for Sally's graduation, and her purse catch had snagged on the tablecloth.

Or the crisp January morning three years ago, when Grace had dropped by Vanessa's. They'd turned on the TV to watch the *Challenger* liftoff. She remembered Vanessa's joke—you sure this is a good idea, Grace?—and their bantering laughter, which lasted all of seventy-three seconds, at which point the space shuttle exploded in a medusa of smoke. Holy shit, people whispered to Vanessa afterward. How could you let Grace watch that? By this point, they were only half-joking.

Still, until her last year of neuro, nothing truly morbid had befallen her personally. Then, abruptly, the Curse had matured.

Dean was her confidant, and hero, during the two years she spent at school. Smart guy, very funny, a good study partner. A serious bicyclist. They'd been lovers for one semester, but that wasn't where they'd belonged. Miraculously their friendship had remained intact, to the point where she'd set him up with Vanessa, her best friend. They'd hit it off—and though Dean was initially reluctant, it had looked like they were moving in together the following fall.

The three of them were in her tangerine orange VW that night, on their way home from a Michael Dukakis event. She could see Dean's face so clearly, could remember exactly what they were talking about: Ronald Reagan's hair. Dean had just seen the president up close, during a speech in Kansas City, and was convinced that Reagan's hair was a plastic headpiece. He'd seen the little square patch, right on the back, with "Made in China" stamped onto the mold.

"It's not just his hair," Vanessa had yelled from the back, looking up from the *Journal of Neurology* that served as her cutting board. "I saw it stamped on his ass." Grace had started laughing, a quick breathless bray, and looked at Dean, who still had a tiny frost of coke on his septum. She wiped her own nose. Vanessa was scrambling around behind her, knocking into her seat. Grace looked into the rearview mirror—"What?"—but her friend was on the floor. "I dropped the bill."

"Forget it."

"It was a twenty!"

Grace craned around for a glance. "Better find it." When she looked back at the road there was something big and dark, looming up in front of her. She jerked the wheel to the right, the car spun, and for a split second the names of all the hormones she'd memorized, from adrenaline to vasopressin, leaped through her mind. Her bug hit the guardrail and flipped.

Grace wore two white scars, high on her left shoulder, from where they'd rebuilt her shattered collarbone. Dean had a wheelchair, and the feeble hope that, if he worked harder at it than he'd ever worked in his life, he could someday walk himself to the toilet.

Vanessa? Nothing. She'd escaped unscathed, but had changed nonetheless. Dean's convalescence obsessed her. She dropped her scholarship and started taking classes in physical therapy, waitressing to pay the fees. It was bizarre, in a way, how she'd reacted to the situation—and awkward, that she'd expected Grace to do the same. For though she never said it directly—no one did—the cause of the crash was clear. It wasn't the deer, or Vanessa, or the packet of coke in Dean's wallet. It was the Modena Curse.

Three months after the accident, as Grace weighed a tray of rat brains in the Behavioral Sciences Lab, it caught up with her. She saw her reflection in a paper towel dispenser—white coat, blue surgical mask, latex gloves—and decided to take the rest of the day off. On the way home—another impulse—she stopped to have her nails done. While she was waiting, she picked up a copy of *Condé Nast Traveler* from the seat beside her. Inside was a feature about Nepal, and the restoration of the Bhaktapur *durbar*. Halfway through, the girl called her in. Grace slipped the magazine into her daypack and finished the story that afternoon.

She'd never thought about visiting Nepal, much less living in Kathmandu, until that day. But something had dropped, and with a nearly atrophied sense of excitement she glimpsed an alternate future for herself: a chance to reclaim the dream she'd had as a teenager, before a pall of guilt and formaldehyde descended over her life. She had wanted to travel the world and make pictures. Suddenly, she wanted that again.

A week later, Grace flew to Europe. She wrote a short note to her father, saying she needed to be on her own for a while and think things through. At the time, she hadn't thought of it as running away. But the days turned to weeks, and she could not find the words to write to Vanessa, or to Dean. She had stood in a hundred phone booths, but could not lift the receiver. After a certain point, the weight of her silence became heavier than her absence. Dean and Vanessa could only think the worst of her: Their concern must have long ago turned to resentment, their resentment to contempt. Not for a moment did she blame them for this.

More than two years had passed since her departure—sixteen months of them in Nepal—but Dean and Vanessa still existed. Did they still wonder where she was, or what had become of her? Did they ever, in their dreams, envision her wandering through ancient temples, sleeping beneath ice-capped peaks, saddling yaks with Khampa nomads? What would Vanessa make of the sadhus, or the sacred cows? How would Dean react to the sight of human bodies, aflame on the cremation pyres?

But there was no point thinking about that now. She only hoped, when she could bear to think about it, that they had stopped wondering about her at all.

I SAID NOTHING. We were holding hands again, had been since she told me about the accident. Grace tilted her head back and stared at the ceiling. The texture was gritty, with shiny little dots. Cobwebs littered the corners.

I followed her gaze. "It's a ceiling that could be anywhere," I said. "Las Vegas, Little Rock, Paris . . ."

"But it isn't anywhere." Grace looked at me, her eyes swollen. "It's here, in Asia. It's the ceiling of my bedroom, in Kathmandu. *Kathmandu.* Sometimes just saying the word amazes me. It thrills me. I'll look at a globe and put my finger on Nepal and say 'Kathmandu,' trying to understand how far away it is. From everything I knew."

"Is it? Do you?"

She shook her head.

I'd never thought of Grace as someone who, like me, had developed an attraction to Tibetan art. But hanging above her bed was a colorful *thangka* that she'd probably bought at Boudha. Framed in silk brocade, it portrayed the Kalachakra mandala: the Wheel of Time.

Of all the mandalas (and there were endless varieties, covering the walls of every gallery and curio shop in Kathmandu), I found Kalachakra the most intriguing. Tibetan scholars said it represented a kind of "time machine." Not an actual machine, in the H. G. Wells sense, but a device for domesticating time and turning it into an ally. Meditating on the Kalachakra helped you visualize a perfect universe: a place where all sounds are mantras and every being is a buddha. In such a universe Time itself is a benevolent engine that, fueled by wisdom and compassion, drives humanity along the road to liberation.

Grace had heard it another way. "The lama who blessed this told me that just *looking* at it," she said, "with the right attitude, of course—is enough to guarantee a rebirth in Shambala."

"Is that the same as Shangri-la?"

"Shangri-la's made-up, I think. Shambala is an earthly paradise that exists *now*. But it's not going to open up for most of us until a few centuries from now."

"Kind of like an exclusive country club."

"I guess so. It's a secret utopia, somewhere in the polar regions, concealed by a cloak of invisibility. Once war and greed are eliminated, and everyone in the world is united, Shambala will be the new world capital."

"I hope they have good heaters."

Grace poured the last bit of wine. It was past ten. "There's something else you should know. I wasn't looking for a boyfriend," she said. "Since I've been here I've avoided any kind of relationship. A week ago I was totally focused, happily riding my bike to the Teaching Hospital, with no obligation to anyone but myself. I don't know why I'm doing this. Or even if it's what I want."

' Maybe you want what everyone wants from a relationship. A kind of redemption. The chance to reinvent yourself in a new place, whatever you had to live through to get there."

"Is that what you want?"

"It's attractive to me, too." I lifted her hair to her earlobes and kissed the tip of her nose. "And so are you. Very." We lay down together, on our sides.

Grace had opened up to me; at least it seemed so. Now it was my turn. I felt a knot of tension grow in my stomach. This was the worst possible moment to create more space between us. But if I was serious about leaving Nepal, I had to tell her. I had to let her know. "I have to tell you something," I heard myself saying.

She propped herself on her elbow. "What?"

"I got a letter from my brother. Two letters, actually."

She'd heard enough about our relationship to know this was significant. "That must make you happy. How is he doing?"

I shook my head. "Not good. He's totally depressed. He was depressed when I saw him, when he stayed with me those two weeks in Oakland, but this is something else. He really seems to be in a very bad place. I'm worried about him."

"What can you do? Can you do anything?"

"I have to try," I said. "But that means going home, at least for a few weeks. And I have to do it soon."

"How soon?"

"Very soon. In six days. March 5. The day before my birthday."

Grace sat up and looked ahead. "I didn't even know your birthday was coming. How long have you known you were leaving?"

"I'll tell you the truth—I'm still making the decision. By telling you, I'm making the decision."

She shook her head. "Well, thanks for telling me, at least."

"Are you okay?"

"What do you think? I'm fine. I mean, yes, I'm sad. What can I say? It's your brother. You have to do what you have to do." She swung her legs off the bed. "We all have to do what we have to do."

A rogue rhythm intruded on our conversation. Grace looked toward the window. Something was happening outside. Through the stillness of midnight, we could hear it: chanting, or yelling. It didn't sound like an organized mob, more like a pack of hooligans.

Grace looked panicked. "What is that?"

"A wedding, maybe? I can't make out what they're saying."

The chorus grew louder. A group of twenty, maybe thirty guys were coming from Hadigaon, just above Grace's street. They were on some political mission, shouting about democracy. But though they could mouth the phrase, they perverted its meaning. For many young Nepalis—whose material urges had been aroused by the influx of Western tourists and films—the concept carried no burden of responsibility. It meant only freedom, without limits or accountability. It included the right to prowl the streets, accosting foreign women and throwing empty beer bottles: an uncontrolled ejaculation.

As if on cue, every dog within a mile started barking. We heard shouting and the sound of shattering glass. They were definitely getting closer, throwing bricks and rocks, breaking windows. What the hell was going on?

In a sickening flash, I remembered: *the blackout.* Everyone in Kathmandu was supposed to turn off their lights from dusk to dawn, as a memorial to the students who'd been killed last month. Those who didn't were assumed to be royalists and dealt with accordingly.

We jumped off the bed. Grace raced down the narrow steps to her front door. She threw the bolt and snapped off the outside light. I turned out the kitchen, bedroom, and office lights. Grace ran back upstairs. We crouched together in the far corner of her bedroom, as far from the window as possible.

The pack stopped outside her flat. There was laughing and shouting, and we heard a few heaved bricks fall onto the road until, with an implosive thump, the sodium streetlight was smashed. Then the protesters marched on, chanting and stomping along the packed dirt road. We heard them stop at the construction site at the corner, gathering more bricks. They rounded the corner toward Chabahil, their voices lost beneath the braying of the pariah dogs.

Grace opened the blinds. Glass shrapnel glinted in the street.

"The Nepali idea of a quiet night at home." She grinned apologetically, as if she were responsible for the melee.

"Life During Wartime," I shrugged, wondering if there was any confluence at all with the Talking Heads song.

"From Bir to Eternity," Grace offered.

"A Farewell to Alms."

There was a pause, filled with background barking.

"The Jana Andolusian Dog," Grace said triumphantly.

If there was any fallout from my previous announcement, it had dispersed Still, I felt shell-shocked. "Six fucking days," I muttered, sitting down.

Grace joined me, and slid her arm around my waist. "You know what that means."

"What?"

She pulled me toward her. "We have no time to waste."

Her bed was a genuine improvement over the Pashupati ghat. We lit two candles, undressed each other, and made love for real.

16

Lhosar

T HE LAST DAY of February 1990 was the first day of 2117: Tibet's Iron Horse Year. This was Lhosar. I navigated a swarm of cows, cars, cabs, and pedestrians, locked my CG125 outside the Dharma Voice bookshop, and walked through the entrance gate into Boudhnath. Bells were ringing, and the air was foggy with juniper smoke.

Though I'd be back in America within a week, I was struck anew by the contrast between my two homes. There is a tension that lingers over the United States, a vibration so subtle and so pervasive that we rarely feel it directly. It is like an atmospheric inversion: as much a part of our environment as the radio waves that knit the air, as invisible as the pollen from our flowers. We emerge into it the day we're born and breathe it while we dream. Most of us spend our entire lives within its umbra, never even suspecting that it exists. As the anxiety that it carries harangues us, we blame ourselves.

But we are not to blame. We are not the sources of this strident signal, but its hapless receivers. I know this because I've managed to escape, now and then, from the grip of that malignant broadcast. Imagine a laboratory rat who has spent his entire adult life in a cage where the wired floor supplies a continuous, mild electric shock. After years of this, the rat no longer jumps and dances; his entire being, mental and physical, has adapted to his condition.

One day a fuse in the laboratory blows out, and the grid on the cage floor goes dead. The rat stands motionless, astonished, unable to comprehend this strange absence of baseline stress.

When I visit Nepal, I know how that rat must feel.

I placed my palms together, faced the eyes of Buddha emblazoned above the white dome, and prayed for the well-being of the people I loved. I prayed for my friends in America; they'd be eating dinner now, or watching *The Simpsons*. And I prayed for Tibet, entering its fourth decade under Chinese occupation. It occurred to me again, as it had so many times during my visits to Nepal, that I was in a place where I could do something that would appear insane in the West: I could stand in the middle of the street, surrounded by fruit sellers and taxis and cows, with motorcycles swerving around me and kids ducking beneath my legs, and pray out loud, with all my heart, without a trace of self-consciousness or an iota of doubt.

NO ONE CAN do everything. At any given moment, any adult individual (assuming a world adult population of five billion) can participate in only 0.00000002 percent of human activity. Even so, I was perfectly happy to be spending the morning at Boudhnath; it had to be the biggest celebration on the planetary calendar.

Pilgrims from all over Asia had converged on Boudha, just as thousands of sadhus had congregated at Pashupatinath four days earlier. Joining the kora, I was amazed by the size of the crowd. A current of humanity flowed around the stupa without beginning or end, a self-consuming snake moving ceaselessly clockwise. The costumes were fantastic: indigo cloaks and crimson silk; intricate striped aprons, the traditional Tibetan chubas, woven of yak wool; earrings and necklaces as thick as kebabs, displaying marshmallow-sized ingots of gold and coral. There were the rich and the poor, babes in arms, gorgeous teenage girls with jet-black hair, crusty old men wrapped in coarse wool. Some of the older pilgrims spun handheld prayer wheels; other ticked off mantras on Tibetan *mallas*. Seen from above, the purposeful mass of humanity might look like atomic particles, whirling inside an accelerator. At the auspicious instant they'd find their target, and prayers would scatter into the ether like quarks.

Boudha dwarfs Swayambhu; it's the largest Buddhist monument in Nepal. Devotees from India, Bhutan, Ladakh, Sikkim, and Tibet itself flock to this site, which was once a way station along the ancient trade route linking Lhasa, Kathmandu, and points south. Fifteen centuries on, it's still the heart and soul of Nepal's Tibetan community.

No one recalls who built Boudhnath. Two oft-repeated legends, Nepali and Tibetan, share the limelight. The Nepali story is typically macabre, reflecting the ancient kingdom's fixation on loyalty and duty. Long ago, a devout ruler built a beautiful shrine and fountain just north of Kathmandu. Some generations later (due, perhaps, to a lapse in naga offerings) water stopped flowing from the sacred spout. The king, a religious man, decided to investigate the fountain's fate. His court astrologers informed him that it would require an offering—human, of course—to get the earthly juices flowing again. The catch was, the king had to sacrifice the most noble man in his realm.

The following morning, under orders from his father, the crown prince arrived at the site of the dry pools. The king had sent him a simple, mysterious command. At the site, the letter said, the prince would find a corpse, wrapped in white cloth. He was to draw his sword and cut off its head at once. The prince saw the body and complied. The instant he did, the fountains flowed again. But when he unwrapped the body, the youth found a terrible surprise: the still-warm body of his beloved father.

The hapless prince, traumatized by his involuntary patricide, withdrew into isolation. After long meditation, he was visited by the goddess Bajra Yogini. She explained the method by which he could atone for his sin: He must construct a huge temple, dedicated to Lord Buddha, on the eastern edge of the capital.

This was not an easy task. As the kingdom was still in drought, creative measures were needed to supply the water used for making bricks. The prince came up with a brilliant idea. Bolts of cloth were unfurled at sunset and left out through the night. Before dawn they were collected, and their moisture wrung out into cisterns. Some still refer to Boudhnath as Khasti: the Temple of Dewdrops.

The Tibetan version is equally far-fetched, but I prefer its focus on self-reliance. Kangma was a pious and clever woman who had moved to the Kathmandu Valley and made a fortune in the goose trade. In gratitude, she decided to build a temple to Amitabh: the Buddha of Limitless Life. All she lacked was the real estate. Kangma was permitted an audience with the king, during which she requested only as much land as she could cover with a buffalo hide. The king, of course, granted her humble wish. Here, Kanga employed the wits that had earned her riches in the goose trade. She slit the hide something like this:

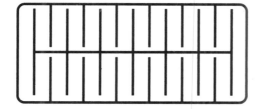

. . . opened it into a narrow hoop (still in one piece, mind you), and encircled a vast parcel of land.

By TEN O'CLOCK Boudha looked like a round, white ship festooned with thousands of blue, white, red, green, and yellow prayer flags. The rising tiers of its plinth were packed with Tibetans: gossiping, praying, practicing dance steps, and untangling lines of flags. A six-foot incense burner—a freestanding earthen censer—poured thick, blue juniper smoke into the air. Light breezes spiraled down from the Himalaya, rippling the flags and dizzying the air with the fragrant smoke.

I circled the plinth, keeping the dome on my right. It would be more fun to be here with Grace, but she'd declined my invitation on the inarguable grounds that she'd get more work done alone. When I'd left Hadigaon she was back in her work room, cleaning her cameras. We made some vague noises about meeting for lunch, but neither of us was eager to obligate the other.

There were plenty of other Westerners on the kora: dharma students, tourists, and oddballs like myself. We greeted each other with nods. Most of them were snapping photos like mad. I'd left my own Nikon behind, without regrets. During my travels I often felt like an obsessed collector, roving the globe with a compulsion to record everything I saw. Without a camera I felt free, able to watch events unfold without the distraction of recording them.

One hundred and eight smoke-blackened buddhas and bodhisattvas, all different, occupy small niches on the upper level of the shrine. I stopped at my favorite: a meditating Buddha in the lotus posture, his right hand touching the earth. The visual gulf between this fit, self-assured figure and his Christian counterpart—the tortured Jesus, nailed to a cross—always startled me.

But did it really happen that way? I recalled the musical laughter of a high lama I'd met at a small monastery, a long bus ride north of Lhasa. He explained that Jesus, during his "lost" years, had traveled to what is now Tibet, studying with local saints and learning how to perform miracles. There was no betrayal, the lama insisted; no Last Supper, nor a crucifixion. Jesus had left Judea by choice and settled in Asia. He'd become a respected sage, known as Issa. Such facts were common knowledge in Tibet. "This Issa, long life!" the old lama laughed. "So many students! And some children also, I think!"

A series of low, earth-shaking blasts—the bellowing of *dungchen*, long copper horns—signaled the start of Lhosar's climactic ritual. The acoustic waves plowed through the atmosphere, beluga whales of sound. I walked to the edge of the plinth, overlooking the kora, and waited.

By now, all four levels of Boudha's stupa were crammed with celebrants. What had been a chaotic carousel of humanity morphed into an orderly procession. Six orange-robed monks led the mass of pilgrims, circling the ancient dome with a framed portrait of the Dalai Lama. Four monks supported his image; two others flanked them, holding yellow parasols over the lifelike painting. Tibetans believe that the Dalai Lama is the human incarnation of Chenrezig, the thousand-eyed, thousand-armed buddha of compassion. The exigencies of the modern world have thrust him into a dual role: He is the political leader of Tibet-in-exile, as well as its spiritual guide. Not only that: He'd once taken apart an entire 1931 Dodge, down to the last cotter pin— and put it back together, without misplacing a single washer.

The procession continued, complete with an elephant; where the pachyderm had come from was anybody's guess. After three circumambulations, the first part of the ritual was completed. It was now time to carry the Dalai Lama's portrait onto the first plinth, for the customary long-life prayers.

As the monks mounted the stairs, though, they were blocked by a squad of policemen. The nearby Tibetans, curious and astonished, clustered around the monks, the police, and the portrait.

Though I couldn't hear the altercation, I knew what was happening: a bit of bullying, courtesy of Nepal's northern neighbor. China had recently learned how easily Nepal's leadership could be manipulated—and the kingdom's large, prosperous community of Tibetan refugees was an embarrassment. Despite shrill protests when any foreign power dared "meddle" in China's internal affairs, Beijing had clearly bought the ear of the palace. The word had come down. Any celebration sympathetic to the Dalai Lama was a tacit and intolerable declaration of Tibetan separatism.

But there were two forces at work here: Chinese outrage and realpolitik. The five Nepali policemen stood among thousands of Tibetans, and let it be said that they never stopped smiling. After a brief exchange, accompanied by much primate posturing and head-wagging, the officers withdrew.

The procession continued up the stars and onto the plinth, where the portrait of the Dalai Lama was placed on a dais. Monks intoned prayers while pilgrims jostled for the privilege of tossing long silk katas over the frame. As this was going on, all the Tibetans around me reached into their pockets and extracted small drawstring sacks or plastic bags. Inside was finely milled *tsampa*: buckwheat flour, the staple diet of Tibet. Somehow, I'd forgotten to purchase this key ingredient. I felt a tap on my shoulder, and turned to see an old Khampa woman with two sleigh-sized teeth grinning at me. Her breath smelled of chang. She grabbed my wrist in her powerful hand, poured a handful of tsampa into my open palm, and closed my fingers around it. Her smile was a joy to behold.

The lamas completed their prayers on a long, low note. There was a brief lull, the eye of a sonic storm. And then a single, jubilant cry welled up with the crowd, building with the roar of an approaching cyclone:

"aaaaaaaaaaaaaahhhhhhhhhHHHH . . ."

At the exact same instant, everyone—each of the thousands of Tibetans and tourists who covered the tiers of the shrine like ants on a wedding cake—hurled their tsampa into the air. Flour filled the air, a fine and nourishing fog, settling on our shoulders, on our shoes, onto the lenses of Sony video cameras; dusting the eyebrows of the monks; frosting the leather handbags of Manangi women; powdering the black-brimmed caps of the policemen, who seemed giddy with relief. Twenty-one seventeen, the Iron Horse Year, had begun.

HALF AN HOUR later, on the flagstones below the dome, I saw Coal and Clarice. They were standing at the edge of a wide circle of Tibetan adolescents. The young men and women wore jeans, white shirts, and black sports jackets. Rocking from side to side, arms intertwined, they crooned a poignant rendition of "We Shall Overcome."

I snuck up behind Clarice and put my hands on her shoulders. "Hey, guys! Walk the kora enough times, and you'll run into your favorite people."

"It's wonderful, isn't it?" Clarice turned around and hugged me. Her loose, blue jacket was covered with tsampa. "Like finding a pin in a haystack. Are you with Grace?"

"Haven't seen her yet. I assume she's out there somewhere. With at least three cameras around her neck. She lives for this stuff."

"Our unofficial historian," Coal chimed in. "In the old days, she would have done engravings. Woodcuts. Can you imagine?"

"Happy Lhosar, Coal-ji. Have you made any New Year's resolutions?"

"Never crossed my mind. Have you?"

"Of course. At every opportunity."

"Well?"

"I resolve to eat more salad, renew my New Yorker subscription, and beef up my collection of Elvis Costello CDs."

Coal narrowed his eyes. "It sounds like you've resolved to go back to America."

I started, dismayed by my transparency. "Wow. Maybe so. But shit, Coal. It's brutal to hear you actually *say* it."

Clarice shot me a pointed glance. "Does Grace know?"

"I told her last night. She didn't seem too bothered."

There was a beat of silence. Coal shook his head, amused by my naïveté. "She's grown quite attached to you, I'm afraid."

I turned to Clarice for verification. She nodded. "We'll all be sorry to see you go. But I think Grace is going to feel rather abandoned."

"I'm surprised. I get the impression she's proud of being a loner. We have fun together, but I don't get the sense she's overly invested in the relationship."

"Maybe your next book," said Clarice, "should be on what you don't understand about women."

I nodded. "There isn't enough ink."

"You've tamed her wild heart," Coal sang. "Just as I've tamed Clarice's."

Clarice rolled her eyes. "Oh, please."

A few tourists had joined the Tibetans, and the singing grew louder.

Deep in my heart
I do believe
We shall all be free someday

Clarice peered around nervously. "I wonder if the police will break this up."

"Not a chance." I shook my head. "There'd be a riot."

"At any rate," said Coal, "it's not a brilliant idea."

"No," I agreed. "But I'm glad they're doing it."

Clarice frowned. "What's wrong with it?"

"It's provocative," I said. "If the Chinese think their noses are being twisted, they'll tighten the thumbscrews on Nepal."

"*Fuck* the bloody Chinese." Clarice smiled, pleased with herself for swearing. "Such a pain in everyone's arse. I wish they'd just go colonize the moon, or something."

"What a lovely thought," mused Coal. "Gazing at the full moon on a warm summer's night and thinking, 'Why, that's a Chinese colony.' What could be more romantic?"

"Well, you couldn't actually *see* them." Clarice pulled at the shoulders of her jacket, releasing puffs of tsampa. "Jeff, have you seen the dead body?"

"No," I said. "What dead body?"

"On the kora. Someone's body. You should see it."

"Why would I want to see a dead body?"

"It's meant to be good luck. To see one." She sneezed, twice. "I don't know why. Maybe it's something to do with the Buddha seeing a dead person before he went off to get enlightened. I don't know. It's quite bizarre, though."

"Highly recommended." Coal wore his droll Brit look. "Not to be missed."

"Just a dead body?"

"That's all. Nothing fancy. You can go as you are, old chap."

"Will you come with me?"

"I think not," said Coal. "You know how it is. You've seen one corpse, you've seen them all."

"See it and come back," Clarice offered. "We'll be right here."

I FOUND THE corpse along the kora, near the wall of the lowest plinth. It lay on its back, covered by a white sheet, face exposed. The body had belonged to a light-skinned man, in his late thirties or early forties. Hundreds of rupee notes and coins had been tossed onto the shroud: contributions, I guessed, toward the man's cremation or sky burial. A policeman stood nearby, charged with the monotonous task of guarding the cadaver and its booty.

"How did he die?"

"*Malai tha chhaina.*" The officer shrugged. "Everyone thought he was sleeping, but he was dead. No one knows."

I regarded the figure. The man's face looked calm, yet pained, as if he had been making a profound effort at concentration as the life ebbed out of him. Although I hadn't known him, it was astonishing to realize that the spirit was gone, and the body an abandoned shell. Left alone, it would

certainly be discovered by vultures, or torn apart by dogs. Such a fate, gruesome as it sounds, is the dying wish of many Tibetans. The body, having consumed its share, might now serve to nourish other creatures. One's
karma could only be improved by such a selfless act.

My mind swam back to an incident that had occurred nine years ago. I
was visiting the East Coast. My brother and I, with four of his friends, had
gone rock climbing on the Shawangunk Ridge. The cliffs were black, and
vertical, but not very high. Jordan and I had climbed very little. I'd scaled a
few walls in the Santa Cruz Quarry; he'd been out with his friends once or
twice. We enjoyed it, but didn't have a lot invested in the sport.

We'd dropped our gear at the foot of a small cliff, maybe forty feet
high. As I knelt down to get a sandwich out of my daypack I heard a cry,
something between a hawk and a seagull. I looked up. A human figure plummeted toward us, clawing the air, and slammed into the ground at our feet.
It was a man in his early twenties. He'd fallen off the cliff, landing flat on his
back. His body was jerking, and blood leaked from his mouth and ears.

The six of us had stood immobilized, terrified, paralyzed. Even Jordan
was in a state of shock. But time was critical. We tore off our T-shirts and
slipped them under the climber's shoulders, back, and knees. Using them
as slings, we carried him nearly a mile, to the ranger station. An hour later,
the ambulance arrived. The climber was loaded in, still unconscious, still
convulsing.

The six of us hiked back to our ropes and packs, all of us shaking. It
was surreal to see our abandoned gear, heaped casually in the flattened
grass. Everyone was silent. We stuffed our jackets and snacks back into our
packs, eager to get away, to leave that unlucky place as quickly as possible.

Everyone except Jordan. He'd put on a fresh T-shirt and was coiling a
rope around his arm. He looked at me evenly.

"Will you belay me," he asked, "or shall I fix my own rope?"

"You're climbing? *Now*?"

"If I don't climb now," Jordan said, "I'll never climb again."

We climbed together. Later that evening, after we returned home, I
called the hospital in Cragsmoor. The climber hadn't survived.

MY ATTENTION REMAINED on the anonymous corpse, stiff and still on the Boudha flagstones. I imagined the eyes drying up, the teeth falling out. What if this was someone I had loved?

A wave of aversion, or pure despair, rippled through me. I turned to walk away, to reunite with Coal and Clarice, but my breath seemed to catch in my chest. A clammy sweat broke across my forehead, and my heart began to pound. It was like pulling a muscle. Before I knew what hit me I was caught in a full-blown anxiety attack. I started to jog, then to run, bumping people aside. My peripheral vision seemed to blur, and I stumbled into someone smaller than me, a woman shouted, a motorcycle footrest clipped my leg and drew blood. I started sprinting, gasping in pain and panic. I knew where I was going, where I had to go, and I raced ahead with dumb conviction, giving my heart a reason to race, burying my gasps beneath an alibi of physical exertion. And then I was indoors, bolting up the monastery steps, tearing off my shoes and lunging toward the heavy curtain that hung like a hide across the familiar doorway.

Chokyi Nyima sat on the long, carpeted couch, chatting with a family of Khampas. They wore dark woolen cloaks, and the men had long, red plaits woven into their ponytails. A dozen Westerners sat on the floor, cradling glass cups. The Rinpoche looked up in surprise as I burst into the room.

"Oh! The giraffe has come!" The Rinpoche turned to the students with a mock earnest mien. "A good man, the giraffe . . ." He smiled and raised his chin at me. "So, some chang . . . ?"

I shook my head, approached, and sank to my knees. I had no kata, no tangerines, nothing to offer but my breathless agitation. Chokyi Nyima looked at me, and his expression transformed.

"Rinpoche." My voice was a dry croak. "Something's wrong, something crazy's got a hold of me, I think I'm . . ."

"NO!" Chokyi Nyima barked, cutting me off. He leaned forward, seized my shoulders, and yanked me toward his chest, throwing an arm around my back. He launched into a rapid, melodic prayer. Every few seconds he would reach an exclamation point, and slap my skull with almost stunning force. I felt the cold tip of his amulet box press against my forehead, followed by a tap from his cloth-wrapped vajra.

After a full minute he pushed me away to arm's length. He peered into my left eye, then into my right.

"Okay? Better?" I tried to talk, but my sense of relief was so great that I burst out laughing. The Rinpoche, unsmiling, placed his right hand on my head. "You don't worry, okay?" He looked into my eyes again, carefully, one after the other. "You don't worry anything. I take care of you."

17

Water Music

A FEROCIOUS TORRENT OF urine, loud as a snare drum, startled me awake. I lay in bed, fuming. Putting the upper flat's toilet directly above the lower flat's bedroom could not have been an oversight. The architect must have fallen off his bench, breathless with laughter as he anticipated the impact of his droll floor plan.

It was 6 a.m. on Friday, the second of March. Four days until my departure. A second bandh, or general strike, had been called by the Democracy Party. Most businesses would be closed. Shops would be tightly shuttered. Driving was forbidden; according to the political flyers handed out on Shivaratri, "no wheels shall turn" (bicycles were exempt from the order, a cute populist touch). Regardless, it seemed, Captain Shrestha was reporting for duty as usual. Come rain, snow, or revolution by the malcontent proletariat, my upstairs neighbor's Boeing would fly to Hong Kong as scheduled.

The strike was good news for Grace: She'd definitely picked something up at the UNESCO dinner on Tuesday. It had taken a few days to hit her, but she was down for the count. The bandh meant a quiet morning, horn-free. I'd dropped by her place last night with a ceramic dish of *dahi* and a course of norfloxacin, but it would be a good thirty-six hours before she could get a full meal down. Laxmi would walk over to Hadigaon around lunchtime, and bring Grace some mild soup. I'd learned through experience that bacterial dysentery didn't reward a lot of socializing.

The upstairs toilet flushed. There followed a scrabble of scratches as Shrestha's Doberman pinwheeled for traction on the smooth upstairs floor. This was a daily routine. In exactly ten minutes Arati, the captain's elfin wife, would enter her kitchen and begin a regimen of spice-pounding that would make my flat shake like the Cotton Club. I remembered the first time I'd seen Arati outside our compound, buying dog chow at the Bluebird Supermarket. She'd been squeezed into a pair of Levi's, her narrow thighs precisely fitting the preshrunk denim. The other shoppers adjusted their chiffon saris and regarded her with suspicion. They couldn't bear the idea that, in this well-to-do, thirty-something pilot's wife, they were seeing the future. Would their daughters dare dress this way? But there was no holding back the new age of fashion. On New Road, teenage boys were already piercing their ears and shaving their hair into absurd mohawks.

My final professional commitment in Kathmandu was scheduled for 10:30 this morning: an interview with Ganesh Man Singh, the gravel-throated patriarch who'd been leading Nepal's banned Democracy Party for three decades. Hopefully, he wouldn't keep me waiting. I had agreed to meet Coal and Clarice for a rather unusual picnic, at one.

The interview with Singh was an unknown. He had a huge stake in this revolution and could not afford to see it written off as a public display of bad manners. Singh would be inclined to inflate recent events, to insist that the recent protests were proof of energetic momentum, rather than episodes of impotent barking.

I wanted to agree. I honestly wanted the Nepali people to demand reform and win their rights by any means necessary. And when they did, when things reached a flash point, I'd fly back to Kathmandu, pencils sharpened, to see that "Revolt in Shangri-la" found its column inches in the sun.

I pulled on a pair of socks and walked, otherwise naked, into the living room. At 6 a.m. it was still dark outside. I lifted the curtain and stared into the swirling fog. There was a sheet of paper on the coffee table, and although I knew what it said, I picked it up again and studied the plain blue ink.

Jordan's third letter had arrived yesterday.

Good God am I in trouble. I feel it today, how there is nothing in me, and how I lack either the strength or the will—and have not the knowledge—to address my problem.

What ails me most about my injury is that because of it I am removed from the human drama. To the subtle soul who would urge that this separation, this enforced distance, might make me a writer, I reply: Yes, except that this injury has robbed me of any desire to write. In fact, it has robbed me of any desire to live. It is as if the Earth itself has turned against me, casting me into exile for the sins I have committed against it.

I do not fear death. I fear the empty hours of life that otherwise lie ahead—a life that seems to me the worst fate for a being on this Earth.

I thought about trying my brother again. Over the past week I'd made a dozen attempts to call him. It wasn't easy, as he probably didn't spend more than twenty minutes a day in his apartment. He came home and went to bed when the university library closed and was up and about by dawn. I'd tried to call him during his sleeping hours, but the international circuits had been overloaded every time. On three other occasions a connection had been made, only to end in unrequited ringing. Jordan had no answering machine.

It was about 7 p.m. in Philadelphia. I dialed Jordan's number, edgy as a high school senior phoning for a prom date, and waited. The satellite link was an oceanic experience: a rich, infinite roar, like the sigh of an enormous seashell, followed by a series of dolphinlike beeps and clicks. My attempt was again terminated by the perky recording, in English and Nepali: "Sorry, but all international circuits are busy. Please try your call later."

"Fuck you," I replied. Busy at 6:15 in the morning? I was dubious, but who knew? Nepalis kept odd hours. At any rate, there was nothing I could do.

The upstairs door opened and shut Captain Shrestha leaving for the airport. On an impulse I threw on my sweats and ran outside. I found him standing in the car park, smoking. He offered the pack as I approached. I declined, but we shook hands, as if we had some understood business together.

"Good morning. Off to Hong Kong?"

"That's right. Business as usual. My copilot's on his way to pick me up. He wants to show off his new Maruti. It's a crap car." Shrestha pulled on the Marlboro and glanced suspiciously at the crows on the wires above us. "Do you have an early deadline?" He knew I worked for the *Examiner*; he and Arati had twice been to San Francisco.

"Actually, I was hoping to talk to you. If you've got a minute."

"Sure. What's up?"

"Tell me something." I tried to sound casual, hoping Shrestha would respond in kind. "For the past two months there have been all kinds of protests here in the valley. A dozen people killed, doctors on strike, the whole city closed down for days at a time. Just last week they arrested the mayor of Kathmandu and beat up an editor. I saw it; I was there."

Shrestha grinned slightly. He was well aware that, like most Westerners, I hoped to see the monarchy toppled. I suspected he felt the same way.

"You pilots know what's going on," I continued. "But you're in an odd position. On the one hand, you work for Royal Nepal Airlines: the royal family, essentially. On the other hand, you've got a broader perspective than most Nepalis. And you know as well as I do that if the people get their act together and support Jana Andolan, the government will be helpless. They'll have to give in, or risk losing everything: trade agreements, foreign aid, tourism, you name it."

Shrestha dropped his cigarette and ground it into the gravel. "So what's your point?"

"That winning democracy will never be easier than it is right now," I said. "But let's face it: Nepal has a thing for authority figures. The only way anything's going to change is when people like you—with high-status jobs and important connections—throw your weight behind the movement."

Shrestha's lips formed a straight line, and his eyes seemed tired. "Here's the situation," he said. "The king is a clown. He and that bitch in the palace have been robbing us blind for years. And what you say is absolutely correct: This is the time. But you know what? The people won't do anything."

"Why not?"

"I'll tell you. You know how Birendra likes to call Nepal the 'Zone of Peace'? Well, the rest of us call it the 'Zone of Passivity.' That's the problem: We're too bloody passive."

"Passive, or scared?" I pressed him. "Let me ask you this. If Ganesh Man Singh himself called for a strike—a total strike, meaning *everyone*—would you fly?"

Shrestha shook another cigarette out his pack. He took a few draws of smoke before replying. "I honestly don't know," he said. "Not if I was the only one taking the risk. You're right. I don't have the guts. I don't want to lose my job, or go to jail. Who does?" He looked at his shoes, then back to me. "But things won't reach that point. The king will make some noise about free press, free lunch, whatever. The India problem will stabilize somehow. People will moan and groan, but they'll accept it."

"I don't know."

"Wait and see. This is Nepal."

I wondered. Shrestha might be right. In some ways, Nepal was a lot like America. The economy might be a mess, the poor might be falling through the cracks, but there were enough comforts and distractions to satisfy the majority. Fruit and sugar were expensive, but they were available. Kerosene was in short supply, but a black market was in place. Yes, the police had arrested and even killed some protesters; homes were being demolished, without compensation, to widen roads; about a nickel of every foreign aid dollar went to the project for which it was intended. But the cinemas and shops were still open. Life could be worse.

"How long are you here for?" asked Shrestha.

"Not much longer. Not even a week."

"We'll call me when you come back. We'll have a beer. Maybe the shit will hit the fan by then. You never know. The Romanians did it."

"And the Americans."

A boxy subcompact pulled in through the gate of our compound. Shrestha slapped my shoulder and dropped his half-finished cigarette to the ground. "Have a safe flight," I said.

"Thanks." He buttoned up his jacket and reached for the door handle of the running car. "So are you going to write about this?"

"I might."

"I figured. Please don't use my name." He jumped into the car, waving briefly as it backed away.

THE MORNING HAD brightened to lavender. I could hear the clomp of cattle crossing the roadway toward the soccer field where they grazed. A bell rang through the fog. I returned inside and switched on the lights, wondering what to do with myself. The logistics attending my departure were settled. Laxmi was paid through March, and the flat's subletters would hire her through April. I'd completed my shopping, picking up everything I'd need for a prolonged stay in America: a dozen packages of Tibetan incense, four block-printed tablecloths, a pair of ceramic candleholders shaped like elephants, a stack of paper prayer flags, and a couple of tubes of Vajradanti (literally, "lightning tooth") toothpaste.

Coffee is something to do. I brewed a pot and carried it into the living room. A cane bookshelf leaned against the far wall, filled with familiar titles. I could read their spines from my seat. It was comforting. The flat felt utterly like home. It *was* home. What was unimaginably strange was the idea of returning to California. After four months in Nepal, the streets of Oakland seemed as distant as the Borneo rainforest.

It suddenly seemed of utmost importance to spend the morning immersed in the sacred ambience of Kathmandu. I picked up my Walkman, pulled a scarf off my coat rack, and set off for our neighborhood shrine.

A THICK MIST clung to the surface of Nag Pokhari. Droplets fell off the golden cobra's snout, plinking into the water beside the square column that served as its support. A single lotus bloomed upon the lake, popcorn yellow in the pale chrome light. By the look of things, the strike was off to a good start. There were no taxis in the plaza, no men in pressed darwa-surwals and black topis bicycling down Naxal to work.

There was only me, sitting under my Chinese umbrella on a damp wooden bench.

Not a hint of life was visible beneath the surface of Snake Lake. If any nagas lived here, they kept a low profile. In all the years I'd lived in this neighborhood, I hadn't seen a single devotee pour any kind of offering into this lake.

Which begged the question: Were there nagas here at all? Or was this an atrophied shrine, the site of an ancient encounter lost to obscurity? Was Nag Pokhari still a holy, percolating abode of snake gods, or a mere historical marker, like the commemorative plaques outside abandoned adobes and New England inns-turned-steakhouses?

I threw a silver *mohar*, a half-rupee coin, into the water. It sank without a ripple. I shuddered, wondering about its destination—and wondered if the very fact of my wondering was perhaps the point. Maybe Nag Pokhari existed, and always had, as a reminder of unseen depths, the serpentine uncertainties of life. Were Nepalis that subtle? I couldn't put it past them. This was, after all, Asia, where things often turned out to be far more complex than they appeared, and even the simplest objects might be onions of spiritual symbolism, their true meaning obscured by layer after layer of metaphor.

A lotus, for example. In America, the word *lotus* has very specific meanings: It's either a flower or a sports coupe. Throughout Asia, however, the lotus—*padma*, in Sanskrit—is the universal symbol of the awakened mind. Rooted in the muck and mire, the determined stalk makes its way upward to blossom in the lush light of day.

The lotus is the throne of the Buddha, and the symbol of his teaching; it is the womb from which Padmasambhava ("lotus-born"), the great Indian mystic, emerged. To gaze at that single blossom yawning upon the dark surface of Nag Pokhari, or to see a lotus anywhere, was to be reminded of meditation's goal.

A lotus is unambiguous. But can the same be said for snakes? Not in Kathmandu, not in Asia, maybe nowhere. In the East and West alike, snakes are charged and variable symbols. It's impossible to see one without feeling a sense of wonder, or dread.

The gulf between Eastern and Western snake symbolism is profound. In the Judeo-Christian tradition, snakes are evil and cunning, promoting the slimy emotions that tempt and wreck our souls. In Nepal, snakes are so well loved they have their own festival. Nag Panchami falls during the summer monsoon, whose sustaining rains are controlled by the nagas.

When one examines the Western prejudice, it's clear how superficial and misdirected it is. Our loathing of snakes seems to date back to a single morning in Eden, when a magnanimous episode of serpentine generosity was falsely cast as a duplicitous dare.

"Ignorance," that archetypal naga cautioned Eve, "may be bliss; but it is also ignorance. God knows this, I know it, and that impressive brain of yours knows it, too. But don't take my word; have a bite of this fruit."

And Eve, whose defiant courage would be twisted into a betrayal of everything high and holy, helped herself.

Was the snake wrong? The snake was right. Yet despite that mythical serpent's sacrifice, something in us that yearns for dependency, and the innocence of the cradle, remains bitter. A snake got us chucked from our little garden, and we've been bashing them with shovels ever since.

The sages of antiquity knew the truth about snakes. Using *gematria* (the art of tagging letters with numerical values), they seeded their language with mathematical ciphers. Secret messages were buried within words, accessible through a kind of linguistic alchemy.

In kabala, the mystical tradition of Jewish wisdom, each Hebrew letter is assigned a number. Every word thus has a numerical value. In his *Introduction to the Study of the Tarot*, Paul Foster Case reveals that, according to gematria, the numerical value of the Hebrew word for serpent—358—is identical to the word for messiah.

It's a shocking affinity, but it makes sense. Both snakes and messiahs, after all, are masters at the art of liberation. A snake literally sheds its skin, emerging as a rejuvenated being. A messiah offers the same opportunity, in metaphor: a chance to invent ourselves anew.

I fished in my daypack and found a Miles Davis tape. Old Miles actually reminded me of a cobra: smooth, regal, and venomous. His playing was circuitous as well, slithering from phrase to phrase with a fluid confidence. Now it rose up and swayed inside my skull . . .

When a Nepali mentions a naga, he or she isn't referring to a garden snake. The classic naga, a snake god, is the hooded cobra: the Arnold Schwarzenegger of the serpent world.

Nagas pop up everywhere in Hindu and Buddhist lore, savvy brokers between the spiritual and elemental worlds. Lord Vishnu, the great preserver of the Hindu trinity, dozes on the infinite coils of Ananta, a serpent-cum-couch, for eight months of the year (during the remaining four, he extricates humanity from its deadlier dilemmas). Shiva, the potent creator/destroyer, source of the Ganges, wears live cobras in his hair. Nagas are the wardens of the monsoon rains, and safeguard the Earth's trove of diamonds, jewels, and underground treasures. And it was Muchilinda Naga, a seven-hooded cobra, who sheltered the Buddha from the sun and rain during his seven weeks of meditation on the banks of the Aroma River.

Nowhere is the Asian respect for serpents more evident than in tantra. In these "secret teachings," snakes symbolize the deepest source of spiritual power. The kundalini lies coiled at our lowest psychic center: the root chakra, located between our legs at the base of our spine. Through specific meditations and practices—like measured breathing, sexual yoga, and the recitation of mantras—we invite that snake to dance. It climbs the spine, electrifying the six internal chakras. It reaches the *ajna* chakra, right between the eyes, then rises higher still, penetrating the cranium. There it illuminates the *sahasrara* chakra, the Lotus of a Thousand Petals, which hovers like a grat above our skulls. When your kundalini hits that point, you know you've arrived: You embrace, with a single glance, all the manifestations of existence.

Once again, you've taken a bite of that big, juicy apple. And again, you have a snake to thank for it.

AND WHAT ABOUT Jordan? Maybe all he needed was a good snake dance: something to revitalize his long-dormant kundalini. I'd be home in less than a week—but I wondered if I might somehow convey, through telepathic alchemy, a real-time blessing from the Earth itself.

Ramana lay on a blanket inside the brick shed beside the shrine house, dozing beside his flea-ridden mongrel. I put my hand on the caretaker's shoulder and shook him gently. The dog growled, but hardly stirred. The shrine-keeper rose reluctantly.

"Ramana . . . Malai naga puja garna manlaagchha."

He looked at me quizzically. What need had a Westerner for a snake puja? Aside from their mythic role in the monsoon, nagas were petitioned when ground was broken for a well, or a house, or when any new construction was about to begin. The offering was essentially a protection payoff, in hopes the local snakes would steer clear of the enterprise. Nonetheless Ramana nodded at my request, and ducked into the tiny brick building. A moment later he emerged, handing me a small brass flask filled with buffalo milk. He topped the rim with a nasturtium, muttering a brief prayer. I handed him a 20-rupee note and returned to my bench.

The mist was beginning to break. Shafts of light shot through the branches of a nearby eucalyptus tree and stenciled the green water. I couldn't see more than a foot down. How deep *was* this pool, anyway? What, or who, lived at the bottom?

Did I really want to know? It was a disturbing thought. As I peered over the pond's edge, I understood something. There is more to this snake thing than the idea of transformation. Snakes have another quality, as well: They abide in the depths. Black water is their domain, and we summon them out at our peril.

So what was Nag Pokhari, then? It wasn't the pathetic pool in front of me, covered with scum and algae. It wasn't the cartoon cobra with a goofy expression and forked tongue, peering archly from its capital. It wasn't the clogged jets ejaculating lamely from the reservoir's corners. It wasn't the benches, or the lotus, or the little temple by the entrance gate. It wasn't even the snakes themselves, assuming that any still lived here.

This domain of the nagas, this Snake Lake, was nothing less than a double-edged allegory for everything ecstatic and horrific about the prospect of liberation. The nagas and their domain are mythic metaphors, warning buoys on the unexplored waters of our psyches. Lacking sufficient wisdom, or the proper training, we plumb these depths with fear and awe: The transition from bondage to freedom, no matter how one approaches it, has a terrifying aspect. We are suddenly responsible for ourselves.

Our best shot, our *only* shot at liberation, lies within the liquid mystery of our own bodies. It's lurking in our depths, dozing in the silt, slithering between the smooth black fingers of the lotus roots, coiled between our legs. Until we plunge in, with a torch in one hand and a flute in the other, we'll never charm it awake.

Ramana watched with amusement as, with a halting prayer, I poured the offering onto the algae-rimmed surface of Snake Lake.

18

Playing in the Bandh

C OAL AND CLARICE met me at the Telecom office. We rode our wobbling rented bikes down the long hill passing the National Stadium and leaned right onto Tripureshwar. Bandh days, despite their implicit menace, had become something to look forward to. It was amazing how even a few hours without trucks and buses could completely clear the air. Not only that; there was a jubilant camaraderie among the scores of people riding bicycles, and a musical quality to their bells.

A kilometer and change down the road, Tripureshwar became Kalimati. "Here we go," Coal announced, pulling over. "A single glorious spot free of cow shit, oil drips, or potholes. I believe I've found God's Little Acre." It seemed as good a place as any. Clarice and I pulled our bikes beside his, carried our daypacks to the middle of the road, and unloaded our supplies.

Clarice grabbed the ends of a bedspread and snapped it flat. The cloth lofted over the pavement, settling like a magic carpet. A puff of air lifted her hair, obscuring her glasses, and she brushed it back with long fingers.

Clarice was, in almost every way, the polar opposite of Grace: private, discreet, deliberate in her movements. She was tall and slender, with a sculpted neck and narrow waist, while Grace's body had the sleek economy of a seal. Adorable and energetic, Grace made me dizzy with desire, but Clarice's poise took my breath away. I knew that Coal knew this. And I think we both appreciated how, in a way, my attraction to his wife gave their relationship an added charge.

The thin cotton bedspread was printed with bold motifs in red, orange, and black: fish, pineapples, and anorexic dragons. Clarice smoothed down the corners and weighted them with our daypacks and sneakers.

"I've always wanted to do this," she said. It was almost a sigh. "Don't ask me why."

"Why, Clarice?" Coal sat cross-legged on the sheet, extracting sandwiches, snacks, and a tall water bottle from his pack.

"For the same reason people climb mountains, I suppose. Because it is here. Because no one else has done it. Isn't that right? Has anyone else done this? I shouldn't think so. Impossible, really."

The idea had been hers: to picnic in the middle of Kalimati, the busiest road in the Kathmandu Valley. On any other day, the plan would have been suicide; even crossing the street was life-threatening. This afternoon, though, the strike had cleared Kalimati of traffic. There were bicycles and pedestrians, as usual, and the occasional scooter buzzed nervously past. But any bus, truck, or tanker that dared the bandh would have its windshield smashed and be set upon by prodemocracy mobs.

Clarice often surprised me. She was pessimistic, almost mocking, about Nepal's prospects for revolution; years in Africa had nurtured her cynicism. Her attitude made her seem conservative. But she was actually a realist, with a keen sense of the absurd. She was also (like all teachers, some more successfully than others) a performer. Her bright earrings, bangles, electric blue scarf, and colorful blanket were a costume, jarring against the gray of the buildings and the blackened road. Clarice would never admit it, but this picnic was performance art: street theater. Her stage was Kalimati, a symbol of Nepal's degradation and dependency; in the center of it, like a distant but reachable island, she was building an oasis of freedom.

"Who's got the cushions?"

"Me." I worked them out of my pack. "I brought four. You want two, Coal? Clarice?"

"Thank you, no, you take it. Where's Grace?"

"She's sick. Some bacterial infection. The worst is over, but she's lying low."

'That's what you get, eating out every night in Thamel." Clarice waggled a finger. "It's worth having a cook."

"It wasn't Thamel; it was some official banquet. She ate shrimp."

"Shrimp?" Clarice shook her head. "Might as well drink the tap water."

"While we're on the subject . . ." Coal probed the sandwiches. "What have we here? Why . . . it's seafood! Tuna, tuna, and tuna. No, my mistake; this third one's tuna. Would anybody care for a tuna sandwich? Jeff? Or perhaps you would prefer tuna?"

"No. Tuna's fine." I turned to Clarice. "What makes us think this canned stuff is safe?"

"Blind faith," Coal answered.

"Tuna. Tuna. Tuna." Clarice repeated the word and raised her eyebrows. "If you say it four or five times you can't believe it's really a word."

"There are words like that," Coal agreed. "I've always thought that *fork* was a strange word. *Fork. Fork. Fork.* Doesn't that sound odd? Who ever came up with such a ridiculous word?"

A taxi honked bitterly, but gave us a wide berth. We watched it weave up the otherwise empty street. A moment later we heard shouts, breaking glass, and the screech of accelerating tires. We stayed right where we were: in the middle of Kalimati, our sheet spread over the worn yellow line, spooning potato salad onto flimsy paper plates. Bewildered Nepalis stared at us from the curb.

"I'm surprised there aren't more cabs," I remarked. "Ganesh Man Singh told me that the government bribed the drivers, with money and petrol, to stay on the streets."

Coal shrugged. "Can't put a price on your health. A driver broke the bandh down by Kamal Pokhari this morning; a bunch of protestors beat the shit out of him. Smashed his windows, slashed his tires, and scratched nasty words into his boot. All within sight of the police station. You could not pay me enough," he declared, "to be driving today."

"What's this about G. M. Singh?" Clarice reached for a tomato. "I thought he was in prison. But you interviewed him, didn't you? How is he? Poor man."

"They released him a few days ago," I said. "He's not in great shape, but he still seems tough. And gruff. What an amazing-looking guy: a big, craggy face, like a proud old lion. And a deep, gravelly voice. Every inch the working-class hero. But this is his last shot, and he knows it. The guy has been fighting for democracy since the 1940s. He's spent years in jail. Now he's on his last leg, and if Jana Andolan flops this time, he's out of luck. Finished. His life's work, for nothing." I reached for a slice of tomato. Clarice held out the plate.

"Did he offer you any words of wisdom?"

"Some." I pulled my journal out of my daypack. "He seemed hyperconscious about the fact that his remarks were for a Western audience. Here's a quote I might use:

> *Fundamentally, we want the right to be heard. If opposing thoughts cannot be expressed, democracy loses all meaning. To reach this goal, we intend to make it impossible for the government to function. But our methods will be peaceful.*

"There you are," said Coal. "And what could be more peaceful than this? A lovely picnic on the tarmac, birds nesting above the Krishna Pipe and Plumbing Concern, a breeze through the power lines. It's paradise. Shangri-la, some might say."

"Here's what really got his goat," I said, holding my place with my finger. "It's so typically . . . *Nepali*. In the old days, when Ganesh Man Singh met with Mahendra or Tribhuvan—the king's father and grandfather—they would greet him with the word *basnus*: a formal way of saying 'be seated.' But when he met with Birendra, the king said *baasa*: 'sit down.' It's the form of address one would use with a child. That's what infuriates these guys the most: the lack of respect."

"Exactly as we discussed last week," said Coal. "The history of conflict is all about humiliation. The sensitive male ego."

"I don't know," Clarice sighed. "I'd like to believe it's all going somewhere. It'd be lovely if Ganesh lives to see some real changes. But Nepalis are too complacent. They've grown accustomed to having their bread buttered by UNICEF, WHO, USAID, the Peace Corps, VISTA, the British Army, and so forth. I know it sounds strange, but as bad as things are in Nepal, at least they're peaceful. It's not like Africa, where you have tribal groups slaughtering each other left and right."

"I agree with Clarice," Coal said, searching through a plastic shopping bag. "Did you see the line outside the cinema yesterday? Thousands of kids. Boys, mostly. Lining up to see the latest Bollywood boob-fest. It's all bread and circuses. Speaking of which, would anybody care for part of this baguette? It's a bit dry, but we'll slice some of this cheese onto it."

"Singh actually talked about that."

"Baguettes? He's even more cultured than I thought."

I found the quote.

The government has carried the country along with it only by entertaining the people from one ceremony to another. There are so many ceremonies in Nepal, where people are exposed to a circus.

"It's true," Clarice said. "Circuses by the dozen." I read on.

We have peace in Nepal—but it is the peace of the graveyard. This is due to the threat of the government. People will shed their fear once the People's Movement gains momentum. The Nepali people are under great economic hardship; this will be the force that pushes them out onto the streets. And nobody knows in what strength.

"Brave words." Coal handed me a yak cheese and tomato sandwich. "I hope the right people hear them."

"Hearing them won't be enough," said Clarice.

She was right. Proclamations from Singh would not ignite the hearts of the masses. The Jana Andolan required a flash point, the snapping of a last straw. Something that everyone, from doctors to rickshaw wallahs, could rally around.

We finished our sandwiches and peeled a few tangerines. More than fifty spectators watched us now, from both sides of the street. No one approached. At one point a man yelled out to ask us, very politely, what we were doing. Coal's nonchalant reply—that we were eating lunch—seemed to satisfy him. He wagged his head and moved on.

Coal asked Clarice, "How long before we get run over?"

"It's two o'clock now. The bandh ends at four. But we should leave fairly soon."

"It's true," I said. "The industrial-type shops will stay closed, but the food sellers and little shops will reopen. People will sneak outside as soon as they think they can get away with it. I doubt any buses or trucks are going to run, but taxis will."

Coal frowned. "What about Thamel? Saraswati's staying at home; we may have to go out for dinner."

"The restaurants should be open. That whole area is pretty much above the law. No one fucks with the tourist economy."

"There's another strike tonight, you know. Same as Tuesday. Lights out," Coal warned. "Else they'll break your windows and tattoo your cat."

"You're going to hide out at home?"

"We're watching *A Fish Called Wanda*. The pale glow of our television, I trust, will be invisible from the streets beyond our compound wall. Join us if you dare."

Clarice collected our trash into a plastic bag and wrapped the leftovers in aluminum foil. "The sun is lovely," she said. "Wouldn't want to do this in summer, though; you'd sink right into the asphalt."

Coal put a hand on my shoulder. "So how much longer do we have you for, old chum?"

"Three days. Can you believe it?" I shuddered with the sudden awareness that my life was about to be turned inside out. "I can't imagine being back in Oakland." My stomach tightened. "Whenever I leave Nepal, I feel like I'm tearing myself up by the roots."

Clarice leaned over and put her hand on mine. "Why don't you just stay?" I looked in her eyes. She was serious.

"I don't know," I replied honestly. "The fact is, I have two complete, completely separate lives." A dog joined us. He was mottled with mange, but Clarice stroked his head and fed him a heel of bread. "When I'm in California, getting ready to come to Nepal, I go through the same thing. The thought of leaving my friends, my flat, my daily routine, terrifies me. There's a great wailing and gnashing of teeth. Then all of a sudden I'm here, absolutely at home, and the thought of leaving breaks my heart all over again." I shrugged. "It's called separation anxiety. I inherited it from my mother."

"Wail and gnash away, then," Coal offered. "We won't think any less of you."

I peered down Kalimati. Typically the road faded to black, lost in a haze of soot. Today, I could see all the way back to Tripureshwar. It had taken just one traffic-free morning for the seemingly eternal pall of pollution to blow away. Just to my right, on the south side of the street, was the Kalimati Clinic. I felt a shock of recognition: We were picnicking at the spot where, two weeks ago, I'd jumped out of my taxi to interview the produce sellers; the very spot where, in 1979, my friend Paul Janes had stopped his bicycle: *This is it.*

"What's that?" Coal turned toward me. I wasn't aware I'd spoken.

"This is it," I said, or repeated. "This is my life. The two of you, Grace, the Nepalis and their discontents. All of this, right here. But one week from now, this will be a dream. I'll be sweating over a pile of tax forms, glued to the phone, stuck in traffic on the Bay Bridge. The West will open its maw and swallow me whole."

"We'll write each other," said Clarice.

"No, we won't. We won't have time. You'll be busy; I'll be busy. The weeks will jump by. And this whole world will disappear from sight, like a postcard that fell behind the desk."

"You'll be back," she insisted.

"Yes. I will. In a month or so, I hope. And hopefully you'll be here, too. And we'll pack a picnic, and celebrate at some grassy shrine."

"And it will be," sang Coal, "as if you never left."

We pulled our shoes back on, and stood up. I crammed the cushions back into my daypack while Clarice shook out the ground cloth. Coal carried the trash. As we unlocked our bicycles, I waved good-bye to the remaining spectators. They waved back, smiling.

19

Heaven and Hell

I'D COME TO the Saturday teaching early, as the Rinpoche had advised. There were no other shoes at all. I placed my sneakers in a corner, covered them with my daypack, and entered Chokyi Nyima's assembly room. I felt sheepish; only three days had passed since the Lhosar celebration and my inexplicable anxiety attack.

Appropriately or not, my display of fragility embarrassed me. Up until Lhosar Chokyi Nyima had viewed me, I imagined, as a self-assured professional, walking the razor's edge of prerevolution politics, taking my dharma on the fly. But I'd blown my facade, betraying a shaky inner core and revealing myself as a potential candidate for the dreaded diagnosis that Dr. Dan was occasionally forced to stamp onto the medical forms of certain trembling, bug-eyed tourists just before they were airlifted back home: PUTTIA. *Psychologically Unfit To Travel In Asia.*

Chokyi Nyima was sitting alone at his dais, perusing a sutra and sipping tea. When he saw me he wagged his head backward. I walked up to him, knelt down, and presented a kata scarf. He held it between his hands, intoned a prayer, and slipped it around my shoulders.

"So. Better?"

"Much better. Thank you, Rinpoche. I don't understand what happened to me the other day. I saw a dead person lying on the kora, just a body. And I lost it. I can't explain why."

"Better not try explain. In Tibet, some people believe seeing dead person good luck. Maybe some other religion bad luck. For you, maybe, bad luck."

"How so?"

Again, he studied my eyes. "Sometimes a lot of things to say, no good to say. Sometimes a lot of things to say, no need to say. Sometimes no need to say, but good to say. This time, no good to say. Understand?" I nodded dubiously.

"Okay," Chokyi Nyima continued. "What I want to tell you is this." I backed off my knees and settled into a trampled lotus. "In Buddhism we have what we call the 'auspicious conditions.' When these things happen together, it is quite good. Quite . . . *rare*. Understand?" I made an agreeable noise.

"First auspicious condition: You have human rebirth. So many possible rebirths! Can be reborn as dog; as fly; as bird; even as tiniest, tiniest, what call? Amoeba! Every living thing must be reborn. But a human rebirth? Very, very rare."

I nodded, familiar with this reasoning. Most East-leaning Westerners take it on faith that any half-decent person will reincarnate, automatically, as a human being. But Buddhist scriptures suggest otherwise. Unless one has practiced the necessary skills and developed an instinctive grasp of the complex dance steps required to transit the Bardo, there are no guarantees.

"Second auspicious condition," Chokyi Nyima continued. "To be born in a time, and place, where Buddha dharma is available. Many other times, many other places, not available! Not so easy to find! Understand? One hundred years before, even you live in America, maybe impossible to find Buddha dharma. One hundred years from now, maybe also impossible. Born in Africa, China, North Pole, South Pole, also not easy to find. Always busy! Always chasing *wawulwu* . . . ?" He made an incomprehensible guttural sound and puckered his forehead in confusion. "*Wrawrlu* . . . ?"

"Walrus," I offered.

"Yes. So. Third condition: desire to study. *Desire*. You hear about Buddha dharma and you think, 'Oh, here's something good. Something *useful*.' You feel the need to learn, some interest to study. Okay?"

I smiled in agreement, quietly amused by how *organized* Buddhism was. Everything was broken into lists and carefully numbered. Such a system would have been very accessible, even to the illiterate people of ancient India.

"Now a fourth condition, very important also. One must find a teacher who can teach. Who is willing to teach. Able to teach. Maybe happy to teach—but that is not necessary! Many good teachers, not so happy to teach! Even Buddha: at first, not want to teach. 'Oh, too difficult, no one will understand, no way to teach.' But it is possible to teach. Difficult, but possible. Okay?"

"Yes, Rinpoche."

"So. These are the auspicious conditions. Even the first one, human rebirth, very rare. If you have all of them, it's like miracle. Isn't it? So how can you not study? How can you not practice meditation? Otherwise this lifetime, this opportunity, is finished. Maybe next time reborn as giraffe. Right? Real giraffe! Then not so possible to change. Not so easy to liberate. Right?"

"Right."

"How many more weeks you stay here?"

"I go back to America the day after tomorrow, Rinpoche."

"Wow! So soon! Then it is very important that you find a good teacher there. Many good teachers there, I think. I will find out. You can write to me, I will recommend. Okay? But please remember the auspicious conditions! Understand?"

"I understand, Rinpoche. Thank you."

"You take this." He leaned forward and tied a red and yellow protection cord around my neck, uttering blessings as he did so. An elaborate knot hung on the loop, reminiscent of the lanyard key-holders that Jordan and I once wove, out of rubbery laces, at YMHA summer camp.

I took my place on the carpeted couch. My mind, oddly, was on Albert Camus. The primary question that any human being must answer, the philosopher had maintained, was whether or not to go on living. If one answered in the affirmative, one automatically assumed a vast responsibility: freedom.

And that, it seemed to me, was precisely what Chokyi Nyima was saying. He was offering, through the dharma, an opportunity for liberation. Living, breathing, and human, how dare I refuse it?

People began entering the room, presenting katas and finding their places. Tea was served. Chokyi Nyima answered a phone call, received a bundle of medicinal herbs from a disheveled Khampa pilgrim, and took a stack of letters from Rebecca. A moment later, a man sitting in the middle of the room coughed: an explosive, hacking cough that startled the Rinpoche. The victim looked lamely to the dais.

"Sick," he explained.

Chokyi Nyima shook his head. "No. Not sick." He returned to his letters.

There was scattered laughter, an awkward moment of cognitive dissonance. A red-haired woman with electric blue eyes and a round, Irish face waved her hand. "Rinpoche . . . why did you say that just now: 'Not sick'?"

Chokyi Nyima set down his pen, handed the correspondence to Rebecca, and settled himself.

"If I *say* 'sick,' he *think* sick, then more sick! Some sick person really sick; some sick person not so sick, but if *think* sick, make more sick. Some sick person very sick, but if *think* not sick, not sick. Sometimes even quite big sick, if you think, 'I'm not sick!' then sickness is cured. Even little sick, if you think, 'I'm really sick!' then make big sick. Okay?"

This virtuoso response drew a smattering of applause. This was the Rinpoche's specialty: delivering gems of wisdom, couched in English primer prose. This particular gem seemed to fit my brother; so much of his suffering seemed to be a self-reinforced condition. I wondered, sometimes, if the key to his cure might be no more than what Chokyi Nyima had demonstrated: a denial of his sickness, shouted boldly into the wind.

Grinning, the Rinpoche called for further questions. The Irish woman waved her hand again. "This has nothing to do with my first question," she warned.

"Okay. I try to give smart answer anyway."

"Well, it seems to me that many Westerners are actually *attracted* to suffering. We put ourselves under a lot of pressure, seeking out situations in which we are sure to suffer. Why is this so? Why would anyone *choose* a life of suffering?"

I stared at her in astonishment; the question seemed perfectly attuned to my own thoughts. The Rinpoche, however, looked at her uncomprehendingly. "That means? Explain."

"Okay. I'm an artist. I design fabrics for a living. I work for myself. Every day I face the possibility of rejection, which makes me feel sad and nervous. Yet I stay with this job. Then, when I do get assignments—when I *am* successful—I sabotage myself. I take on more and more work, until I get completely stressed-out. Do you understand? It's as if I'm not satisfied unless I'm suffering somehow."

"People make themselves busy in order to be famous, in order to get rich," Chokyi Nyima observed.

"Yes, but what if it's clear that you're going to be neither famous nor rich, but you keep doing it anyway?"

"Then, habit. You are caught in a bad habit." The Rinpoche answered quickly, then stopped. He considered a minute before continuing.

"There's a difference here," he said at last, "between West and East on some level. Westerners seem to get a better education from a young age, so they are eager to use their skills to become successful. In this part of the world, many people cannot even read or write. So they do not get caught in the same way. But they get caught in other ways! Some are deeply interested in their reputation, in having a respectable image in other people's minds. Very, very important. For others, having money is enough. But here is one funny similarity I have discovered." Chokyi Nyima leaned forward, and the students craned toward him. "It seems much more painful to be unsuccessful, than there is pleasure from success." There was a murmur of assent.

"Understand? When good things happen, it is never enough. For example, when a businessman makes a good deal—a big deal!—that is just how it should be. Good—but maybe next will be better! But if a deal fails, it's very, very painful. A really big disaster! The same is true with one's reputation. If you get credit for something, that is good, a sweet feeling! But if you get blamed or criticized? Terrible! So terrible! Isn't it?

"Why is it," he asked, "that mind can never be filled, or satisfied? Why is it mind cannot be satisfied, with attainment of any kind? Why? Why? Hmm?"

He surveyed the room, Sphinx-like. They were a bit odd, these riddles posed by the Rinpoche. If you guessed wrongly, everyone would chuckle at your foolishness. If you were right, you came off as a pompous ass. The room, accordingly, was silent.

"Because mind is empty. Always empty. There is no way to fill it up. No matter how much success—money, job, get famous, get girls, get boys—no matter how much, mind is never satisfied! Simple as that." Chokyi Nyima looked down and furrowed his brow, as if he'd suddenly found himself at the edge of a precipice and had no choice but to leap forward.

"But how can the mind be empty? This is very important, so please listen well. Are you ready? Okay: *Mind has no beginning. Mind has no end.* But the world of phenomena, and our five gross senses, confuse us. This is very difficult to understand, but very important. If you need proof, please try this." Chokyi Nyima inhaled dramatically. "Take a deep breath. Relax. Now begin searching your mind. Searching, searching your mind. Where does mind begin? Where does mind end? Can you find mind's beginning? Can you find mind's end?"

We sat in silence, earnest in our collective search. This went on a few minutes. There were no shouts of "Eureka!" or any satisfied sighs of success. The mind, I discovered, turns out to be a good metaphor for the universe, or vice versa. It is impossible to establish a limit, or to think beyond it, but it is possible to imagine it curved: a topological paradox in which any given direction takes you back to your starting point. At any rate, the Rinpoche's lesson was well taken. If something is without beginning or end, no amount of stuff will fill it up. There is infinite room for distraction, attachments, and suffering.

"One more question?" Chokyi Nyima leaned forward, studying the attentive faces. An elderly Swiss man spoke out. He sat by the back of the room, hands on his knees like an obedient schoolboy. "Many times, I hear talk of Buddhist hells and heavens." He spoke in a thick accent. "But do Buddhists really believe that hell exists? Or heaven, for that matter?"

The Rinpoche nodded vigorously. "Good question," he obliged. "Many people think this. I'll try to explain.

"This condition into which we are born—the cycle of existences, of death and rebirth—is called samsara. So long as we are generating karma, there is samsara. There is rebirth. Karma has a complicated meaning, but usually means *deed*. Action. Action is important; but most important is *intention*. Good intention, bad intention. Good karma, bad karma.

"Now, human beings all look similar. We all have mouth, eyes, nose. We all see that mountain is mountain, sky is sky, moon is moon. We all accept things that way. This is called general karma.

"Individual karma is not like that. How you see, how she sees, may be completely different. Different interests, different likes. Books, music, even food. So. We're all human. We all have similar karma. Similar, but not the same. Okay so far?"

"Yes, yes, yes," the Swiss man said dismissively. "I know this. But my question is, what about the hell realms?"

"Listen, I'm telling you! In Tibetan Buddhism, we talk about six karmic realms: *gods, demigods, humans, animals, hungry ghosts,* and the *hell realms.* Each realm has its own special, how do you say, *trait*. For the god realm, the trait is pride. Everyone is proud, conceited, very self-satisfied. The demigod realm is quite similar—but there the trait is envy. Jealousy. Always spying, spying, trying to find a weapon, trying to defeat someone else. Jealous.

"In the animal realm, it is very different. Their trait is ignorance. Not knowing samsara, not knowing karma; just living and dying, eating and shitting. Underneath that, we find hungry ghost realm. In this realm, no one is ever satisfied. The special trait is greed. In the hungry ghost realm, they say, creatures have huge stomachs—but their mouths are the size of a pin. They want more and more, but can never be satisfied.

"Okay. Are you ready? The hell realm. Here, the trait is anger. Anger is the worst emotion. The human being has so many problems already that getting angry, we say, is like building up the fire under a boiling kettle. So we call this place, where everyone is angry, the hell realm. Burning, torture, misery. Everyone in terrible pain, always very . . . *furious.* A very bad place. Okay? Understand?"

There was a vague suspense in the room, wondering if the questioner would challenge the Rinpoche again on this point. But he remained silent.

"So. One final realm. The one realm I didn't mention. Hmmm? What about the *human* realm? Human realm comes between demigods and animals. What is our trait?"

"Desire," Rebecca blurted half-consciously.

"*Desire.*" The Rinpoche nodded. "Humans feel desire. Desire can be negative: wanting this, lusting for that, a strong attraction to objects, people, reputation, money. Like the artist lady said before. But desire can also be a good quality. If the desire for liberation is strong, it can create a powerful attraction to Buddhism. A strong attraction to meditation and dharma practice. So desire can also be very positive. Very useful. For this reason, a rebirth in the human realm is the best."

He raised his arm and jabbed a finger at his inquisitor. "But your question—I didn't forget!—do these realms *really* exist, or not?

"Maybe if you search some kind of outside place, like in the sky or underground, they won't exist that way. But you will find that our *inner* experience visits all six of those realms—arrogance and jealousy, ignorance and greed, anger and desire—every day. And not even in one day! In one hour! In ten minutes! Our minds continually go up and down, up and down, from heaven to hell."

I remembered Chokyi Nyima's earlier words: *We are demons; we are buddhas. We contain the cause of samsara; we contain the cause of nirvana.* Here was a parallel concept: that we unwittingly manifest, many times each day, the conditions that either edge us toward liberation or drag us into despair. The purpose of the Buddha's teaching, I was beginning to understand, is to train our minds toward cultivating the former, despite an inexplicable attraction toward the latter.

"So. These six karmic realms exist," the Rinpoche concluded. "But not outside. They exist right here." He tapped his chest, then his head. "No need to search elsewhere. God realm and hell realm, animal realm and hungry ghost realm: all here. All inside. Okay? Satisfied?"

The Swiss man was satisfied. I was satisfied. We were all satisfied.

"Good. Then for today, finished."

A few people stayed behind to ask personal questions. I stayed as well. When the last student had left, I approached Chokyi Nyima. He smiled with what seemed, in my eager mind, to be special affection.

"So, Giraffe, please travel well. And practice well! Both important."

I took his right hand in both of mine. "Thank you for everything, Rinpoche. Meeting you has been a privilege." I looked into his eyes. The lama's calm, amused face seemed absolutely familiar, too familiar, certainly, for our relatively brief acquaintance.

"Don't forget to write," he said.

"I will. I promise."

"And next time you come Nepal, you see me first thing. Understand? Go through customs; put bag in room; go to toilet; take shower; then here. Any other thing, don't do. Okay?"

He squeezed my hands and released them. "*Kali pei.*" It was the traditional Tibetan farewell: Go slowly.

"*Kali shú,*" I replied, completing the exchange. Rest easy. I blotted my eyes with the corner of my kata, pressed my palms together in a final salute, and left the room.

20

The Boxer

FROM A DISTANCE, the field appeared to be filled with clean, white laundry: sheets and towels, blouses and undershirts, clipped onto clotheslines and billowing around a weathered old farmhouse. As my perceptions shifted into Nepali, though, I realized what I was seeing: acres and acres of white prayer flags, flapping from dozens of strings and poles.

I pulled up on the loose gravel and set the kickstand. Grace got off the motorcycle and stretched, her joints a bit stiff after two days in bed. The village of Pharping was just ten miles south of Kathmandu, but the bike was small and the road an acned expanse of potholes, fallen rocks, and dung. The trip had taken the better part of an hour; even I was saddle-sore. It felt good to be on my feet again. Grace led the way eagerly, skipping along a brick path toward a distant wooden farmhouse.

This was our farewell outing, the last time we'd be together for an unknown spell. Grace had chosen this destination; it was one of her favorite places in the valley. We walked until we reached a series of narrow dirt dikes separating dry rice fields. Grace continued on a zigzag heading toward the ancient, apparently empty dwelling.

"Who lives there?" I asked.

"A very high lama." We jumped down into a paddy to let a boy pedal by. His one-speed Hero was balanced expertly on the high, narrow hump of dike. "His name is Urgyen Tulku. That's his monastery, up there." She pointed across the road, to a gleaming white building on a nearby hill. "Have you met him?"

"No . . . I've never even heard of him."

"Really? He's Chokyi Nyima's father."

"His father . . . ?" What surprised me most was the notion that the Rinpoche had parents at all. It had never occurred to me. "Is there any chance of meeting him?"

"No, he's at Nagi Gompa for the month, giving Lhosar teachings to the nuns. But sometimes you can find him here. He's a trippy guy. He looks like one of those old lamas from *Magic and Mystery in Tibet*: the guys who could levitate, and melt ice with their inner heat."

Entering the lama's property, we stepped into a vast kinetic sculpture. Bolts of white fabric hung in rectangles and squares, block-printed with prayers and mantras, dancing like pearlescent flames as they filled the air with a deafening gallop. The Tibetan word for prayer flag is *lung ta*—"wind horse"—and many actually bore the image of a strutting colt. Others portrayed Tara, the protector goddess of the Kathmandu Valley; Chenrezig, the overworked bodhisattva of compassion; and Padmasambhava, who had subdued Tibet's animistic gods and made the high plateau safe for Buddhism.

The wind swelled, and the stampede with it. I stood still, imagining the prayers swirling upward in dizzy corkscrews. Blessings filled the air like snow, or fallout; we inhaled them with every breath.

Scraps and rags from tattered flags littered the ground, snagged on brambles and stones. I picked up a stray flag and flattened it out against my jeans. A block-print of Tara was visible on the cotton gauze. I wanted to keep it. Would that be a sin?

Grace was a few yards away, picking up what looked like a strip of torn cloth. She turned toward me and shouted, "Take a look at this!"

It was a perfect snakeskin: a gossamer stocking as brittle and translucent as winter frost. She lifted it toward me in her outstretched hand, applying the slightest pressure to keep it from blowing away.

"That's fantastic," I said, wishing I'd found it first. "Maybe it belonged to a nagaraja—one of the original snake kings who migrated from the lake when Manjushri drained it with his sword." I touched it lightly. "It's an amazing omen . . ."

"Of what?"

"I haven't the slightest idea."

"It's yours," she said. "If you can get it home in one piece."

"Really? Don't you want to keep it?"

She shrugged. "I thought you liked snakes."

"I do, I do . . ." I took it from her hands and cradled it between my cupped palms. We walked together into the nearby village, where a shopkeeper sold me a cardboard tube. He watched with amusement as we slid the molted naga skin into the cocoon.

GRACE AND I had dinner plans that evening at Rhoda and Kunda's. My packing wasn't quite finished, but it would be bad manners to cancel. Grace climbed onto the motorcycle seat behind me. Her left hand gripped my belt; her right balanced a pie. "I know you've never met Rhoda," she said. "But do you remember meeting her husband, Kunda Mainali? The journalist?"

"Of course. It was the same day we met—at the doctors' strike, two weeks ago. He'd told me you were friends with his wife. I'd had no idea she was American."

"A New *Yaw*-ker," Grace added. "Yeah, they're a strange couple. She's pretty manic, and he's . . . I don't know, almost shy. They met at school, in the States. But I have no idea how they got together in the first place. Her parents are very Jewish. I'm sure they were thrilled."

"His parents were delighted, I'm sure. I mean, their grandchildren will have American citizenship." I kick-started the bike, and away we went, chugging up the road toward the overgrown shrine at Bishalnagar.

Rhoda and Kunda lived in an airy one-story house in a small but beautifully planted compound surrounded by a low brick wall. Vines draped into their yard. The inside was decorated with large wood carvings, two framed color photographs by Mani Lama, and thick, expensive Tibetan carpets. Rhoda had prepared a classic expat meal: "buff" lasagna with mushrooms and spinach. Grace contributed an apple pie; I'd supplied a liter of *elaichi pista* ice cream.

Unavoidably, the main topic of conversation was politics. It seemed obvious the Jana Andolan had hit a pocket of stale air. The bandh itself had been a success. But the anarchy that followed, with its lasting memories of broken windows and smashed streetlights, was a very bad sign. There were strong suspicions that the roving bands of troublemakers had actually been *mandaleys*, thugs and hooligans hired by the Palace to discredit the movement. If this strategy continued, there would be trouble. The majority of Nepal's population were poorly educated farmers, small merchants, and hill dwellers, who would quickly equate democracy with chaos.

Kunda, born in Kathmandu, had been sent by a well-connected uncle to study in New York for two years. The same uncle had secured him a post at the *Shaligram*, where Kunda, quasi-reluctantly, was creeping slowly toward the editor's chair. Like most people who read the newspaper every day, he had a bleak take on recent events.

"Whether or not Jana Andolan succeeds, Nepal will face unrest and political confusion," he declared. "For a decade, at least."

"That's a cynical view," Grace mumbled, refilling his glass from a two-liter bottle of table wine. "Let's hope it's not a self-fulfilling prophecy."

"People in this country don't understand the concepts of leadership and democracy," he shrugged, spooning ice cream over his pie. "It's simply not part of our tradition. There's no precedent of give-and-take, and no concept of political compromise. Political compromise in Nepal, a hundred years ago, meant beheading your brother instead of poisoning him. Compromise for this king means . . . what? Putting out his cigar before going to bed?" Kunda drained his wine. He'd been mixing it with ice, but drinking steadily. "Agreeing to rent the latest Meg Ryan video, instead of his beloved Bruce Lee?"

"Shhhhhh!" Rhoda slapped his arm. "The house could be bugged."

"*Enter the Dragon!*" Kunda shouted, casting his vote to the hidden mikes. "Go with Bruce!"

"You won't think it's so funny," said Rhoda, "when they deport *me* and make you stay here."

"She's uptight," Kunda confided to Grace, "because she won't drink while she's pregnant." He tipped a defiant splash into his glass. "Here's the basic problem. Democracy in Nepal could mean *anything*. Right now, the only opposition comes from the Congress Party. Ganesh Man Singh. He's safe, and predictable. But they aren't the only activists in the country; far from it. For now, the other banned parties have put away their differences, to create the illusion of a united front. But this is only temporary. If there *is* a revolution, and democracy *does* become the law of the land, who's to say the communists, or socialists, or even the Maoists won't disrupt the process—or, God help us, win an election?"

"*Maoists?*" Grace was incredulous. "I thought they went out with twenty-mule teams."

"In this country," Rhoda said, "they still have twenty-mule teams."

"They're a fringe group," Kunda assured us. "Small, but passionate. And well organized."

I helped myself to a piece of pie. Pie, it occurred to me, hadn't been part of Nepal's tradition, either—and they'd certainly gotten that right. "It's highly unlikely that a fringe group will get any traction here, much less win an election."

"Probably." Kunda nodded. "But the communists and socialists aren't extremists. What if they win a majority and decide to nationalize the hydro-electric and mining? How will Nepal's neighbors react? Relations with India have never been worse. China, as you know, has closed its grip on Tibet; they're already starting to pull strings on this side of the Himalaya."

"So what are you saying?" Rhoda asked. "That democracy is a bad thing for Nepal? You want to keep bowing to this useless king?"

"Of course not." Kunda spanked his ice cream with the back of his spoon. "All I'm saying—for the benefit of our esteemed foreign correspondent"—he nodded at me—"is that if democracy *does* come to Nepal, it will have its own learning curve, just like all the other imported gadgets. Electric heaters, power saws, Toyota sedans, they all appeared practically overnight, and Nepalis made all kinds of tragic mistakes learning how to use them. Democracy will be the same. After ten or twenty years, we may get the hang of it."

"The main problem with democracy," Grace speculated, "will be getting people involved. Most of Nepal's population is illiterate, and lives far away from the population centers. I don't see how they'll learn to make intelligent decisions."

Rhoda shook her head. "I think that argument is overused. People can be intelligent without being literate. Many illiterate people are surprisingly shrewd. They'll understand the issues, believe me."

"But what about logistics?" I asked Kunda. "When we talked at the strike, you said that even if you published an article, people wouldn't be able to read it because they speak different dialects. What will that mean for campaigning? Not to mention the difficulties of having fair elections in remote villages, days from anywhere. How is anyone supposed to campaign? Or *vote*, for that matter?"

"Those are two different things. Yes, it's true, the different dialects and remote areas make it difficult for the movement to reach a flash point: a moment when everyone bands together, and by sheer force of 'people power' overthrows the king. But once the country is liberated, voting won't be a problem. Even now, we have a very effective political infrastructure. You'd be amazed at how politicized the people are, even in remote villages."

Rhoda had rented *Brazil* from the British Council library, but I had a full night ahead. I helped with the dishes and said my farewells. Grace left with me. We rode to my place, waking up the Shrestha's hell-hound. Inside the flat, we drowned out the barking with a tape of gamelan music.

Grace had been unusually quiet all day. She used the bathroom while I scanned the chaos of my bedroom. Socks, books, toiletries, incense, brassware, pashmina scarves, statues, prayer flags, trekking gear, cassette tapes, notebooks, computer batteries, travel pillows, film canisters, and newspaper clippings were strewn across every surface, waiting for the sleight of hand that would enable them to fit into my suitcase. It was too much to face. I considered leaving all of it behind. What liberation that would be! To travel without baggage, unfettered as the wind. The aspiration seemed as unlikely for me, in this particular lifetime, as enlightenment. I suspected that they were related.

Grace opened the bathroom door, vanquishing any illusions I might have had about a productive night of packing. She was wearing a satin teddy, black stockings, and a musky, infinitely erotic perfume that reminded me of my high school girlfriend.

"Hi." She leaned against the jamb, flaunting an irresistible silhouette.

"Whoa. Where did you find that outfit?"

"Where do you think? I brought it with me."

"How come I've never seen it before?"

"You talk too much." She moved to the nightstand, lit a candle, and shivered. "God, it's freezing in here." She jumped onto the bed and threw the blanket over herself, scattering my folded shirts across the floor. "Hey, sailor." She wiggled her toes. "Wanna have some fun?"

I lit a kerosene heater and carried it into the bedroom. Grace lost the blanket, and the room warmed up fast.

MAYBE IT'S NERVES, but it had become a tradition: Every time I visit Kathmandu, I spend part of my last night walking the streets. It's a final, intimate immersion into the city: my way of saying farewell. At midnight, as Grace slept, I slid out of bed and dressed.

Despite Friday's strike, there was no curfew. I moved briskly, shivering slightly until the heat pooled inside my jacket. My legs carried me past Nag Pokhari; past the pointy, guarded gates of the Royal Palace; down Tridevi Marg through Thamel; and past the empty, fluorescent-bathed bandstand in the center of Chhetrapati. I gave a wide berth to a pack of dogs, and spied two young bulls nosing at vegetable scraps.

A frantic dust bowl by day, Kathmandu is transformed at night. The shadowy ancient lanes, garnished with pipes, wires, and poles, call to mind Allen Ginsberg's "Sunflower Sutra": the busted, rusty funk of worn-out industrialism, reflecting humanity's natural slouch. I traipsed past crooked tenements propped up with bug-eaten struts, the delicately carved lattices askew in their window frames, past illuminated signs hawking cigarettes and soy milk, instant noodles and the Cosmic Language Institute. Someone poured a bucket of slop out a window, and I leaped backward, narrowly avoiding the amoebic splatter. From a tiny room, high in one of the cramped buildings, a radio blared Hindi film music. An infant's cries filtered from another. What is life like for these urban Nepalis, nestled so close together

that the sound of every conversation, argument, squeal of laughter, or moan
of passion is public knowledge? Have they developed an inner ear-lid that
allows them to shut it all out, hearing nothing, self-conscious of nothing?
Or is each *guthi* a single, intimate family, codependent and cocounseling, a
vast human apiary?

Sodium streetlamps washed out some of the ancient magic, but cast
an eerie, off-Broadway glow upon Asan Tole. A woman in a dark shawl
wandered from temple to temple, offering flame and receiving blessings. I
stopped at the Annapurna temple and gave myself a red *tika*, a chalky bene-
diction over my third eye. Then I just stood there, awed by the transformation that midnight visits upon these usually overcrowded squares.

A few blocks onward I'd had my fill. I took a narrow lane that led
back toward Kantipath, and dog-legged toward the Clock Tower. It loomed
above Rani Pokhari: the Queen's Lake, a man-made reservoir that, though
shallow, was popular for suicides. The clock chimed 1 a.m.

One moment I was alone on the avenue; the next, a deranged-looking
man stood in the middle of the street. He was in his late thirties, under-
dressed for the chilly night. His face was covered with bruises. He walked
straight toward me, blocking my path, and stopped.

"Excuse me, sir. Would you like to fight?"

"What?"

"I wish to fight you." He squared into a boxer's pose, arms up, sucking
in his belly. "Please . . . Let us fight."

Back home, the encounter would have made me take flight. Here, oddly,
it didn't feel threatening. I regarded the man gamely, wondering what twist
of karma had thrown us together on this particular night.

"I can't fight you now," I said. My ostensible opponent looked so crest-
fallen that I felt the need to blunt the sting. "But thank you, sir."

"Thank you." The man lowered his arms. "Thank you very much." He
stepped courteously aside, and I continued on my way.

The valley, characteristically, had tossed me a metaphor: the bat-
tered young warrior, emerging briefly from the shadows, desperate to be
a contender but unable to channel his energies. I turned around and saw

that the man had not moved. He stood poised beneath the Clock Tower, shadowboxing the moon.

GRACE WOKE UP as I slid back into bed. She wasn't aware I'd gone out at all.

"Hey . . . how do you feel? About leaving?" She pressed up to me, her hands folded against her chest.

"It hasn't sunk in. I keep thinking it's a huge mistake. But those letters from Jordan really spooked me." I felt her nod; there was no way to contest that imperative. "Anyway," I said, "I can't imagine I'll stay away for long. I seem to belong here."

"You do." She touched my nose. "Maybe you'll come back with your brother."

"That would be amazing." I stroked the clipped hair falling across her cheek. In her eyes, glowing in the dark, I saw something I hadn't seen before.

"I'm going to miss you," she said quietly.

"I'm going to miss you, too."

There was a moment's silence.

"What about Carlita?"

I remembered the last letter I'd received from her, three weeks ago. There was little pretense at affection. What had come through most strongly was her angry doubt that I would return and ambivalence about whether or not I did. I'd wanted to reply reassuringly, but everything I wrote seemed false, and I never mailed the letter. And then I'd met Grace. Altogether I'd acted abhorrently. Visiting the scene of that wreckage was not a happy prospect.

"I would say we're pretty much the past tense."

"Is that your conclusion, or hers?"

"Probably both of ours, by now."

"I guess you'll find out." Another, longer silence. "If I ask you a question, will you tell me the truth?"

"Yes."

"Are you really coming back?"

"Of course. I always come back."

"That's not what I mean." She drew a slow breath and took my hands into hers. "Would you come back for me?"

I studied her face in the darkened room, knowing what it had cost her to ask.

"I would," I said. "I will."

We kissed, and kissed again. I drew my fingers across her shoulder blades, tracing the smooth, white scars from the accident. She wriggled upward, bringing her neck to my mouth. The perfume she'd put on earlier commingled with a deeper, irresistible scent. We met and merged and rocked together, sending the lumpy comforter to the floor. When we fell asleep, her face was in my hands.

I didn't know where I'd be in a day or two, but wherever it was, it wouldn't be as good as this.

PART II

During

21

Happy Birthday to You

"IT'S GORGEOUS OUTSIDE," Paula called out from the flat's tiny kitchen. "Why don't you guys go up on the roof?" The old North Beach apartment, tucked into a block-long lane that didn't make it onto many San Francisco maps, had a small, flat roof with a panoramic view.

"In a couple of minutes . . . *Damn!*" Gina Rosa, Paula's six-year-old daughter, was teaching me to play Tetris. Her eye-hand coordination left mine in the dust. She shrieked with glee as I lost another round, the awkward geometric shapes moving too fast, colliding, rarely a fit.

"Let me," she demanded, grabbing the Game Boy out of my hands. "Watch." Her fingers danced effortlessly over the tiny keys.

"I want that game. As a birthday present," I said.

"No way, José!" She pranced into a corner and turned her back to me, geomancing with single-minded concentration.

It was the late afternoon of March 10, 1990. I'd been back in the Bay Area four full days, but hadn't been able to reach my brother. Paula and Mark, who lived in the flat above Carlita's, were throwing me a small birthday party. Carlita orbited the dining table, distributing a gamelan of goblets and flatware. I'd arrived half an hour ago, but aside from our long and almost wistful welcome-back hug, we hadn't had a moment alone.

"I think that was a hint," said Carlita, referring to Paula's suggestion. "I'll go up with you. Let me grab a sweatshirt. Paula, sure you don't need any more help?"

"No, no. Go to the roof. It's almost never this clear."

"Take my jacket." I slipped it over Carlita's shoulders. "Paula? Where's Mark?"

"Downstairs, probably. In the studio."

I'd met Mark and Paula in 1979, during my first visit to Kathmandu. Paula and I were teachers at ELI, the American English Language Institute. Her partner, a shadowy figure who never showed up at ELI parties, was a painter. That August, the American Cultural Center sponsored an exhibition of his work, and I dropped by after class. I hadn't expected much, and found myself in awe. The canvases were hypnotic and surreal, like nothing I'd seen before. They conveyed complex, hallucinatory thoughts, opium dreams of travel. One showed a richly textured rear view of three Thai monks climbing the stairs of a golden pagoda. There was something deeply disturbing, yet somehow revelatory, about the image, but the painting was so well balanced that I couldn't put my finger on it. After a few minutes, I got it: One of the monks had no head.

A guest book in the gallery invited comments. I was lavish in my praise and left my number. That evening Mark called, and we spoke for hours. During the five months I stayed in Nepal, we saw each other several times a week. He and Paula (as extroverted and spunky as Mark was private and morose) had continued their travels long after I'd returned to America. When they returned, a full year later, they called me: They'd gotten married in Australia, and had settled into this North Beach fourplex, owned by Mark's family.

Six years later Carlita, a Spanish teacher from Tucson, moved to San Francisco. She was a dark-eyed beauty who could have been cast as a tough but vulnerable south-of-the-border barmaid. Carlita loved teaching, but her secret passion was sculpting: creating whimsical assemblages out of religious fetishes, barbed wire, and other semifound objects. Mark had seen her ad on the Art Institute's housing board and called her for an interview. Two days later, she was living in the downstairs flat. Within a week she'd bonded with Paula, who had introduced us. It seemed an inspired match. How could I resist a woman who had created a mosaic of Ganesh out of the shattered shards of a ceramic Jesus?

Carlita and I ducked out the back door and carried our glasses of wine to the roof. It was nearly sunset. We stood facing northwest, toward the Golden Gate and its bridge. The weather was clear, but a foghorn blew. A seagull, or goose, passed above our heads. Fisherman's Wharf lit the waterfront while, further east, the sky mirrored the Ghirardelli sign's ruby glow.

Carlita seemed affectionate, but guarded. I knew she was unhappy I'd waited this long to see her. I'd told her I needed to decompress, get my feet back on the ground, unpack, and sleep, but she'd waited long enough. My failure to leap into her arms must have seemed like a sign of something hidden, which it was. We'd spoken on the phone a few times, and she'd set up this dinner. But her usually effusive spirit was held in reserve. I wondered if she, too, had taken a lover while we were apart. We'd discussed the possibility before I left, deciding it wouldn't be the end of the world. The understanding had seemed like a good idea, a sort of emotional and physical safety valve, but neither of us had raised the obvious question: What if one of us actually fell for someone else?

Of course I'd tell her about Grace. But it was important to pick the right time. In Nepal everything had seemed clear; it was as if no other world existed. My life in America—Carlita, Jordan, my familiar Oakland routines—had faded into abstraction, impossibly distant. But now everything seemed dizzy and scrambled, and Nepal itself unreal. Grace, Coal, and Clarice were a universe away. The idea that their lives were continuing without me, in a radically different time zone, was profoundly disorienting.

This state of mind was not unfamiliar. Despite years of traveling, I was more susceptible to culture shock than ever. Each time I visited Nepal I immersed myself more deeply, opening my cynical shell to a little more of the magic and mystery. Returning to the United States meant reacclimating myself to a world of spiritual anemia, existential doubt, and political decay. The equation was tenuously balanced by fresh onion bagels, live jazz, and a community of like-minded friends, many of whom had lived in Nepal themselves. But neither Max Roach concerts nor ripe avocados could compensate for the fact that I felt more at peace in Nepal than anywhere else. The question that followed on the heels of that realization ("Why don't you just *live* there?") was one I could not answer, though my reluctance seemed to revolve around vague concerns about health and my career as a writer. As deeply as I loved Nepal, as closely as I had bound the kingdom's fate with my own, it was not my country. The place in which I was most at home was a place to which I did not belong.

I'd promised Grace I'd come back. But when? And how? And what would I do in the meantime?

"I'm thinking of driving to Utah," I remarked. In fact, the idea had just entered my mind. It was a sudden compulsion, a need to make some plans, to ground myself. "Go hiking in Bryce, or Zion, or somewhere."

"Sounds like fun." Carlita leaned against me, her arms folded inside her leather jacket. I slipped my arm around her waist, remembering the feel of her hips, her body against mine. An immense longing filled my chest. Who was it for?

The moment for me to add something, to include her in my plans, lengthened. She stared ahead. "Did you get hold of Jordan?"

Carlita was good at this: the art of subtle admonition. It was the East Coast I should be racing off to, not Mormon country.

"Not yet. I tried a couple of times, but he doesn't have an answering machine. But I talked to my mother. She said he'd called a couple of days ago to ask when I was coming home." I'd reread his last letter on the plane from Hong Kong to the United States; its urgency had not diminished with time. "It's weird he hasn't called me."

"Does he usually remember your birthday?"

"He does. Last year he sent me a first edition of Rilke's *Sonnets to Orpheus*, in German."

"I didn't know you spoke German."

"I don't."

The buoy sounded again. Now we could see the fog rolling in, swirling between the towers of the Golden Gate Bridge. Due east, Berkeley sparkled.

"So," Carlita said.

I nodded. "I'm not all here yet," I said, sensing a precipice opening in front of me. The time and distance between us seemed too wide to fill with explanations.

"What was her name?" Carlita didn't move away, but after a moment she turned her head, and I felt her eyes on me.

"Her name is Grace." I watched the fog; the upper levels of the orange towers were already hidden. "But it isn't just her. It was a very intense time. Did you read my stories?"

"Of course."

"Well, it's crazy. The whole place is ready to crack. Like an earthquake fault. Being there, living there, working with Grace and my friends . . . it was like being in a different dimension." I shook my head, annoyed with myself. Articulating the experience would explain nothing; it could only diminish the mystery that kept me somehow connected to that world.

"Do you even want to be in this one?" It was a fair question, to which I had no instant answer. "Because if you don't, this would be a very kind and honest time to admit that to me."

"What I think I want," I said carefully, "is to be okay with being here. But the transition is painful. It's as if I've traded one dream for another. I was completely, 100 percent invested in being in Nepal. But it was time to leave, and here I am."

"What you're saying is that I didn't figure in this decision at all."

"You were part of it. Jordan was part of it. Part of it was just impatience. It's hard to explain, even to myself." It was so much easier, infinitely easier, to stay in Nepal than it was to return there once you'd left. "Carlita, we've spent an awful lot of time apart. I thought I'd be better at readjusting, but all I feel right now is a sense of . . . *disorientation*. Literally."

"What do you mean?"

"Well, I'm not in the Orient anymore."

Carlita pondered this, nodding. She was trying to be supportive, heroically so. "Maybe what you need is shock therapy."

"That sounds extreme."

"*Culture* shock therapy."

I looked at her for the first time since we'd been on the roof. Her eyes were hopeful, tentative. "I like that. How is it administered?"

"The usual way. You lie in bed and grit your teeth." She giggled. I found myself highly receptive to this change in focus.

"I see. Is the treatment center open this evening?"

"I think something can be arranged." She turned her body toward me. "Do you have insurance?"

"No. Is it expensive?"

"Very. You have to promise to forget Nepal, forget whatever-her-name-was, forget the big news earthquake . . . I even want you to forget about your brother. Just for tonight. As an experiment. Can you?" She looked at me with a shy, vulnerable smile. "Can you do that?"

The thought of it broke my heart. "I can try."

"Seriously. I'd like you to stay. If you want to."

"Carlita . . . Of course I do. I just don't know if I'm ready."

We heard a series of thumps on the stairs: Mark, jogging up from his basement studio. "Hey you two! Dinner!"

Paula yelled up the stairs. "You ready to come down?"

"Are we?"

"I guess so." Carlita rested her hands on my shoulders. Her eyes were cool, and she seemed to have decided something. "Happy birthday," she said, and gave me a distant kiss.

THE MEAL ENDED with a cake, a mocha mousse monstrosity that Mark had decorated with the all-seeing eyes of Buddha and a tactful minimum of candles. Gina stared at it, enraptured. Everybody sang while I grinned awkwardly, standing behind Carlita and gripping the back of her chair. There's something disarming about being sung to, privately, by a group of people; nothing in our mammalian or reptile memory contains an appropriate response. I blew out the candles, forgetting to make a wish. Mark took dozens of pictures, but soon realized there was no film in the camera.

We drank espressos and shot the breeze about Nepal. A few years ago, when Dr. Dan returned to Kathmandu after a couple of months back home in Portland, he joked about his visit to America. "Everybody wants to hear all about Nepal," he said. "For exactly five minutes."

It was a different story in San Francisco, where so many people had spent extended periods of time living or trekking in Asia. Mark and Paula were hungry for details about the People's Movement and ravenous for news about the social scene. Though eight years had passed since their last visit, we still knew a few names in common. Jenny Klein, for example. Here was a nice Jewish girl who spoke Hebrew, played a mean game of Scrabble, and taught Advanced English with Paula at the ELI. One day she failed to report for her classes and was never heard from again. Paula remembered the unanswered phone calls, the alarm and mystery surrounding her disappearance. "It seemed she'd vanished from the face of the Earth." I was able to provide the juicy intelligence that Jenny had become a born-again Christian, entered into a polygamous marriage with a Turkish juggler, and was now living in Goa, expecting her third child.

Then there was Nat Montgomery, a mutual friend who'd achieved fleeting fame by mountain biking from Kathmandu to Everest Base Camp (truth be told, he carried the bike most of the way). Montgomery had moved to Hong Kong, where he'd fallen in with a band of expatriate gold smugglers working the Nepal–Hong Kong trade. He had amassed a small fortune, then made the mistake of diversifying. Montgomery had been busted by bloodhounds while carrying a kilo of Nepali hashish through customs at the Geneva airport. He was four years through a seven-year sentence in a Belgian prison, contemplating the error of his ways on the gymnasium's exercycle.

Having thus entertained my hosts, I was ready for fresh information about the Western world.

"Same old same old," Mark confessed, sucking mousse off a candle. "Good old status quo."

"Speak for yourself," Paula said. "I started night school. Teaching English as a Foreign Language. It's a two-year program at S.F. State. And guess what? We're reading from the *Ramayana*. Didn't you say your brother is studying Sanskrit?"

"Sanskrit, Arabic, you name it. All at the same time. It's unbelievable. I don't know how he does it. I learn a few words of Nepali and lose all the French I ever knew."

"Open your presents," Gina demanded.

"Already?"

"She has to go to bed soon," Paula explained.

There were three gifts on the table. The first, from Mark, was an out-of-print folio of black-and-white photographs: the Himalaya, as they'd appeared in the 1930s. Paula had wrapped a bottle of port in a rice paper print of the goddess Saraswati. Carlita had already given me my "official" present, a set of champagne glasses, before the meal. This second present had to be something unusual. I shook the box; it rattled. "Don't shake it too hard!" she warned.

Inside was a folk art sculpture of a snake, made of wired-up bottle caps from Mexican beers. "This is fantastic," I said. "Did you make it?"

She shook her head. "I bought it from a local artist. I don't know if you realize it, but every letter you wrote me had some mention of snakes."

"My neighborhood was called Nag Pokhari: Snake Lake."

Mark picked up the serpentine assemblage, which would have been about two feet long uncoiled, and bent it into a striking pose. "This is great." He set it on the table and shook it from side to side; the caps rattled convincingly.

"It's a rattlesnake," Gina declared, blasé. "We saw one in Golden Gate Park."

"Really?" Paula grinned. "We saw it at the aquarium, honey."

"It's in the *park*, Mom!"

"You've got me there."

I found four small crystal glasses in the pantry and uncorked the port. "Mark?"

"Certainly." A telephone rang, its muted chime coming up through the floorboards.

Carlita rolled her eyes. "That's mine. Sorry." She left the table and ran down the back steps. I poured out the port. Less than a minute later Carlita returned, looking concerned.

I handed her a filled glass. "Do you have to leave?"

"It's for you. Your mother. She sounds strange."

"My *mother*? Why's she calling me at your place?" I looked at the wall. "It's almost ten in New York."

She shook her head. "Wait for me," I said. I set down my own glass and hopped down the wooden stairs.

Carlita's bedroom was at the front of the flat, facing the street. A street-lamp glowed just out of sight, defining the facing buildings with sharp shadows. I sat on the bed and picked up the receiver.

"Hi, Mom. This is a surprise."

"Jeff?" Her voice sounded choked.

"Mom, what's wrong?"

"It's Jordan," she said. The words seemed to cost her enormous effort. My heart leaped into my throat.

"Jesus, what's wrong?"

Silence radiated from the receiver, a black vibration that surrounded my head like a cloud of wasps.

She whispered, "The worst thing you can imagine."

"For God's sake, Mom, just tell me what happened."

"He shot himself."

"Oh, my God. Oh, my God." But I held on. She hadn't said it yet, not really. It could have been an accident. Fucking around with a gun. Posturing, posing, playing on the edge. The thing discharged. Some kind of grazing wound. In the foot, maybe, or, worst case, the torso. Internal bleeding, intensive care. Tomorrow, first thing tomorrow morning, I could be on a plane. I could already see the tubes coming out of Jord's nose, feel the thick, flat hospital bed against my knee, hear the respirator. He'd missed his heart. I'd stand beside the bed and hold his hand. Tomorrow I could be in New York. Crazy fucker. But he'd pull through. He'd be okay. My crazy little brother.

"Oh, God," I begged. "Is he all right?"

"Jeff?" My mother's voice was an incredulous whimper, and I squeezed my eyes shut. "He's dead."

22

Emptiness

NONE OF IT existed.

Not the brief apparition of the Sierra Nevada, whose bleached peaks gnawed the sky. Not the lapis eye of Lake Tahoe, or the impossibly straight highways drawing their nails across the Nevada sands. The Rocky Mountains did not exist. There were no fields in the whole expanse of Nebraska, vast even from the sky

It seemed that clouds exploded from horizon to horizon, like popcorn strewn across an infinite glass tabletop, throwing animated shadows against millions of acres of farmland, but I knew better. No cities interrupted the monotony of the landscape, and no one lived in them. The empty blue swimming pools and red clay quarries and schoolyards full of yellow buses formed an illusory rainbow.

The paradox presented by my own apparition in the midst of so much emptiness was a puzzle of no interest. What *did* interest me, and served as my personal vine—dangling above an unthinkable abyss—was the Buddhist doctrine, so urgently stated by Chokyi Nyima Rinpoche, that nothing and no one was "real." Not the world, and not myself. The vivid physical presence I had known as "my brother" was a serendipitous accumulation of atoms: parcels of pure energy, temporarily bound together by barely understood forces. These atoms themselves were separated by vast tracts of space; you could drive a truck between them.

Who, then, was I grieving for? Jordan had never existed.

Yet it seemed that he had.

I REMEMBERED OUR last encounter. It was in San Francisco, late July. Jordan had jettisoned himself from my Oakland flat and taken a room in an unremarkable Victorian on Twenty-fifth Avenue. We had reconciled, to a degree, and met for lunch at a Greek restaurant on Clement Street. He had expressed reservations about moving back to the East Coast. I tried to convince him to stay in San Francisco, but he was committed to completing his graduate degree in linguistics at the University of Pennsylvania.

"Well, if it doesn't work out, you can always come back here." We were alone in the car. I was driving him home. A tall black man pulled a convoy of bottle-filled shopping carts along the broad avenue, singing a pop song at the top of his lungs. Jordan studied him as we passed by.

"There's money to be made by the man with enterprise," Jordan remarked. "This is why I find it so difficult to abide the common street-beggar, a member of which species assailed me as I made my exit, last night, from the Balboa Theater. The fellow requested 'spare change.' To which I replied, in commiseration, that it was spare indeed."

I pulled up next to the curb in front of my brother's house.

"Need any help packing?"

"No. Save a few cartons of texts, I've accumulated remarkably little in the way of material comforts. A futon, a lamp, some dried cheese, a rasher of bacon, and goblet of cold, clear water. These, and a Spartan toilet kit, suffice."

"Don't forget your running shoes," I added.

"Right . . . and a scrap of cloth to cover the loins."

I chuckled at this self-parody, which seemed to define more and more his default behavior. He opened the passenger door and regarded me evenly. I looked at him in turn. People usually guessed that we were brothers, although our resemblance had declined with age.

"I wish we'd spent more time together. It was an incredibly busy summer, with my new book and all."

He nodded peremptorily, permitting the alibi.

"Come back after you graduate," I said. "I really think the atmosphere here is healthier than the East Coast's, psychologically and physically. And you already know a lot of people. I needn't tell you that my friends are your friends."

Jordan bowed his head in acknowledgment and extended his hand. I grasped it. He looked at me for a long time before releasing his grip. "Farewell," he said, swinging his legs out of the car. When he closed the door, I quickly rolled down the window.

"Take care of yourself!" I shouted. "Call me if you need anything."

"Yes." He hesitated. "Thank you for everything."

I watched him turn his back and climb the short flight of steps to his front door. It opened and closed. I would never see him again.

I LEANED MY head against the airplane window and wept. There was nothing for it: no secret of self-control, no imagined Buddhist cure. My brother had killed himself. And the most awful thing was that it was still so *fresh*. Three days ago he was alive. I could have called him on the telephone. I could have spoken to him, heard his voice. He would have spilled out his plans, and I would have stopped him. Of this I was certain. I would have done anything, gone anywhere, to prevent my brother from taking his life.

I wished that my heart could fly out into the atmosphere, wished that my horror and grief could burst out of me in a single wild tide and be expressed, complete, done with. But there was no such end in sight. And I understood, from my limited knowledge of such things, that the shock and pain I now felt were the first frost of a coming winter, the length and darkness of which could not be measured.

The enormity of my dispensation struck me full force, and I was surprised by how much satisfaction it brought. There is simply nothing more tragic, I realized, than death. Every play, every book, every film that relies on tragedy relies on death. Only the victims and circumstances change.

There are the huge deaths, the vast genocides that sweep through nations. There is the unspeakable horror of watching everyone you know and love die, and the guilty longing to follow them into the grave. There are the deaths of children, but all deaths are the deaths of children. There are the poignant deaths of misaligned lovers; the senseless deaths of colliding cars and plunging buses; the maniac street-corner deaths; the righteous deaths; the swift, dreamlike deaths on plummeting airplanes; the long deaths and short deaths; the heroic deaths and holy deaths. There are useful deaths and useless deaths, the "friendly fire" and sanitized collateral death that we read about in the newspapers. The good guys kill the bad guys, the bad guys kill the good guys, and each side writes its own tragic libretto.

I recalled a cold and moonless night in 1984: the night after my father's funeral. My cousin Susie and I drove aimlessly through the Long Island suburbs. When we reached the north shore, my bladder began to throb.

"There's no place to take a leak," I observed in a panic.

Susie pulled to the curb in front of a posh estate that looked like a set from *The Great Gatsby*. She leaned over and pushed my door open. "Your father just died," she said. "You can piss wherever you want."

The memory made me laugh sharply, startling the already uneasy passenger beside me. No need to explain. My condition raised me, for the moment, above social convention.

But there would be liabilities as well. Facing my mother at the airport, for example. And I would be expected to say something at the funeral. Afterward we would sit shiva at my mother's house in Ossining, propped on little stools, receiving an endless stream of guests who meant well but couldn't possibly know what to say. What *could* they say? I didn't know what to say to my own mother.

After the formal grieving period, there would follow an era of sad logistics. Calling Jordan's friends, closing his bank account, sorting through his possessions. Most of the latter, I imagined, would be found in his apartment in Philadelphia. I remembered that he kept private journals; it was imperative I find them before my mother did. My motives included, irrationally, a desire to conceal my brother's sexual dysfunction—but there was more. The fact that Jordan despised our father was no secret to me. I could only imagine what his personal writings might say.

He could really be a bastard. And now he had shot himself. He'd put a gun to his head and pulled the trigger. I wondered if he thought even once about our mother, our sister, or me. The sheer frustration of not being able to slap him across the face made me dizzy. It simply wasn't possible that I couldn't ask him these questions, that I couldn't grab him by his arm and say, *Why, you fucking melodramatic asshole? Why'd you give up, you spineless coward? Why didn't you call me, you selfish prick? What good is it going to do you now, moron? How dare you do this to yourself. How dare you do this to me.*

The clouds above, the earth below. Snow still dusted Ohio, untouched on the flat roofs of shopping malls. We flew above the worn knobs of Appalachia. Freeways ran like fuses through the powder. Now there were cities amid the fields, tracts of evergreens, parklands with meadows of dormant wildflowers. Soon the entire hemisphere would erupt into spring. My brother was dead, but the world looked the same from the air.

23

Egyptian Wing

O N THE MORNING of March 15, a sparrow landed on a squat bush outside of the Chase Manhattan Bank in Ossining, New York.

My mother and sister were with the bank manager, terminating my brother's accounts. I waited in the parking lot and leaned back, etherized, against the side of my mother's Camry. The sun was glorious, its full electromagnetic spectrum beating against the receptors in my skin. Light filtered through my eyelids, displaying a boundless persimmon sea.

When I looked again, the bird was still there. It cocked its head and watched me, studying my features. We watched each other. Then came the rush of recognition, and I caught my breath: *Is that you? Jord? Could that be you?*

We had buried my brother the day before, and I was already wondering where he might turn up next. There's a wonderful sense of democracy in the idea of reincarnation. When someone you love has died, the whole world becomes a stage for their potential reappearance. I had recognized Jordan in a dozen potential forms: the raccoon raiding the trash cans outside my bedroom window, the dragonfly hesitating over the small lake on my mother's property, the sleeping baby draped over a mother's shoulder in the Ossining Bakery.

But none of these scenarios could be accurate. It took longer than a week, supposedly, to be reborn. It required some forty-nine days for the soul to complete its journey through the Bardo and migrate into another form. This period, right now, was the crucial time: the period of passage. My brother was not perched on a shrub in Ossining-on-Hudson. His soul would be navigating that terrifying realm of flashing lights and deafening explosions, beginning its journey from the ineffable place we call death to the ineffable place we call life.

I'd learned all this, but couldn't help myself. I saw him everywhere.

MY BROTHER'S MEMORIAL had been held in a Long Island mortuary, an hour's drive from Ossining. It was a small event. We'd arrived early, at my insistence. There was something I needed to do.

Folded in the pocket over my heart was a silk kata scarf blessed by the Dalai Lama. I'd received it some years ago, when His Holiness had visited San Francisco. Now I would place it around Jordan's neck, and pray that its potent blessing would ease his journey through the Bardo.

But as I entered the empty assembly room and saw the closed coffin, displayed in perfect solitude before rows of empty padded chairs, I collapsed against the door frame. My sister stood beside me, trembling so much she could barely speak.

"Are you going to open it?"

"I have to. I must."

"I can't look." Her face was white as aspirin. She left me, moving to a seat near the middle of the chapel.

The shiny box. My brother was inside of it. All I wanted to do was lift the lid, place the kata around his neck, and kiss him good-bye.

But there was a problem. Jordan had shot himself in the head. Through the back of the head, actually, with a hollow-point bullet that had blown his face off. There was now apparently something in its place, though I didn't know what. I knew only that the mortuary had billed my mother hundreds of dollars for "cosmetic restoration" fees.

I've seen my share of horror movies and have felt my heart race with terror as crypts or coffins or spaceship doors creaked open to reveal gelatinous blobs, psychotic killers, or the blank eyes of the undead. I've waltzed with death myself, losing my footing on Himalayan precipices or careening out of control on icy New England roads. Three years earlier, during a night dive in the Solomon Islands, an underwater current nearly dragged me away. I've been thrown from motorcycles, cornered by forest fires, and trapped amid a school of hammerhead sharks. But at that moment, standing beside Jordan's closed coffin, it seemed I had never known fear before. My heart pounded in my chest, and my legs were clay. My entire body seemed gripped by a stupefying narcolepsy. All I wanted was to lie down and sleep. My dead brother's face was three feet from my own, but I dared not look. I dared not open that box.

I held the coffin lid by the edge with the fingers of both hands, steadying myself, sensing its weight. Debra sat behind me in the pews. I took a deep breath and lifted.

Inside lay an unfamiliar dummy with a waxen, painted face. Jordan's cadaver was dressed in a natty suit and tie, its chest artificially inflated. His eyes were too far apart. His nose, my brother's proud Medici beak, had been flattened. The lips, so adept at smirking, described a piously straight line. His eloquent hands, their nails neatly trimmed, lay beside him. A rolled-up towel propped his neck.

The face bore no look of suffering, or any expression of peace. It was utterly lifeless, and completely anonymous. The embalmers had tried to restore him, but the feat was beyond their skills. Better, I thought, to have left the wound. This caricature was more awful, in its dishonesty, than no face at all.

I stared, paralyzed by revulsion. I couldn't touch him. There was no question of lifting his head, or putting anything around his neck. My kata hung limply in my hands. At last I draped it across his breast, tucking the silk fringes under the lapels of the jacket.

This was what was left of him. My strange brother, solitary navigator of the dense worlds: those neutron-stars of philosophy, ancient languages, linguistics. My brilliant, irreplaceable brother, insane prankster, pitiless critic, divine comic, desperate clown. Here lay hammer and anvil, calculator and goose quill, athlete, Athenian, ass. My brother, Imitator of Sheep. My impossible little brother.

He was really dead. He would be dead for the rest of my life. My wife, if I married, would never know him. Our children would never meet him. We would never trek in Nepal together, never picnic at Point Reyes, never again send each other birthday cards. There was no one else alive who had shared my childhood so closely, or who knew me more intimately. I realized, for the first time, how utterly alone I was.

In a moment I would close the coffin and say farewell to Jordan forever. But first I reached out and touched, tentatively, his cheek. It was cold and firm, like neoprene. And then I kissed my fingertips. I kissed them as if I had touched something holy, although I knew beyond any doubt that what lay before me was nothing but an empty husk. I closed the lid.

My mother was in the mortuary office, sitting stiffly in a wooden chair while a clerk totaled the bill. She turned to look at me as I walked in. I shook my head.

"I wanted to say good-bye to him," I told her. "But he had already left."

WHEN THE FUNERAL ended, my sister and I caught the Metro-North to Grand Central. We hopped on the Lexington line and emerged at Seventy-seventh Street, gasping at the city's fin-de-siècle beauty. It was the first time either of us had encountered strangers, or been around crowds, for days. I found it vivifying. It was a joy to be back among the living, ascending onto Manhattan's spring streets. We turned uptown and continued the final half mile on foot.

The Met is always crowded, often chaotically so. Debra didn't know the place, and stumbled into stunned agoraphobia as we entered the echoic enormity of the Great Hall. I took her hand and led her along, beelining toward the galleries Jordan had loved the most.

The bookish sobriety of the place seemed to forbid speech. We wandered reverently among the Cycladic harpists, beheld the marble warriors and Greek sphinx, and peered into dimly lit showcases loaded with ancient necklaces. Finally we reached Gallery 25: the bright and spacious atrium housing the Temple of Dendur. Debra walked directly toward a low wall containing a still, rectangular pool. She sat down and pulled off her boots.

"My feet are killing me."

I sat beside her and looked at her feet, comical in wasp-yellow stockings. At twenty-seven she was quite beautiful, with a radiant smile and thick auburn hair that glinted copper in the sunlight. She had a sharp sense of humor and could grasp the most oblique concepts instantly. But in other ways she was surprisingly unsophisticated, lacking the self-confidence of my other friends her age. Unlike Jordan or myself, she had spent her adolescence adrift, bereft of a sense of direction.

It wasn't surprising. Most of my sister's life had been spent in a spiritual and intellectual vacuum. As the youngest of three, she'd been left to contend with our parents' discontent, long after Jordan and I had made our escapes. Her search for approval and acceptance took all the wrong turns, landing her in a witches' brew of drugs and alcohol. The self-destructive cycle had carried into her twenties, where she'd bottomed out in a crazy marriage that lasted three weeks.

But all that had changed. Over the past five years, she'd pulled herself together. Debra had found a steady job, started therapy, and was dating her grade school sweetheart. She'd even discussed turning her supernatural rapport with animals into a pet-grooming business. It seemed far-fetched, but I'd heard crazier things. The point was, she had her dreams; she could imagine her future.

I pulled some change out of my pocket and handed her a quarter.

"What. Am I supposed to make a wish?"

"It's an option. Jordan and I did, the last time we were here."

"I can't picture that." She seemed completely astonished. "When? What did he wish?"

"It was five years ago. I don't know what he wished for. I asked him; he gave me a very earnest look and answered in ancient Greek."

"He's incredible." Debra leaned forward and pinched yellow nylon off the soles of her feet. "I know it's sick, but I can't believe he's dead. I can't accept it. It's like a dream. I *feel* like I'm dreaming. Even being here, sitting here with you. It's like nothing is real. Do you know what I'm talking about? Am I going crazy, or what?" Tears fell onto the cement floor between her heels. She looked at the coin in her palm, twisted around, and flung it into the shallow pool. It gulped and sank. I followed suit.

"What did you wish?"

"What did *you* wish?"

"Are we supposed to tell?"

"You don't have to if you don't want to."

Debra took a breath. "I wished that this doesn't kill Mom," she said. We were silent for a moment, then she turned to me.

"So? What did you wish?"

"I wished that someday, somehow, I can write about him. He deserves to be written about."

"He does," she said. "I can't imagine how you would do it, but he definitely does."

The atrium was spacious, but cold. Debra put her boots back on, and we left the ruins of Dendur, walking through the Egyptian galleries. As we entered the room containing finds from Dynasty 21, I stopped in my tracks, drawn magnetically to a dimly lit mummy. Staring at the desiccated shape threw a switch in my brain. The full impact of the recent days struck me like a blow, and I groped for my sister's hand.

"Jeff? Are you okay?"

She shook my arm. "Do you want to get out of here?" Debra's palm was sweating; she, too, was spooked. "Come with me," she said. "I feel better when we walk."

I followed her into one of the adjacent galleries. Two long papyri, excerpts from the *Egyptian Book of the Dead*, filled one entire case. In the other were ornate coffins, the paint as fresh and colorful as if it had been applied by David Hockney. One of the wall cases held canopic jars, scarabs, amulets, and some fragments of what must have once been larger bas-reliefs. It was here that we stopped. Debra pointed to a small sandstone carving. It portrayed a small bird and a single hieroglyph. I read the card:

QUAIL CHICK PLAQUE

PTOLEMAIC PERIOD (332–30 B.C.)

"Do you recognize that bird?"

"It looks familiar . . ."

"That's what Jord gave Mom and Dad once for Hanukkah," she said. "That very thing. They must sell reproductions in the museum gift shop. It's weird"—I felt the familiar force of my sister's telepathy at work—"but he had this thing for birds. Did you ever notice? He was, like, infatuated with birds. I thought that was kind of cool, because he actually reminded me of a bird. The way some people look like animals. Do you know what I mean?"

We left the gallery, making our way toward the exit. "I was thinking about that just this morning," I said. "While you and Mom were in the bank. I had the strongest feeling that if he comes back, he'll be a bird. It would make perfect sense."

"Do you believe in that? In reincarnation?"

"Yes," I said. "I think so. It makes sense to me that things should work that way; that consciousness is never wasted, and never disappears. But I also believe in karma: that your situation completely depends on the positive and negative actions you've performed. Not only in this lifetime, but in your previous lifetimes as well. So while I hope Jord comes back again, I have a feeling that committing suicide really screws up your karma."

"Why? I mean, what if someone's really sick, or in constant pain?"

"I don't know what the policy is on that. The point is that getting a human life, being reborn as a human being, is incredibly rare. One book I read said you should imagine a single lifebuoy, floating on the surface of the ocean. In all the ocean, there's one turtle. What do you think the chances are that the turtle, coming up for air, will pop through that ring?"

"What do I think? Zero."

"Well, not quite. But incredibly small. That's how likely it is that, of all the possible rebirths, you end up as a human being. It's an amazing opportunity—because only as a human can you meditate, study, and behave in ways that change your karma. Killing yourself doesn't change anything. All you've done is wasted your human rebirth. Who can say when, or if, you'll get another one?"

"I disagree." My sister unhesitatingly took on the Buddha. "I don't accept that Jord's life was wasted. In any way. Period. Sorry."

We left the Met, walking through Central Park. Debra's boots clonked on the walkway. There were jugglers, joggers, and women pushing strollers. A volleyball sailed wild, bouncing by our feet. A Chinese man sold Good Humor bars to a pair of skaters, their legs splayed for balance. Pigeons clouded the path. The air was pure Manhattan ambrosia, perfumed with sweat and ambition, a lick of exhaust and the Hudson, mowed grass and muck, cotton candy, the exotic scat of the zoo.

We strolled in silence, welded together by grief and solitude. Sometimes Debra would shake her head, and at those moments I knew exactly what she was thinking, because I was thinking it, too. Our nagging question, the tormenting, overarching *Why?* pervaded the day like mist; but beneath its vapor hung the even more inscrutable *How?* How did you ever find a way to forsake this sweet, sweet planet, Jordan? How did you bring yourself to shut off the trees, grass, ducks, bicycles, and squirrels?

How could you close your eyes forever to the clouds sailing above the skyscrapers, to the hot pretzels laced with sweet mustard, to any or all of the infinite rest of it? And could *anything*, any sweet final memory of this world you barely knew, any hope or scheme or itch of curiosity, any seductive wink or lustful embrace, Baroque fugue or cello concerto, telephone call or sudden visitor, have kept your finger off that trigger?

We crossed Central Park South near the Plaza, jaywalking between hansom cabs, to meet Fifth Avenue. I was looking in the window of Saks, captivated by a line of handbags studded with huge fake gems, when Debra called to me. She was standing by a newsstand on the corner.

"What's up?"

"Look!" she said, pointing to the cover of a newspaper. "There's something about Nepal."

I dropped a few coins into the rack and opened the *Times*. There was little new in the story, just an update on the stalemate between Nepal and India. But it was a reminder that my other home still existed, so far in time and space from this one.

A strange thought gripped me. Jordan and I had both left our worlds. I wondered if, like a determined ghost, I'd be permitted to return to mine.

24

An Apartment in Philadelphia

THERE WAS A coffee shop next to my brother's apartment building. I sat at a red Formica table, drinking jasmine tea. On the walls of the café hung framed photographs of Hollywood starlets: Jayne Mansfield, Lana Turner, Marilyn Monroe. Refilling my cup from a tiny Pyrex pitcher, I wondered if these vampish images, which Jordan was forced to confront every time he stopped in for a bagel, were sources of torment to him.

My mother and sister were on the nearby campus. They would join me in an hour and a half. What I had to do between now and then was finish my tea, go next door, introduce myself to the building manager, and gain entrance to my brother's apartment. No one had been in the room since his suicide, with the exception of a police detective and the medics who had removed his body seven days ago. It was my responsibility to do whatever was necessary to ensure that my mother and sister could enter the studio without fear of what they might see.

The air was cold. Every time I had a birthday, for the rest of my life, I'd remember this anniversary. But my brother's timing had been an act of compassion, not cruelty. He had phoned our mother three days before his death, asking when I'd be back from Nepal. "In a day or two," she'd replied. It had finally dawned on me: He'd waited. It was not his choice that I'd flown home on my birthday.

The lobby of the apartment building was cavernous and dim, the floor polished-granite inlay, the overhead lamps opaque with a half century of moth wings. One entire wall was filled with old brass post boxes, their perforated doors tarnished green. Rococo trim scampered around the ceiling. I liked the place immediately. Some distance away, two Louis Quinze armchairs flanked a circular marble table with a reading lamp rising, stalklike, from its center. A middle-aged woman sat in one of the chairs, leafing through *People*. She folded the magazine and placed it on the table as I approached.

"Mrs. Walsh? I'm Jeff Greenwald."

She took my offered hand in hers. They were thin, but warm. "I'm so, so sorry." She had a triangular face, with large black eyes and small lips. "I'm so terribly sorry."

"Thank you." I had learned, at last, that there was no better reply.

"He lived on the fifth floor." Her voice reverberated slightly. "We can take the lift."

I followed her into the elevator. The door closed in front of us. We emerged into a slightly musty hallway. An anemic rubber tree sat on a table with fiddlehead legs. Maroon carpeting covered the floor. Mrs. Walsh led me down a short hallway and into a little alcove. Three doors faced the space; she paused in front of room 603. The keys were in her hand, but she didn't unlock the door.

"You know that no one's been in there since . . ."

"Yes. Yes, I do."

"It hasn't been cleaned up."

"I understand." I reached out to touch her elbow, but she took my hand.

"If you like, I'll go in first," she said. "Or I can wait out here. Or of course if you prefer, I can just unlock the door and leave you by yourself."

"You're very sweet." I released her hand. "I'd like you to unlock the door, and let me go in when I feel I'm ready."

"Of course." She slid the key into the deadbolt. "If you need anything, I'll be down in the lobby." She turned her wrist. There was a definitive snap, which resonated in the foyer. Then she removed the key and left me alone.

I placed my hand on the doorknob. Adrenaline pounded in my temples. It was almost comical, to be so frightened. So frightened by a room. As frightened by this closed door, in fact, as I had been by Jordan's closed coffin.

I tried to objectify my fear by envisioning Asian traditions. In Nepal I'd have watched Jordan's body burn to ash, heard his skull pop. In Tibet his body would have been carried to a hilltop, hacked to pieces, and fed to birds of prey. Now he was in the ground; there was only this room, this apartment in Philadelphia. The room where he had shot himself. What was the worst thing I could imagine? Bits of brain on the floor? An eyeball in a corner? All of this was just stuff. Empty stuff. It had belonged to my brother, but wasn't a part of him anymore.

Yet the truth was that, Buddhism or bravado notwithstanding, such a sight might be too much for me to handle. I recalled the anxiety attack I'd suffered during Lhosar. Though I hadn't known it at the time, it now seemed obvious that my reaction to that corpse, exposed on the Boudhnath kora, had been a premonition. I'd always been squeamish. If there was anything gruesome in the apartment, it could set me off—and this time, Chokyi Nyima would not be here to save me.

This was a risk. Even so, I had no regrets about turning down Mrs. Walsh's offer to remain. My visit to the spot where my brother had ended his life was a pilgrimage, but it was also a labor: a reconnaissance of the naga's den. Like the descent into Shantipur, it had to be performed alone.

I faced the door. It stared back blankly, its stenciled numbers an unknown area code. *Was there a keyhole?* I wondered absurdly. *Somewhere I might peek in, first?*

A distant memory surfaced: the one and only camping trip I'd ever taken with Jordan, fifteen years ago. We had stood side by side, naked, at the edge of an alpine lake, anticipating the icy rush that a momentary surrender to gravity would shoot into our veins. Too wimpy to plunge, I dipped my toe in the water. Not Jordan; he snorted at me in exasperation, then dove headlong into the lake. His lean body knifed through the water, emerging sleek and blue on the far side.

"It's like bathwater!" he cried out, arms wrapped around his shaking torso. "It's like a fucking Turkish bath in here!"

I turned the doorknob and stepped inside the room.

THE FIRST THING I noticed was the blood. The mattress caked with blood, so dark it looked like chocolate; the streaks of blood thrown recklessly across the wall; the broad puddle of dried blood, the deep brain blood of my brother, cracking on the lath floor. A crumpled white sock lay next to his ruined pillow. I closed the door behind me.

The room was surprisingly bright and pleasant, nothing like the mortuary's pall of mourning. I recognized my brother's smell, mingled with stale milk and laundry. A single, large window faced an open courtyard and, beyond, an unremarkable cityscape. The window opened easily, and a breath of spring air rushed in. It occurred to me that the weather had been very different a week ago: cold, windy, maybe even raining. The change of seasons was so dramatic, so vivacious on the East Coast. After sixteen years in California, it was the only thing I missed.

In Kathmandu, I'd bought a sheaf of 1,008 small paper prayer flags. They were intended as a gift for an artist friend. Now I took a handful of them from my jacket pocket and scattered them over the bloodstained bedding. The victims of violent death, Tibetans believe, sometimes loiter at the site of their demise, seeking solace or direction. If Jordan's spirit returned here, it would find useful tools: prayers of wisdom and compassion, potential passwords for the difficult journey ahead. Nothing I could do or say would bring my brother back to life, but it seemed possible that I could expedite his Bardo experience. It was better than nothing.

When my prayers were finished, I went into the bathroom, returned with two large towels, and used them to cover the bed and floor.

It was remarkable, how everything in the room had acquired an air of sanctity, as if I had walked not into my brother's apartment but into a museum. His jeans and V-neck undershirt draped carelessly across the single chair; the saucepot, wooden spoon, and pasta strainer in the sink; the teacup full of loose change; all seemed eternal, immutable. Jordan's address book sat on the desk, next to the phone, opened to the letter C. I picked up the receiver and hit "redial." The phone on the receiving end rang twice, and a woman answered.

"Good afternoon, Sheriff's department."

I hung up, feeling foolish, and wandered into the bathroom. His toothbrush. I ran my thumb across the bristles. A quart of Listerine waited in the medicine cabinet, along with a bar of Mennen Extra Dry, Barbasol shaving cream, and a flask of Drakkar Noir cologne.

"'Tis a nocturnal scent," Jordan had explained as I recoiled from him one night in Oakland. We were on our way out, and he reeked. "Meaning, literally, 'black dragon.' For 'tis the Latin noun *draco*—ostensibly the source of this brand-name neologism—which forms the root of *dragon*, first employed in the thirteenth century. Though one might also admit 'black serpent' or even 'beast,' *ergo*, night beast' . . ."

"Jord, we're going to a Ravel recital, not a vampires' ball."

"Nonetheless: an irresistible draw."

"I'm repelled," I parried.

"Quite so," Jordan nodded. "To repel one's competitors, whilst simultaneously attracting the female of the species, is the aim of male display behavior."

I replaced the cologne, returned to the main room, and began looking for my brother's journals. There were footsteps in the hall, then a knock. It was hesitant, but firm enough to make the door swing slightly open. A tall black woman with beaded cornrows took a step into the room and looked at me incredulously.

"You're his *brother*," she said. I nodded. She walked directly to me, encircled me in her arms, and laid her head against my chest. Her scalp smelled of musk and tobacco.

"I'm Monica," she whispered. "In 605. Next door." She backed away a few feet, looked into my eyes, and gripped my hands. "Last Friday," she said, "just before nine in the morning. I was rushing to work. I saw him. He was standing right outside the room, in the hallway, staring at nothing. Just nothing. I looked at him and thought, 'Monica, this guy is hurting. He needs something. Maybe he just needs a hug, or someone to say something to him.' But I was already late for work and I didn't stop. I didn't stop. Oh,

Jesus." She embraced me again and began weeping. "Oh, God, I'm so sorry. I should have realized. I should have known."

I held her tightly. My brother, the report said, had shot himself at eleven. Monica would have been the last person to see him alive.

"It's all right," I whispered. "No one could have known."

I was not mouthing words. It had already struck me, and would do so many times again, that nearly everyone I knew—my colleagues, my friends, my lovers—could one day throw themselves from a bridge or swallow an overdose of pills or shoot themselves in a sunny bedroom, and I would receive the news and mutter to myself miserably, *I should have seen it coming.*

But there is no question, I understood, of seeing it coming. It is already here. It comes with the territory. Human beings suffer. We have our episodes of abstract dread, profound loneliness, sickness, self-loathing, despair. We all notice how close death is, how casual an invitation it requires. Chokyi Nyima had spoken of the precious human rebirth, and the four auspicious conditions: ideas meant to underscore the momentous value of each human life. But my brother hadn't studied Buddhism. He had read Thomas Mann and Søren Kierkegaard, Friedrich Nietzsche and Albert Camus. The ultimate question, for him, was not about devoting his life to liberation; it was whether to continue the act of living at all. Had he read *Zen Mind, Beginner's Mind* or *The Experience of Insight* and bought a meditation cushion, he might have spent his adult years cutting through his preconceptions about life, love, and the mind. Instead he bought a pistol and blew his mind away. The greatest tragedy was not even the act itself, but his ignorance. It was the only solution he had imagined.

WHEN MONICA DEPARTED I resumed my search for Jordan's journals. Three of them, spiral notebooks dating from 1980, were in plain sight, on a shelf beside a Greek lexicon. I would read these later. What I wanted right now was the most recent volume. I found it in a blue daypack, hanging from a nail inside the hall closet. Unlike the other journals, this one was bound, with a black plastic cover.

The pages were covered with my brother's angular, insectlike scrawl. My heart pounded as I browsed ahead, moving inexorably toward the place where the blue ink would end and the empty pages begin. When I found the spot, my ears were ringing, and a patina of sweat covered my neck.

The last words my brother wrote had been entered on the seventh of March. The entry consisted of one sentence: *I cannot bear even once more to wake to sorrow.*

Closing the book, I stared at the wall above his desk. Suddenly it astonished me, how utterly *blank* the room was. There were no posters, no photographs, no tchotchkes or souvenirs. There were no vases, plants, or candleholders. Not even a calendar hung on the wall.

This was entirely out of character. Jordan had loved art, and his other rooms had always been papered with prints: Rembrandt, Leonardo da Vinci, Gustave Doré. Here, after six months, he still hadn't gotten around to decorating. Was that it? Or had his appreciation of beauty atrophied to the point where nothing at all could bring him solace? It was then, at that moment, that I understood how completely he had introverted. Somewhere, he had taken a wrong turn into the maze of his intellect and had never found the way back out.

But here was something new. Sitting on the white laminate bookshelf was a hand-thrown ceramic mug, lapis blue. Behind the mug stood a Valentine's card, illustrated with a Jim Dine heart. I picked it up and read the brief inscription:

To my sweet friend Jordan
who has won a place in my heart
Love
Lindsay

I replaced the card and moved to the desk, where my brother's address book still lay open. There were five names under the letter C. The most recent addition was Lindsay Cohen.

I lifted the receiver and dialed.

25

Lindsay

THEY'D MET AT the campus racquetball club: the intense graduate student, lean and muscular, and the Amazonian architect sweating through her Lycra top. She wondered if the thick hair under her arms bothered him, but on their first date he put her mind at ease: "I like earthy women," he'd told her. "Women unafraid to carry lambs under their arms."

She was two years older than Jordan. Her three-story house, set behind an iron gate in a rough but up-and-coming section of Philly, had cost her $1 when she bought it as part of the neighborhood regentrification program. Now, ten years and $45,000 in renovations later, it was hers free and clear.

We climbed the carpeted stairway to a large dining room. The table was set; between the stoneware plates sat a large brown bag.

"I ordered Chinese. They make it with no MSG. And we can have herbal tea. Is that okay?"

"Perfect. Thanks." I wandered through a broad passage into the adjacent living room. Lindsay had good taste, and was well traveled. Russian lacquers were decorated a low Chinese table; it wasn't the kind you bought at boutiques. A row of ancient, dirt-caked clay oil lamps, evidently excavated by either herself or someone she knew, were displayed on wire mounts atop a low bookshelf. Framed Henri Matisse posters from the Musée d'Orsay hung above the sofa.

"This is a beautiful place. You've got some lovely things. Have you been to Russia?" I spied the piano. "My God . . . that Steinway . . ."

"I know. It belonged to my grandmother. Isn't it amazing? She gave me my first lessons when I was eleven. But it needs to be tuned. Do you play?"

"No. I wish I did." I returned to the dining room and stood, resting my hands on the back of a chair. Lindsay had migrated into the kitchen. Her voice emerged, twangy with echo.

"I've got . . . let's see: peppermint, chamomile, Cranberry Cove, Almond Sunset, Orange Spice . . . Constant Comment . . ." The refrigerator door opened. "Juice, Diet Coke . . . unless you'd prefer a Calistoga. Or a beer. I think I . . . well, there are two. You can have a Budweiser or an Amstel."

"Amstel, please. I'm sorry, I should have brought wine. I wasn't thinking."

She returned to the dining room with a Diet Coke and my beer and a handful of serving spoons. "Never mind," she said. "This is the first day I've been able to think for a week."

We hadn't shaken hands, or touched; nothing. "Lindsay . . ."

She put what she was holding down on the table and came up to me with unexpected urgency. The instant we embraced, she released a flood of tears.

"*Christ*. I was hoping this wouldn't happen. *Shit*." She let go. "I'm sick of having swollen eyes."

"Does it help to cry?"

"It did at first. Now it's, like, sneaky and uncontrollable. I'll be waiting at the bank, or drawing at my desk, and all of a sudden I'll think about Jordan, and bam, I'm gone. What about you?" I said nothing. She pushed back and looked at me—we stood eye to eye—and laughed a little. "I'm sorry," she said. "I'm being selfish. Just hold me for a minute. Okay?"

WHEN LINDSAY HAD first opened her front door I'd experienced a moment of perceptual vertigo. For a split second the motive for my brother's infatuation seemed absurdly clear. *Lindsay looked exactly like him.* Their resemblance was so striking that I knew she must resemble me, as well. What would it be like to make love with a woman who could be your fraternal twin, or conversely, to embrace a man who so nearly mirrored your own features?

He was tall, maybe even five foot ten, with the kind of lavish, curly hair universally coveted by women who don't have it. In better times, I imagined, she had an easy laugh; her face had the right lines. It was a sweet face, bright and intense, clearly accustomed to expressing the full range of emotions. In this respect she would be the polar opposite of Jordan, whose entire emotional range could be represented by a small array of Noh masks.

"We were magnetically attracted," Lindsay said quietly, filling a mu shu pancake with vegetables and plum sauce. "I thought he was the handsomest man I'd ever met. He was absolutely the smartest. I mean, I'm no dummy, but half the time the things he was saying went . . ." She sliced her hand through the air above her head. "And that was when I could get him to speak English!"

We told stories and laughed, mostly, falling back again and again upon our disbelief. She shared his letters with me, even the most personal ones. I was astonished by the vulnerability of his writing. It was a side of my brother I'd never seen.

But resonating within his prose, one could hear a steady chord of theatrical melodrama, as if even his love letters were part of a scripted exchange, borrowed from some doomed classical romance. He had flown his soul like a kite, spinning out string until it got so high and wild that he'd lost control.

I trickled soy across the skin of an egg roll. "Lindsay . . . How did you find out?" Her whole body seemed to contract. "You don't have to tell me."

"No, No, it's okay. Give me a second." Throughout the evening her tears had fallen and stopped, her face clouding and brightening and darkening again like a monsoon sky. Lindsay got up, went into the bathroom, and came back with a Vicks inhaler. She drew the vapors deep into her nostrils.

"It was last Saturday night. The ninth. I'd been at a party for one of the women in my office; she's leaving to open her own office in Maine. It was a great party, our boss had hired a band, and we'd all chipped in and bought her a paraglider. We were drinking a lot, and at about three in the morning I called a cab. By the time I got home the place was spinning. All

I wanted was to get into bed and collapse. But the light on my answering machine was blinking. Which was weird, because I'd left for the party pretty late—about ten.

"So I turned it on, and the message said, *Lindsay Cohen, this is Detective Moorehouse from the Philadelphia Police Department. We have a suicide note addressed to you from a Jordan Greenwald.* And that was how I found out."

The blood drained from my cheeks. "That's . . . it's horrible."

"You can't imagine."

I picked at my chicken and broccoli and managed to ask, after a minute, if Lindsay would show me Jordan's note. She nodded. It was a copy, she said apologetically. The police had kept the original.

March 8, 1990

My Dearest Lindsay,

I want you to know, first of all, that you bear no responsibility for my death. Since my mishap ten years ago, the thought of suicide has been with me constantly—a grim companion, to be sure, and one who, after a time, left his traces upon the lineaments of my face and in the inflection of my voice. Through the awful length of days, I summoned strength from the hope of recovery and from that only. Last month, however, I learned that any change beyond my present condition is most unlikely. It was then that I bought a pistol.

All these years I attempted to conceal my spiritual decline from others; but never, not by pages read or miles run or hours spent in picture galleries, could I conceal it from myself. I know that you, too, perceived in me a certain want of spirit. Its cause, though you may not believe it, resides in the flesh. Knowledge of this insuperable obstacle, particularly as it keeps me apart from you, has made my life at last intolerable.

The German poet Friedrich Hölderlin ends one of his poems with the line, Einmal lebt'ich, wie Götter, und mehr bedarf's nicht: "I lived once like the gods, and ask no more." When you and I lay together, Lindsay, I, too, *knew that blessèd life. It is to you, then beloved, that I owe the greatest happiness I have known on this earth—the greatest happiness, I think, that anyone could know.*

I do not believe in a life after death; but if there is one, be certain, my darling, that I shall watch over you from that other world.

Sweetie, please remember, you bear absolutely no responsibility for my act and I have not for a second held you responsible. It results rather from long, long unhappiness. In a letter to a friend I wrote that my chief dread was that you entrust yourself to me and I fail to make you happy. You foresaw that when we parted; I foresee it too, not only in your case, but in the case of any woman. I am altogether too unhappy to continue; I long for an end to consciousness.

I am writing these lines in what I believe to be my last minutes (an hour). How pleasant it is to think of you, darling! From the day we met I have thought of you without cease. And again I have the opportunity to tell you that I love you.

My dear, dear friend, I bid you farewell. I do not know what to write except that, in this difficult hour, I am glad to reflect that I did not conceal my love, and that my attentions brought you pleasure a while.
Love,
J.

I finished the letter and set it on the table, humbled. The kata and prayer flags I'd left on Jordan's corpse and around his room were trinkets. Lindsay's love was the single gift, I knew, that might truly redeem my brother's spirit and save him from the lowest rebirths.

"When was the last time you spoke with him?"

"Thursday night. He called me about going on a bike ride Sunday. I told him I didn't know if it was a good idea. We'd stopped seeing each other about a week before, and I was feeling conflicted. It was so tempting just to see him to hold him." Her voice broke. "But I knew it wasn't right. I knew if I saw him again I'd lose whatever ground I'd gained. I mean, look, I'm thirty-five. And I was really sure he was *it*. When we first met. I thought he really might be the one. Your brother was really such a wonderful man, but he just . . ."

We sat in silence. I became aware of the hour: the Metroliner back to Manhattan left at 10:30 p.m. But there was something I wanted to know, a piece of information I needed before I could leave the house.

"Lindsay, can I ask you a personal question?"

She nodded, but said nothing.

"For a long time—for years—my brother complained of a sexual problem. It was the root of his despair. The only time I heard him talk about killing himself, it was related to that issue. Supposedly there was a moment, when—during sex, almost ten years ago—he felt what he described to me as a sharp pain in his penis. That was the 'mishap' he wrote about in his note." I was tempted to stop there, but realized I still hadn't asked the question. "I understand that it must have been terribly frustrating, even humiliating, for you as well. But what I need to know is, how bad *was* it? I mean, do you think he was beyond help?"

Lindsay looked at me directly, neither blinking nor wavering, while I spoke. When I finished she pulled her hair away from her face with both hands and threw it back over her shoulders. Then she placed her hands on her knees.

"Can I be equally frank with you?"

I nodded, flushed.

"Sex was not a problem," she said.

"What?"

"Jordan was wonderful in bed. He was a wonderful lover. He had no sexual problems at all."

I couldn't speak. The room quivered and spun, as if she had hit me over the head with a frying pan.

"It was *out* of bed that our problems arose. Jordan just couldn't relax. He couldn't let go. He had this mask of formality that he put on, always, the minute he got up in the morning.

"I used to shake him"—her voice seemed to arrive from a great distance—"and beg him to loosen up. But it wasn't something he could shake off. He had spent too long building that persona, that wall. And he couldn't let it down, not even for me. So I asked him to see a therapist. I gave him $1,000 to cover the first few months, the trial run. But he only went once.

"Sex was not the problem," she repeated, shaking her head. "If he could have been as intimate and loving out of bed as he was in bed, we would never have split up."

26

The Wind Tunnel

THE FIRST FEW weeks after my return to Oakland, friends came by every day. We'd sit on the purple futon in my living room or congregate around my dining table, the memorial candle burning, and talk about death and transfiguration. Beyond the window, city buses and bottle-filled shopping carts jostled down Fortieth toward Telegraph. I served chips and salsa. A photograph of my brother sat on my writing desk, his ironic gaze banishing the nightmare memory of his mortuary death mask.

Familiarity can be like a cream. The fabric of my own everyday life, viewed through the filter of Jordan's suicide, took on an iridescent sheen. I felt beatified. Fabulous things happened. Dying plants bloomed back to life in my presence. Fortune cookies blessed me. Strange cats pressed their muzzles to my shins. I found money everywhere: $20 bills, two or three at a time, balled up in careless post-ATM configurations.

Sex was an exception. I gave Carlita's "therapy" an honest try, suppressing a longing for Nepal during our time together. Our couplings were primal and efficient, keeping a connection alive without bringing us closer. We knew how to have fun together. But when we were apart, my thoughts turned to Grace, with an odd mixture of craving and concern. Half a dozen attempts to phone her had ended in frantic busy signals or scratchy recordings, in Nepali and English, about overloaded lines. It often seemed that Nepal, like James Hilton's Shangri-la, was a phantasmagoric world. Once you left, you no longer had access.

And my life in Oakland was full. Every day—answering the telephone, standing on line at the post office, shopping for coffee at Piedmont Grocery—I received sacraments of sympathy and concern. Somehow, everyone knew. People touched me, usually on the arm or shoulder, and asked: *How are you? Are you all right? How's your mom?*

They were tough questions. For despite the oddly luminous quality of my life, I was *not* all right. I could not honestly say that I was doing well, or that my mother or sister were doing well. I could not state that we had come to terms with Jordan's death, or that we ever would.

How are you doing? people asked.

And I answered: It's like a wind tunnel. The kind used to test experimental rockets and jets. Engineers place a scale model inside a wind tunnel and turn up the fans. For the jet to survive, its shape must divert the winds around its surface. If there is a design problem—any aerodynamic flaw—the model disintegrates.

The strongest blast had hit me when I'd lifted the lid of Jordan's coffin. My frame had shuddered, trembling with dangerous vibrations, but had not gone to pieces. My mother and sister faced equally powerful gales from different angles, and they, too, had survived. Everyone who experiences a suicide must turn toward the wind in his or her private way.

For some, the strategy is anger: rage at the fool who has thrown away his own life and brought so much suffering to others. For others it is uninhibited grief: days of sobbing, lamentation, the flushing out of pain. I chose the shape of an explorer: investigating, reporting, sublimating my own grief into the excitement that accompanies a journey of discovery. I read Jordan's journals, perused his letters, spent hours on the telephone with his confidants, professors, and lovers. I roamed through this labyrinth of mysteries with awe and compassion, in search of I knew not what. If this was a quest, it was toward an indefinable goal.

By the end of my third week in California, I realized the goal was not indefinable at all. I had begun to sense its edges.

My desire was to find the True Cause. I wanted to convince myself, beyond a shadow of a doubt, that Jordan's suicide was *unavoidable*. I wanted to know that there was no other way for events to unfold, that nothing I might have said, and nothing anyone could have done, would have arrested his cancer of the spirit.

IF A TUNNEL is long enough, and dark enough, it might as well be a cave. The first days after Jordan's death had found me stumbling blindly. But as my investigations progressed, there was gradual illumination. I began to know Jordan as never before. Immersed in his writings, communing with his friends, I found the intimacy that had eluded us as adults. It never felt like a one-way street. We were in constant communication, my brother and I, through channels both subtle and direct.

Others, I learned, had shared this experience. Loved ones die, and after the initial shock, we realize we've been given the responsibility—and privilege—of keeping them alive. It's not a matter of reading their mail, riding their bicycle, or wearing their clothes. It has nothing to do with the stuff they left behind: the structure of objects and friendships, which crumbles like a neglected road in the Amazon rain forest.

It's about *becoming* them, in an almost organic way. We absorb the essence of our lost ones, drawing their best attributes into our own lives. If they were kind, we swell with their goodness. If they were pushy, we extract their decisiveness and will. In the case of Jordan, I felt my neck elongating, my eyes becoming more keen. I grew funnier, but more cynical; sharper, but less self-revealing. I felt a strange attraction to Virgil Fox recordings and Berlitz language courses. I picked up rare books, running my fingers along their spines.

My mother and I walked into a bakery in Tarrytown, looking for a fresh Jewish rye. After the clerk had sliced the loaf and slid it into a waxed bag, I stuck my nose in the sack and inhaled deeply. "'Tis the aroma of freshly baled hay," I declaimed, "with a hint of sweet manure. One needs only a sharp cheese—or a jar of schmaltz." My mother looked at me in astonishment, as though I'd channeled the deceased. She was right: I was seeing my brother from the inside, looking out.

At other moments—visiting museums, listening to music—I heard his sharp, critical commentary in my ear, heard it as if he were speaking the words himself. One afternoon I dropped into the Strand bookstore, looking for an English version of Rainer Maria Rilke's *Sonnets to Orpheus*. But a ghostly admonition—*There is no such thing as a translation*—hustled me along.

My brother's quality of observation, his provocative opinions about art and music, took root within my personality. The vow I had made in Kathmandu, a seeming eternity ago, had been fulfilled. We were brothers at last: on his terms, not mine.

His JOURNALS WERE heartbreaking, but the precision of his entries amazed me. He would write a paragraph, rewrite it on the following page, and then write it again, changing a single preposition. But if the writing was lovely, its message was devoid of hope. Jordan had known for years that he was going to kill himself. I found entries penned five, six, seven years ago that might just as well have been written the morning he took his life. There were months on end when Jordan did not believe he could live another day; long summer evenings when he stood on bridges near Cornell University, feeling the wind rise up the gorges and imagining the rush of air against his falling body.

The language of his suffering was theatrical, and unapologetically classical. His journals and letters overflowed with testimonies of unrequited love, phrased in the cloying, overripe language of Victorian tragedy. Even his most despairing entries seemed to have blossomed from the pen of a nineteenth-century dramaturge:

> *If I must die, good; I've lived enough for ten men, for a hundred, for a thousand men. When I laughed the sky, the stones and the long grasses laughed with me; no one had ever laughed as I did. When I fell into despair not a thousand generations of men could speak a word to succor me. When I sought for truth I could have moved the planets, and the stars. In all I did I kept to truth and courage.*

The words were overblown but, coming from my brother, they rang true. Jordan *longed* to die, and to die tragically. He had nurtured his pain for years, like an exquisitely twisted bonsai. His death, like Yukio Mishima's, was ultimately a performance: a self-fulfilled prophecy, crafted for its pathos and impact.

I was fascinated by the accounts of Jordan's relationships. One of the more unsettling things I learned about my brother was that, despite the earthshaking intensity of his feelings for Lindsay, he had chronicled a nearly identical courtship a few months before, with a woman named Kate. Before Kate had come Jennifer, and Daphne, and Britta.

The evolution of these affairs was remarkably similar. Each began in a flash followed by overwhelming infatuation and immediate decline. This final stage was an epoch of lamentation and woe, which Jordan painted in the blackest hues. The reason for the breakup was always the same: his "physical problem."

ONE MORNING IN early April, making a pot of coffee, I wondered what Jordan had been doing just over six years ago, on my thirtieth birthday. I found that journal: a spiral-bound, single-subject notebook. As I leafed through it, I realized I had missed something. When I'd first read it, the journal had seemed to end about halfway through. After a gap of ten pages, though, the writing resumed.

There were only a few entries, undated. The first few were reflections on Cornell and his linguistics courses. But then Jordan returned to his malaise, which was still in its early stages. He wrote of his misery, and of his conviction to see a specialist. But then came something new:

> I could pretend I had been selected by the gods to suffer, and make a noble story of my woe. But a more candid view suggests that one evening, hidden, fearful for the shame of my act, I did myself injury while abominating myself.

It took a few minutes for the meaning of this confession to sink in. *Abomination!* Jordan's use of that word, with its biblical roots, changed everything. In the abstract, it applies to a broad spectrum of nastiness, from bad table manners to two-headed calves. But applied to an *act*, the implications of sodomy, onanism, and homosexuality are inescapable. Jordan was the most literal writer I had ever known; he would never use a word without a full awareness, and intention, of its meaning. With that realization, the puzzle pieces of my brother's suicide began moving into place.

I returned to his other journals, looking for the places I'd marked as revealing or intriguing. The word *abomination* had appeared only once before, so casually that I'd glossed over it. The setting was a dorm party, in the room of an older student. A night of drinking had progressed into what sounded like an orgy, an experimental free-for-all where *I myself*, Jordan had written, *did not shy from the abominations that followed.*

When I'd first read the entry, I thought my brother was being funny. It had not occurred to me that the other students might have been men.

The paradox of my brother's sexual "problem" made sense to me now. The incident he described was not merely an event; it was an event horizon that he had irrevocably crossed. At some point in his high school or college years (or before, although I never had a clue), Jordan must have discovered that he was gay. But he was not, for many reasons, one of those fortunate men or women who absorb this truth, face the challenges of coming out, and emerge into a proud or private ownership of their sexual identity. For my brother, the aberration was intolerable. Despising our father, dependent on our mother, and terrified of the judgment of his friends (and, very possibly, his brother), he smothered his cravings. He regressed into his studies, modeling his public persona after the virile, heroic figures of ancient texts. But his self-proclaimed virtue was a facade: a cardboard cutout, like the model of King Tribhuvan paraded through the streets of Kathmandu.

Was the suppression a conscious process? There was no way to know. But it seemed incredible that someone would put himself through so much suffering. Jordan would weather countless romantic disasters, steel himself for endless sexual disappointments, rather than face his true orientation. He dared not partner openly with men, but pleasured himself covertly. Maybe he *had* injured himself during one of these autoerotic episodes, but I no longer believed this injury was the cause of his "numbness" around women.

If you would know me, Jordan confided in one entry, *look to Thomas Mann*. Though his own copies of Mann's work were in German, I found summaries of the two he mentioned most often. The isolated, superior protagonist of *Tonio Kröger*, torn between life and art, clearly inspired my brother's lifestyle. But it is Gustav von Aschenbach, the tragic hero of *Death in Venice*, who provides the key. In the novel, the renowned author falls in love with Tadzio: a young boy. His infatuation with the youth, which von Aschenbach desperately conceals, costs him his life.

Jordan, like Mann, was no misogynist. He adored women and was adored by them. But they were never more than abstractions, toppling awkwardly from the pedestals he erected. Lindsay and Kate, Daphne and Britta; all were objects of worship, showered with verses and gifts, pined after like unattainable goddesses. But they were not his true partners. Their emotional needs defied his understanding. Jordan's letters to them, like his suicide note to Lindsay, were eerily similar, blending the archaic prose of John Milton with the longing of Rilke. They read like exercises, essays for a course in romantic love. It was the one subject he could not master.

There was a final entry on the page that followed the confession of his injury. It began with a brief paragraph I'd encountered several times in his later journals: one of those phrases that he kept refining, over and over again, as if by adding or omitting a comma he could make his meaning absolutely precise. Here, at its very first occurrence, it made exquisite sense:

O you who read these words! Never deny your true nature. For I have done so, and it has destroyed me.

The word *deny* leaped out at me, just as *abomination* had. If an abomination is an event, denial is a path: a road away from the heart's desire. Chokyi Nyima had described desire as a double-edged sword, a force that can overwhelm us or prod us toward liberation. But denial is a barricade that stops everything and halts all forward motion. To deny a crime is to reject the possibility of forgiveness, but to deny yourself is to abandon all hope of acceptance. This was what happened to Jordan. Unable to accept who he was, terrified by his self-discovery, he had pulled that lever. His capacity for arousal, for joy on any level, shut down.

Jordan, who claimed to value honesty above all things, had lived a lie. To explain his passionless encounters with women, my theatrical brother —an expert at mimicking the lame—had invented his own disability. For nearly ten years, the myth of sexual dysfunction had served as his alibi.

Jordan was not a coward. What had stopped him from declaring him-self, shamelessly, defiantly? Did he really believe that my mother, my sister, and I would reject him? Every gay person I knew had navigated that bardo: the dread and exhilaration of coming out. Some had been embraced by their families; others had ongoing issues with narrow-minded parents and friends. But they had lived, and sometimes died, on their own terms.

This, I knew, would be the enduring mystery. I'd never know why Jordan couldn't step into the world, at peace in his own skin. Maybe it was because he despised modern society, with its "faith healers," careless translations, and jazz. His sensibilities were locked in an era long past, when homosexuality was a public scandal and a personal mark of shame. Or maybe it was just him, the way he was made. It could be that facing his "true nature," which he saw as profoundly flawed, was beyond his ability. Some people are so good at manipulating what's on the surface, you never realize how terrified they are of looking below. It's one thing to imagine the presence of nagas, multiplying in the depths of the earth; it's another to know you've buried them there yourself.

PART III

After

27

Kunda Mainali vs. the Leeches

THE MORNING HE heard about Nagarjun, Kunda Mainali was filling in at the National Desk. The *Shaligram* had zero redundancy; if a single editor took the day off, his entire department was at loose ends. With events heating up in Nepal's capital, a lapse in national coverage was impossible. Mainali had been relieved of the Friday Supplement, which he customarily put together on Wednesday, and thrust into Birendra Rana's high-profile position. "King for a day," he had smiled to himself.

He was sitting behind Rana's ancient oak desk—a relic from the British Raj, no doubt, dragged over the hills by coolies to Kathmandu—editing a story about yesterday's bandh. It had been the second general strike in the kingdom in two weeks, and certainly the most violent. The past week, from March 8, had been a nonstop nightmare marked by gang rapes, scenes of hired thugs beating up striking students, and to cap it off, the discovery of six headless corpses in the Sindhuli forest. Nearly eight thousand citizens were now in prison, and at least thirty people had been killed in the escalating violence. None of this seemed to concern King Birendra; he was at his lakeside hideaway in Pokhara, due back tomorrow.

Kunda pored over the copy, despising his sudden responsibility. It was the *Shaligram*'s official mandate (and, therefore, Rana's) to sanitize the bandh—or, better still, overlook it altogether. During the past month the world press had lavished unusual attention on Nepal, publishing unflinching reports on the kingdom's turmoil. His own newspaper, meanwhile, had cast the Jana Andolan as the rabble-rousing of criminal elements, funded and inspired by foreign forces. Ignore it, professed the *Shaligram*, and it will go away.

This kind of propagandizing was a cinch for Rana, who came from a wealthy family with strong palace ties. But for Mainali, who'd cut his teeth covering the Donald Manes scandal in New York City, it raised bile. He was staring at the copy, staring *through* it actually, when Meera Khanal came charging in.

"They've sold Nagarjun," the reporter informed him. Her eyes blazed with the delight of a good scandal.

"Sold it? Who?" The question was rhetorical. Nagarjun, the sacred hill that towered over the northwestern rim of the Kathmandu Valley, was the property of the king; it had been part of the wedding dowry presented by Queen Aiswarya's father in 1973.

"Birendra! Who else?"

"Well who the hell did he sell it to?" Mainali heard a trace of his barely acquired New York accent. "The Brits? The Japs? Germany? How can you sell a damned national park?"

"No, no, not like that." Khanal laughed, and her horn-rimmed glasses leaned askew. She adjusted them with the end of her pencil. "No, what happened was this: Birendra sold it back to Nepal itself. The statement says he returned it to the 'People of Nepal,' with some typical bullshit wording about 'the rights and responsibilities of posterity.'"

"How much?" Mainali's gray eyes narrowed; Birendra's strategy was already clear to him.

"Fifty crore. About $16 million U.S. He's already approved the withdrawal from the National Treasury."

Kunda nodded. His thin, feminine hands were pressed together in a prayerlike mudra in front of his mouth. A chewed-up pencil stuck up like a yellow obelisk between them.

This was it, then. This was really it. With the democracy movement gnawing the strings of his hammock, Birendra was taking no more chances. Sixteen million was a lot of money. It was enough, probably, to pay off what those in the know cynically called the "Royal Life Insurance": a private island in the Maldives. Unbelievable. But what could Mainali do? If he ran the story, he'd lose his job, possibly wind up in prison. And even if he *was* to risk everything, and print a full exposé—who would believe it?

The problem was, Kunda didn't know where the average Nepali, the so-called man in the street, stood in relation to the king. There was angry talk, dissatisfaction, yes. But that was among the educated, the literate: professionals, businessmen, university students, Rhoda. Their circle of friends. They had no trouble believing the rumors that filtered down, layer by layer, from the heights of Kathmandu society. Stories about the king's brothers, and their links to gold smuggling and drug trafficking; about the shooting of Padam Thakurathi, a journalist who had exposed the palace mafia; about torture and rape in the prisons. But their talk was discreet, for they also knew of the Public Security Act, under which any Nepali citizen could be thrown into prison for eighteen months without trial.

When you interviewed the activists or listened to their speeches on the weed-choked lawn of the Technical University it was easy to imagine that every citizen of the valley, from computer engineers to cart-pullers, felt a common sense of disgust with the royal regime and its self-serving domination of the country. But this was an illusion. When all was said and done, the throne still commanded enormous respect. People on all levels of society—even the opposition leaders!—regarded Birendra with barely suppressed awe. In some ways the sentiment was healthy, a collective yearning to set aside caste and clan differences and unite under a single, traditional symbol. But too much of that deference was based on the insidious belief, conditioned over centuries, that the king of Nepal ruled by divine right. To millions of Nepalis, Sri Panch Maharaja Birendra Bir Bikram Shah Dev was not a man, but a god: a direct incarnation of Lord Vishnu, eternal preserver of the human race.

The king himself had been conditioned to believe this, as well. And his role as divine, omnipotent monarch was nourished and sustained by every single person who kowtowed within the royal aura.

What would it take, Mainali wondered sourly, for people to shrug off this ancient mantle of superstition? How could they see the royal family for the bloodsuckers they were? He leaned back until the front feet of his chair tipped off the ground.

"We can't use it, can we?" Meera Khanal still stood before the desk, shamelessly reading a personal letter on the edge of Mainali's desk.

"No," Mainali said. He pointedly picked up and turned over the letter. "But write something up anyway. I'll try to interest Reuters." He frowned, nagged by the thought of giving the story away.

"But first, try to find out where that money's going. It went out of the Treasury, but ended up where? Listen, does your mother's uncle still work at the Home Ministry?"

"Better than that. My stepbrother's a VP at Rastra Bank."

"Great. See what you can find out. Use the phone in Sports."

AFTER MEERA LEFT the room, Mainali doodled absently on a yellow notepad. He made a squiggly line, thickened it into an elongated S, then doodled a few more alongside it. Suddenly, with a wave of revulsion, he realized what he was drawing. His reaction was strong enough to make him stop, grimace, and hide the doodle beneath a thick layer of scribbling.

Twenty-eight years ago—good God, was it that long ago?—Kunda had made a pilgrimage to Tengpoche Gompa with his mother. It was quite a trip; they'd taken the overnight bus to Jiri and walked ten days to reach the famous monastery, perched on a lofty saddle almost twelve thousand feet above sea level.

They spent about a week in Solo and Khumbu, visiting sacred sites and taking a day-hike in the hopes of glimpsing Sagarmatha: Mount Everest. On their return walk toward Jiri, as they were descending the long hill outside of Namche Bazaar, his mother tripped over a sharp rock and cut her foot. It didn't seem like much; but by the time they reached the village of Ringmo, four days later, the wound was so badly infected that she could no longer put her weight on it.

The families in Ringmo were sympathetic, and there was much tongue-clucking and head-wagging. There was a health post at Junbesi, they said. But no one volunteered to go. There was only one solution: Kunda would have to walk, alone, to Junbesi. There he could hire a porter or, at the very least, return with antibiotics. He was six years old—and Junbesi was five hours away, through thick jungle. The sky threatened rain.

His mother was a relatively modern woman, but she held to a few old-fashioned beliefs. "Don't go if it rains," she had warned him. "Wait. The wet will bring out the leeches. They're demons; they'll suck your blood right out of your body and hang your skin from the branches of a tree."

Kunda had never seen a leech; they rarely appeared in the Kathmandu Valley. He imagined them huge as snakes, with sharp fangs and glowing red eyes. They were genuine monsters, creatures of nightmare. But his mother was growing feverish. When she fell off to sleep, he put a few things into his small rucksack and left the tiny inn.

At the edge of Ringmo, an old man sat on a tree stump, rolling a cigarette. His eyes were misted over with cataracts.

"Eebaji, pani aunu parchha?" Elder, will it rain?

"Er, babu! Pani pardaina! Gaam aundaichha!"

Kunda found it hard to believe that the sun would emerge from these clouds. They stuffed the sky like gray feathers. But age was wisdom, and with the old man's assurance and twenty rupee coins in his pocket, he set off.

The old man was right. The clouds backed away, and sunlight poured through the treetops. But an hour later the sky darkened again, and now Kunda heard thunder rolling up from the valley. The first raindrops hit the leaves above his head soon after, as he descended to the river. The last tea-house was far behind him; the next, hours ahead. He contemplated going back to Ringmo, but remembered the old man's guarantee. Maybe the rain was concentrated behind him.

The drops fell harder. Now they were pounding the leaves, cascading down to soak the trail and the forest floor. Thunder rumbled all around him, impossible to locate; it came from all directions at once. A stick got jammed into his thong, and as he stopped to pick it out he saw a mud-brown leech, narrow as a noodle, writhing up his ankle. Seized by fear and disgust, Kunda snapped at the creature until it balled up and rolled off. Another leech fell from the leaves above, landing on the back of his hand. He shrieked and slapped at it as it twisted like a miniature cobra; in the meantime, two more leeches crawled onto his foot.

Kunda started to run, gasping for breath. From every leaf, from the mossy tree trunks and carpet of fallen leaves, from the branches above his head and even the clouds themselves, the forest filled with leeches. Kunda stopped every few steps to scrape them off, but every time he did so, half a dozen more would appear on his shirt, his arms, his feet. He began to run blindly, in a panic, racing through the rain as the creatures crawled into the soft spaces between his toes, behind his ears, beneath his collar. He could feel a leech on his forehead, see a black wriggle on the side of his nose. He slapped at his face and raced ahead, shrieking. What if he fell? He imagined himself fainting, covered head to toes with leeches. They would suck him dry and display his skin, like a rabbit pelt, from the limbs of the spongy trees . . .

"*Chiya, sahib?*"

Mainali jumped, startled by the tea boy. The cheap pencil he'd been holding snapped in his hands. "*Danyabat.*" He plucked the glass of milk tea from the cup holder and handed the boy a rupee. He held the glass with both hands, sipping slowly as he recovered his composure.

The leeches hadn't killed him, of course. Junbesi had been closer than he thought. The locals had laughed riotously at the sight of the crazed little city boy, exploding from the jungle with a fattened leech above each eye. They'd removed the harmless creatures and flicked them away like dead mosquitoes before feeding Kunda a hot meal. Kunda's feet, neck, and back were pocked with tiny round wounds, which the man at the health post swabbed with alcohol. They gave him a full dose of antibiotics in a smart plastic bottle and sent him back toward Ringmo in the clear, sunny morning with a group of porters.

That was it, after all: a few little nips. A little lost blood. And no more fear of leeches. He had never listened to his mother's tall tales with the same gullibility again.

How much blood would it take this time, he wondered, to prove that the leeches at the end of Durbar Marg could also be resisted? How many more years of fear and intimidation before Nepal's people realized that this self-styled deity was just a stocky, middle-aged man with a weakness for Irish whiskey, Cuban cigars, and Bruce Lee videos?

Mainali nursed his tea. He craved a packet of biscuits, but didn't dare leave the office. He began snooping through Rana's desk, hoping to find some kind of snack. There was a packet of roasted soybeans in the right-hand drawer, and he popped a few into his mouth.

The issue, Mainali admitted to himself, was more complicated than getting rid of the king. Despite everything he'd said to Rhoda and her friends, he was terrified of democracy.

It wasn't democracy itself, of course; that was an abstraction. It was the way the system would be interpreted by Nepalis. Political parties had been outlawed in Nepal since 1960, when Mahendra, the current king's father, had banned them. Mahendra had imprisoned hundreds of people, including the activists who'd helped his own father, King Tribhuvan, reclaim Nepal's throne from the corrupt Rana families in the early 1960s.

For the older generation, living in the middle hills and the mountains, democracy was synonymous with instability. It meant a loss of cultural values, a challenge to traditional authority, and a blasphemous insult to the god in the Palace. The scenes they associated with "democracy" were of stone-throwing students, battling helmeted police.

But it was the kids Mainali was most worried about. They'd grown up without any concept of what democracy was, or the civic responsibilities it carried. They did, however, have a twisted idea of its perks, based on the excesses of Western tourists and the racy images in smuggled Hollywood videos. For many teenagers—the disco crowd, the self-styled punks, the New Road cowboys—democracy was a form of anarchy. It was a ticket to the world of material affluence and social arrogance that visitors from the "free world" had flaunted in their streets for thirty years. And those guys were relatively benign. For others, Mainali knew, democracy was the right to break bottles in the streets, harass women like Rhoda and Grace, and run down the streets in packs, heaving rocks through windows.

And it wasn't just that. It wasn't just his immediate apprehensions about what the first few months, or even years, would portend. He'd often talked with Rhoda and his friends about how democracy could succeed in Nepal, how even a spinach farmer in Simikot could watch his vote be counted. But there was a flip side to this coin. With the middle hills and

Himalayan villages so spread out, the largest single voting bloc would be
the Terai: the hot, flat, southern lowlands that slouched unceremoniously
into India. To the casual visitor, much of the Terai was in fact indistinguish-
able from India. If those cities, which held nearly half of Nepal's population, wanted closer ties with India, the rest of the country would be swept
along. The average Nepali's greatest fear—"Indianization"—would be realized. Neither the middle hill tribes, nor the Sherpas of the Khumbu, nor the
Newars in the Kathmandu Valley would stand for that. Nepal would burst
apart like a rotten squash.

What a marvelous dilemma, thought Mainali. Stagnation . . . or
anarchy?

Back at Hunter, a Haitian friend had lent him a book by Woody Allen.
There was one particular line that he had noted down; it seemed remarkably cogent.

"Mankind stands at a crossroads," the comedian had written. "In one
direction lies total destruction; in the other, utter despair. Let us pray we
have the wisdom to choose correctly."

Kunda Mainali drew a long breath and slapped the mouth of his empty
tea glass with his right palm. It made a high, startled noise, like a tightly
tuned drum.

The Newars had their share of sayings as well. He remembered one his
uncle had taught him: "He won't carry the load, because it hurts his back—
but it breaks his heart to pay someone else to carry it."

Recalling the proverb was enough to make Mainali wince. He, all his
friends, even his parents, had lived with broken hearts for years. Maybe it
was time for Nepalis to start developing their back muscles.

Meera Khanal rapped at the door and walked in, a pencil between her
teeth. She opened her mouth and let it drop onto her notepad, then flipped
it into the air and caught it in her right hand. Mainali raised an eyebrow,
impressed.

"What've we got?"

"Okay, here's the scoop. No one knows where the money went. But I
called in some favors at the Home Ministry anyway, and guess what?"

"Go on."

"Next week, the United States Army is sending in a military transport plane via Pakistan. The contents will be one Sikorsky helicopter—ideal for an evacuation—and two escorts. Total price: $14 million, U.S."

"What an uncanny coincidence." Mainali breathed deeply and stared at the doodles on his notepad. He'd heard enough. It was time to deal with Kathmandu's little leech problem. He felt calm and resolved; an odd state, he reflected, for a man about to forfeit his job.

Mainali picked up the phone. He punched the code for the print shop. Static. He tapped the cradle and tried again. On his fourth attempt the call went through. The line was so bad it sounded like he was talking to someone on the moon.

"Deepak? Kunda Mainali here. I'm on the National Desk today. Yes, it's going well. Thanks; listen. No, just listen to me. *Hold the presses*. That's right. Yes. We have a bit of late-breaking news."

28

Critical Mass

O N THE NIGHT of April 4, I got home from a late showing of *Dead Poets Society* to see the light blinking on my answering machine.

Hi there, it's Paula. Hope it's not too late to call. Listen, if you get this and have a shortwave, try to find the BBC. Or I think it's on NPR here in the city. There's a lot going on in Nepal. I thought you should know. Anyway, hope all's well. Give us a call. Gina misses you!

I didn't have a shortwave, but I had DeLauer's. The all-night newsstand had been a fixture in downtown Oakland since 1907 and stocked an amazing selection of international newspapers and magazines. It was a short drive at midnight, and by the time I got out of there I'd dropped 20 bucks on newsprint.

Back home I made a pot of tea, put on an Ali Akbar Khan CD, and planted myself on the living room carpet with the *New York Times*, the *Washington Post*, the *International Herald Tribune*, the *Financial Times* of London, and the *Times of India*.

Paula hadn't been kidding: Nepal was big news. Two centuries of repressed rage was surging through Kathmandu in peristaltic waves. I pulled out a notebook and made a chronology of the month since my departure.

Nearly everything had happened within the past week. On Saturday, March 31, more than ten thousand demonstrators had marched through the streets of Patan, Kathmandu's neighboring city. The protestors attacked a police station and tried to burn down the mayor's office. Women threw buckets of water from windows to neutralize the tear gas, while volunteers ran through the crowds distributing onions (which, strangely, help to counter the gas's weepy effect). Two people were killed in the melee. That evening Nepal's foreign minister, S. K. Upadhyaya, handed his resignation to the king.

On Sunday, the king fired nine other ministers who backed Upadhyaya's view. Meanwhile, a coalition of banned political parties held a rally in Patan's Nag Bahal ("Snake Square"), building crude barricades to keep the police at bay. Kathmandu's physicians staged a wildcat strike, refusing all but emergency calls, to protest the arrest of seven doctors. They weren't the only high-caste professionals who'd been tagged by the Palace; scores of college professors and activist attorneys had also been dragged off to jail.

The following day—Monday, April 2—at least fifty thousand people, many armed with hoes or scythes, converged in the unassuming village of Kirtipur. Their plan was to march across the Bagmati bridge, and into Kathmandu. Every strata of Nepali society was represented: shop owners in black topis, banner-waving schoolboys, mothers with babes in arms. The police fired into the crowd, killing or wounding more than thirty people.

Among the casualties was Bijaya Maharjan, a twenty-five-year-old college student. He was rushed to Bir Hospital, where he died on arrival. A police squad raided the ward, demanding his body. The government, clearly, did not want the nature of his wounds, from lead dum-dum bullets, to reach the press. The doctors refused to surrender the corpse. When the body was taken by force, medics lay down in front of the police vans. That afternoon, as Maharjan's funeral procession swelled through the streets of Patan, police tried to drive a bulldozer through flaming barricades of Nag Bahal in an attempt to rescue more than three hundred troops being held by the demonstrators. They failed. Jubilant mobs overturned the bulldozer and set it ablaze.

Reading these stories was intensely frustrating. Until now I'd kept my spirit afloat, weathering waves of regret and professional jealousy for my colleagues still in Nepal. As desperately as I wished to be in Kathmandu, I'd remained reconciled to my situation: the harsh and indefinite process of dealing with Jordan's death. But a short dispatch in the final newspaper I opened—a Reuters dispatch in the *San Jose Mercury News*—capsized my raft.

In an unprecedented protest against the killing of civilians, all 165 pilots of Royal Nepal Airlines had staged a wildcat strike.

In just four weeks, the chain reaction I'd long awaited had taken place. Nepal had reached critical mass, and I was ten thousand miles away.

There was no hope, I knew, of calling my travel agent and booking a seat on the next available flight to Kathmandu. I couldn't afford it; the expenses for the New York trip had drained my account. But even if I could—even if I borrowed the money, made the necessary bookings, and got myself back to Nepal in a week—there was no way I'd get my story.

Journalists rely on their intuition. Mine told me I was too late.

29

New Year's Day

THE REVOLUTION WAS televised. I'd followed it all, from start to finish. The April 6 Massacre; the dusk-to-dawn, shoot-on-sight curfew; and finally, on the night of April 8, the king's capitulation. It had taken half a million weathermen, but the Palace had finally figured out which way the wind was blowing. Nepal, the world's last divine monarchy, was a democracy at last.

As *Week* ran Larry Prince's spectacular photographs of the victory parade, hundreds of thousands of Nepalis dancing down Ramshah Path and Durbar Marg, banging aluminum dekshis and throwing red powder into the air. Women and children waved banners in triumph. Everyone was singing, laughing, and smiling.

Nepal had burst into bloom. Suddenly, irrevocably, and without me. *Jivan yestai chha,* as the locals say. Life is like that. Our imagined personal destinies are mere inventions, myths that can be rewritten by our own hand, or anyone else's, in an instant.

I swung out of bed and drew my curtain for a bead on the day. It was the fourteenth of April, a fine spring morning in Oakland. At this moment, on the other side of the world, the citizens of the Kathmandu Valley were celebrating Nawabarsa: Nepali New Year. In Bhaktapur, a tinderbox town eight miles east of the capital, the festival was just warming up. The town's citizens would be pouring into the streets, lighting candles, and whacking drums in honor of Bisket: a yearly ritual commemorating the slaughter of

two demons who had taken the form of nagas and hidden themselves up the
nose of a beautiful princess. Bhaktapur's male population would soon begin
their traditional game of tug-of-war, straining on heavy, hard-woven ropes
in an attempt to topple a giant lingam: an eight-story-high phallus, carved
from a single tree and erected the previous afternoon. Each team would pull
with all its might, rocking the flower-topped pillar from side to side. When
it crashed to the ground, the demons/snakes were destroyed. The year could
begin anew. Tonight's celebration would be electric, full of triumph and
metaphor. The snakes had been vanquished indeed.

It was over. And nothing could make up for the fact that I'd missed
it. Every third sentence that came into my mind, it seemed, began with the
words *If only.* If only I'd reached my brother from Kathmandu. If only he'd
trusted me with his secret. If only he'd held out another month. If only I'd
stayed in Nepal a few more weeks. Jordan would still be alive—and I'd have
the front page of the *Examiner.*

No use think this, Chokyi Nyima would say. I carried my round cushion into the living room, set the timer, and assumed the position. Since
returning from New York I'd been "practicing" almost every day. I didn't
have much in the way of technique; it was simply a matter of folding my legs
and giving my mind a rest. It shouldn't be a struggle. The idea, as I understood it, was to make no effort.

Nothing is more difficult, I was discovering, than making no effort. But
no one said it was going to be easy. *That's why they call it practice*, I told
myself. It made sense; why should learning how to liberate your mind be
any easier than learning how to play the clarinet?

Despite its frustrations, the exercise was useful. It was the only thing
that reminded me of my life back in Nepal. Meditation awakened a physical memory. As I sat on my cushion, I could imagine that I was still a traveler, away from the desperate sales pitch of Western civilization.

Some sessions were more fruitful than others. Today's was not. The
timer's bleep roused me not from purified awakening, but from a daydream
of Carlita's rump, bouncing like a hot pumpkin against my loins. It was a
painful image; we hadn't had sex for weeks. Like steam on the windows of
an old Chevy, the passion of my first weeks home had evaporated, and the

inevitable return to the Familiar Questions had not served our love life very well. Carlita was ready for a real partnership, and vocal with her opinion that Jordan's suicide had now replaced Nepal as my open-ended excuse to avoid the issue of commitment.

On one hand, she was right. Dealing with Jordan's death did not create the ideal mind-set for reevaluating our relationship. I hadn't asked her to come to New York with me, so the event didn't serve to deepen our connection, or bring her into my family. The whole mourning process was something that had distanced me from her. On the other hand, I could hardly feel guilty about grieving, or for taking as much time as I needed for myself.

The upshot of this was that we seemed to have broken up, more by default than intention. For one thing, I simply didn't know how long it would take to refocus my attention on her. For another, I had no idea where I was going from here. Carlita's intuition had been wrong: Despite any pretense at reintegration, my heart was still in Nepal.

Which brought up the issue of Grace. Sexy, sensitive Grace. I hadn't spoken to her, not once, since I'd been home. I'd tried—but more than a week had passed since my last attempt. Neither Carlita nor Jordan was a credible alibi. The truth was more selfish: I wanted to keep my two lives separate. I'd come to enjoy the way Nepal hovered at the back of my mind like a delicious secret, an imaginary friend. To reconnect with that world from here would break the spell and make Nepal somehow . . . *ordinary*. Kathmandu was my Shangri-la, not a prize to be carried home.

But that myth had been shattered and laid to waste. Eight days ago—on the afternoon of April 6, Pacific Time—I'd been eating a bowl of vermicelli at Pho 84, a Vietnamese eatery downtown. A television was blaring CNN from the wall above the cash register. I glanced up, riveted: It was a segment from Nepal. The camera moved inside a hospital, where a few exhausted doctors tended to the wounded. The next instant, a staggering apparition appeared: Grace. It was her, absolutely. My heart bucked against my ribs. She was standing in a hospital hallway in her bra, holding a rag, her face splattered with what must have been blood. The moment was so unreal that I wondered for a split second if the entire month I'd just lived through—Jordan's death, Carlita, California—had been itself a dream, about to shatter into wakefulness. But it

was real. Grace's lips moved. Then the camera swept sideways, panning a corridor lined with bodies.

There was no more footage of Grace, but the point had been made.
As soon as I'd gotten home I'd picked up the phone and dialed the thirteen
numbers that would reconnect us. A breathless series of clicks, then static. I
tried again and again. On my fifth attempt, a familiar recording chided me
in singsong Nepali. *"This line is not in service. Please try your call again
later."*

And I had, for a few days. But in Nepal, when they say a line is not
in service, you can take them at their word. The utility pole might have
been knocked down by a Tempo. The phone itself might have caught fire.
Or a crow may have landed on the outdoor wires, shorting out the entire
neighborhood.

Now, as I sat on my cushion, the CNN image replayed in my brain:
Grace's eyes wide, her expression dazed and disbelieving, as if she had
looked into the camera's lens and seen me sitting there, bolt upright, staring back at her with a broccoli floret in my chopsticks. What had she felt at
that instant?

Six weeks away from Nepal is not a long time, by expat standards.
People come and go, gone for the monsoon or the winter holidays, returning
two or three months later to a community that barely remembers they've
been away. It didn't matter what Grace had felt in that moment. She hadn't
forgotten us, and neither had I.

The days since my brother's funeral had rattled by in a single instant,
like a tray of surgical tools spilling down a laundry chute. A catastrophe is
a gateway. It leads out of, and back into, the world. One is sucked into a
vacuum, but can reenter the atmosphere wherever one chooses.

A year and a half ago two friends of mine, a couple from L.A., drove to
Venice Beach for a picnic. At midday, the quality of the sunlight changed.
They looked up to see a giant cloud, tinged with gold, blackening the sky.
Within minutes, they knew the cause: Granada Hills was ablaze, roaring
beneath a wildfire that would deform steel, implode television screens, and
reduce their neighborhood to a scorched mesa of stumps and cement. They
returned to find that their house, and everything in it, had evaporated. Family

photographs, an impressive record collection, six new wineglasses, two vintage guitars, their hard drives and shoes and toothbrushes, had been released as energy and reduced to their component elements. All they owned at that moment were a car, two pairs of sunglasses, and the clothes on their backs.

The first month after the fire was a gauntlet of despair, disbelief, and logistics. But as the shock receded and the element of choice flowed back into their lives, my friends did something amazing. They climbed the crow's nest of calamity and from that unobstructed perch viewed their entire lives with detachment. Their careers, their friendships, even their marriage, were reassessed with an unblemished eye. The inspiration was to complete what the fire had started: to annihilate the unneeded, creating their lives anew.

My brother's death was a similar disaster: an opportunity to reinvent myself. So far, I had not done so. Like Jordan, whose personality had penetrated mine, I had shouldered the burden of denial.

I abandoned the cushion and rose on popping joints. A few feet away, above the fireplace, a copper Ganesh danced above a blackened oil lamp. Beneath it lay a fragile veil: a rattlesnake skin I'd found at Point Reyes, almost identical to the one that Grace and I had brought back from Pharping. I lifted it with two fingers and carried it to the window by my desk. Catching the light, the surface was opalescent; a moiré of colors that changed and rippled, defying resolution. It looked like a mythic map: a diaphanous diagram, etched onto naga skin, that might contain my destiny.

I stared at it intently, trying to recognize a familiar shape. Suddenly, the blinds rattled. A gust of wind flew into the room, snatching the gossamer skin from my hands. It corkscrewed upward, disintegrating into a million rainbow flakes. They snowed on my carpet and made their way up my nose. I sneezed powerfully, and my ears seemed to pop. In that moment, something was released—surrendered as powerfully as that burning corpse at Pashupati had given up its soul.

The future was clear. I had to return to Nepal. My initial hope, of getting back in time for the revolution, was obsolete. But the pull was no less intense, and my motives no less urgent. Grace was a big part of my decision, but she was not the only part—for this would be a spiritual journey, as well.

I needed to see Chokyi Nyima, and speak with him about my brother. The Rinpoche, I imagined, would provide the last piece in a puzzle that had begun in Jordan's Philadelphia apartment. Suicide is a grave sin, even in the Tibetan Buddhist tradition. But Jordan's life had been a rich canvas, filled with good works, insight, and a genuine love of the planet. I needed to hear, from Chokyi Nyima himself, that this case was an exception: that Jordan's tragic exit would not blacken his karma and condemn him to endless rebirths in the lower realms.

These were my aspirations. Unfortunately, my financial situation stood in the way. The trip home had been expensive, and I was broke. It would take at least two months of lucky freelancing to raise enough money to return to Nepal.

I sliced a banana into a bowl of Grape-Nuts and ate breakfast while staring at my calendar. A busy weekend lay ahead, but none of it amounted to much. Since my birthday I'd been coasting, bedeviled by the notion that any sort of enthusiasm, or inspiration, was somehow blasphemous. Like Jordan, I'd become estranged from my true nature. If *going* to Nepal was out—for the time being—it didn't mean my life was over. I could still cultivate the things I'd seen, the lessons I'd learned there. But how?

Thinking this way is like rubbing a lamp. As I recalled the events of the past months, trying to see them in a larger context, the seeds of a book began to germinate at the edge of my cerebral cortex, a book that would explore the worlds I'd visited since February. They were linked, somehow; the idea hovered just beyond my consciousness, like a naga glimpsed in a murky pond.

And then it surfaced, with the thrill of a childhood dare.

I poured my cold coffee down the drain, boiled fresh water, and loaded a filter with fresh grounds. While the first cup was brewing I put five John Coltrane CDs on the carousel, and opened a spiral notebook.

BY EARLY EVENING I'd filled forty pages. The more I wrote, the more I wanted to be in Kathmandu—with its crooked wooden buildings, clouds of incense, and sacred cows shitting nonchalantly in the streets; for Coal's irreverent humor, and the foggy, cold mornings in bed with Grace. I longed for the Saturday teachings, and the view of the Great Stupa through the Boudhnath gate. That was my home. That was where I belonged. I knew it. And the size of that knowing was big, with muscled arms and cobra tattoos, and it pounded on the door of the universe while my own narrow hand sketched out a rough outline and recalled snippets of dialogue.

There's nothing like a beginning. It fills the bloodstream with energy, sucking away ghosts like a cosmic Dustbuster. But the body has its own demands. I threw together a turkey sandwich, opened a Sierra Nevada, and leaned against the sink, eating off a paper plate. The phone rang, an unwelcome interruption.

"Hello?" My mouth was full.

"Hi, I'm trying to reach Jeff Greenwald."

I swallowed with effort. "Speaking."

"Great. Hey, listen, my name is Joe Robinson, I'm an editor based down in San Diego."

"What's up?"

"Well, it's kind of exciting. I'm planning to launch a new magazine this fall. The theme is adventure travel, and we're putting together our premier issue. I like your work, and want to know if you're available for an assignment. The downside is we can't pay very much, aside from travel and expenses."

"Mmmm." The promise of even modest income was beguiling—but between planning, travel, writing, and editing, these jobs consumed several weeks at least. "When would you need me to go?"

"As soon as possible. Our issue has to be wrapped by mid-May. And the story's time-sensitive."

"I see." I pondered in silence. The inspiration for the day's work felt like a gift. I'd turned away from a few such gifts in the past; they tended to sneak out the back door.

"Hello?"

"I'm still here," I said. "Listen, Joe, I appreciate your call. But I'm sort of involved with another project right now. Where, exactly, do you want me to go?"

"Here's the deal," Robinson said. "As you might already know, there was just a huge revolution in Nepal . . ."

30

Life During Wartime

THE COOL, BRIGHT days were over. By late April, Kathmandu had lost the charms of spring. Dust and exhaust from a thousand trucks and buses rose into the atmosphere and paused, suspended between pressure and gravity. The sky wore a metallic sheen. In February, on a good day, one could see the brilliant snowcap of Langtang, forty miles to the north. Now you were lucky to make out the finial of Swayambhunath on the valley's western edge.

Women shopped for goat and chicken with bandanas pressed against their faces. Commuters biked to work wearing particle masks. The whole city had become a giant, clogged nostril. It would remain so until July, and the first of the monsoon rains.

These seasonal doldrums did nothing to dampen Nepal's air of liberation. The changes were subtle, but they were hard to miss. There was optimism afoot, a sense of giddy possibility. A weight had been lifted from the nation's shoulders. In the grassy field near Snake Lake, kids played soccer with louder shouts; young couples window-shopped on Durbar Marg, holding hands. The vegetable market in Asan Tole brimmed like a cornucopia, with baskets of tomatoes, peppers, and cauliflowers spilling onto the pavement, surrounded by women in vivid purple shawls. The Nepalis walked taller. They'd made world headlines and won the prize of self-determination.

But the situation was far from perfect. A curfew was still in effect. Random acts of violence by royalist thugs claimed several lives each week. Democracy had not made anything easier; on the contrary, it had provoked profound confusion. People had no idea what to expect. Many had believed that the word *democracy* itself, like an incantation, would be enough to transform their lives. When they returned to work, they were astonished to discover that nothing had changed. In fact, things were worse. Prices were rising, and His Majesty's government, lax at the best of times, had no incentive to ease the situation. The interim prime minister, an ethereal activist named K. P. Bhattarai, seemed as shell-shocked as the next guy.

The afternoon of my return to Kathmandu, as I rode home from the market, my taxi was temporarily blocked by a procession. Hundreds of people marched down Ramshah Path, carrying red banners and chanting in Nepali.

"What are they saying?"

"'*Fulfill our demands*,'" the driver informed me.

"And what are their demands?"

"No one knows." He shrugged. "Even they do not know."

Even so, it was wonderful, amazing, to see the well-ordered procession, composed not only of men but also women and children, making its way down the road without fear of reprisal.

My first afternoon in Kathmandu was a riot of logistics: organizing my flat, finding a new didi (Laxmi had moved into the service of a German diplomat), reclaiming my motorcycle. By early evening I succumbed to jet lag and dropped into a poppy-sleep of utter exhaustion.

The next morning, my first full day back in Nepal, I phoned Coal. Neither he nor Clarice was remotely aware of what I'd been through the past two months. Few of my friends in Nepal, I realized uncomfortably, even knew I'd had a brother.

"How's Grace?" I asked. "Have you seen her?"

"Have you not called her yet?"

m anxious about talking to her, for some reason."

"Oh, I think you have a very good reason. She told us she hasn't had a word from you."

"Coal . . . believe me . . . I tried. Right now I just need to let my brain catch up with my body. I'll call her tomorrow and invite her for dinner." I added, too quickly, "You, I can see tonight."

"Why, that's a lovely invitation. Very hard to resist."

"I'm sorry. I really do want to see you. And Clarice. If you can do it. It'll help me get grounded."

"As you like." He suggested we meet at the Ghar-e-kabab, a posh Indian restaurant managed by the Annapurna Hotel.

ROUNDING THE CORNER onto Durbar Marg I was struck by how ordinary, how business-as-usual, everything appeared. Cars were double-parked along the curb. Nirula's Ice Cream was open, filled with tourists and well-to-do Nepalis. My eyes canted downward, looking for bloodstains, but the faded red blotches on the sidewalk were probably pan juice.

Arriving a little after seven, I shivered with a full-body thrill. A uniformed doorman let me in, and I took the narrow steps two at a time. Strains of an evening raga filtered down to meet me. The restaurant, with its plush seats and low-wattage chandeliers, was dim and crowded, but Coal called out my name. He and Clarice sat in a semicircular booth, below a Mughal-style painting of a princess feeding a deer. Grace sat with them. She greeted me first.

"Hi, asshole. Thanks for calling."

"Welcome home," Coal smiled. "Isn't it lovely to be back?"

Clarice stood up. "It seems you were never gone." She kissed me chastely on the forehead.

I slid in next to Grace and moved to kiss her on the cheek, but she turned peevishly away. I felt a pang of resentment toward Coal for bringing her here and forcing our encounter before I was ready. But here we were: another reminder that life in Kathmandu was a continual process of improvisation.

Coal poured me a glass of beer and asked how things had gone back home. I drew in my breath, considering how to answer. There was no need to be cagey, or apologetic.

"Not as one might wish." Slowly and precisely, I narrated how the past two months had unfolded on my side of the world: from the phone call that had interrupted my birthday party to the funeral in New York; from my search for meaning in Jordan's journals to the unexpected assignment from the adventure travel magazine. It took a while. I spiced the narrative up with funny anecdotes, so they'd know I wasn't an emotional cripple.

Mostly, they were quiet. Grace felt along the bench seat and found my hand. Coal discreetly ordered dinner. When I finished my story, it was clear there was a gulf between us—as if our scattering in early March had been a shipwreck, and the currents of the spring had washed us up on different islands.

Grace's hand kneaded mine nervously. "I'm sorry about my comment," she said. "When you first came in. But I do wish you had written to me."

"Me too. I'm sorry," I said, meeting her eyes. "I missed you. I just didn't know where the whole thing was taking me. I didn't know how to fit this life in with that one."

Our appetizers arrived: vegetable samosas, shaped like miniature throw pillows. The mood picked up. Grace talked about the wild anticipation, and ceaseless activity, during the days leading up to revolution. It seemed that, for both of us, the spring had been a pivotal chapter.

"I saw you on TV," I told Grace. "On CNN. You looked like a wild woman."

"You did?" She seemed stunned by the news. "During the marches?"

"No, it was in Bir Hospital, afterwards. You were helping the doctors."

"Oh my God. What was I wearing? Did they show my brassiere?"

I remembered vividly, but managed a merciful lie. "I think it was a head shot. Why?"

"No reason." She traced the rim of her beer glass. "Well, welcome back to Nepal. *Jai* democracy!" Coal and Clarice joined the toast. We clinked glasses, careful to make eye contact.

Three waiters delivered our feast: tandoori chicken; eggplant curry; round, savory onions; sweet mango chutney; hot buttered naan. All for the price of a Big Mac and fries. The blind sarod player looked like a South Asian Ray Charles, his dark sunglasses reflecting the small, hot spotlights as he sweated and nodded on his dais.

"What was this about your brassiere?" Clarice asked.

Grace shook her head. "It's not as interesting as you think."

"On the contrary," said Coal. "Anything about the female breast is of immense interest: to men in general, and myself in particular."

"Can you believe," Clarice interjected, "That it's nearly May? Come June, we'll have been in Nepal five years."

I tried to remember where I was five years ago, but my mind drew a blank. Coal, however, lit up.

"Imagine that," he said. "And to think that, five years ago, I was an aspiring mystery writer. It's astonishing, isn't it, how the finger of fate has its way with us. Who could have predicted that, by 1990, I'd be the Ralph Lauren of Nepal's fashion industry?"

Grace snorted. "Come on, Coal. Give yourself a little credit."

"But it's so very true. I wrapped up a sale today; a big one, too. The great continent of Australia. Land of boomerangs and Vegemite. An amazing coup, I bashfully admit. But I'm sure you'd be bored by the details." He allowed a beat for protest, then turned to me. "So you're back at Snake Lake?"

I shrugged. "It's fine. It's not as idyllic as your place, of course. But the Shresthas moved to Fiji. So I don't have a rabid dog on my roof anymore."

Clarice turned to face her husband. "Have you heard? There's talk of load shedding. No electricity from 5 until 11 p.m., beginning the first of June."

"Jesus! No. You're kidding. Fuck. Well, I'd better pick up one of those 100-watt generators when we're in Hong Kong. I've got to keep the sewing machines running until half-nine. And the lights! *Fuck!* The lights! That's 250 watts at least . . ."

"You're going to Hong Kong?"

"In a few weeks." Clarice paused, tore a handkerchief from her purse, and sneezed violently, three times. "Ucch. Excuse me. We're actually going to Beijing, by way of Hong Kong. Coal's idea of a vacation."

"Come on, it was your idea as well."

"It was not."

"Anyway, what could be more restful? Bicycling along the avenues . . ."

"With millions of Chinese."

". . . and touring the great silk factories, namesake and inspiration for the legendary Silk Road."

"Exactly. It's a business trip; don't pretend otherwise."

"Coffee?" The waiter gathered our plates, as obtrusively as possible.

"Yes, please. With milk."

"No, thanks," Coal said. "Not for me. Anyway, boys and girls, we have to go if we're to make it home by nine. Ah, curfew. Another of the many pleasures, the innumerable pleasures, of life in Kathmandu."

"I'm going to the loo," Clarice said. "Don't leave without me."

Grace picked up her bag. "I'm going, too."

We watched them cross in front of the sarod player and disappear behind the bar. The waiter brought my coffee. It was strong and sweet.

Coal coughed. "May I ask you a personal question?"

"Of course. You can ask me anything."

"It's been less than two months since your brother's suicide. I gather you were quite close. Your story about what happened was fascinating, of course, but it seemed a bit—and I hope you don't take this the wrong way—perhaps a bit *removed*. Aloof. Have you really come to terms with his death?"

I found this touching; Coal had waited for the girls to leave before stepping out of character.

"No. I haven't. That's one of the reasons I came back here so quickly. I need spiritual counsel. But I haven't seen Chokyi Nyima yet."

"It's a bit of a crapshoot, seeing these lamas."

"That's true. The problem is, I don't really know what I *want* from him. I don't know what I expect. Coddling and reassurance aren't exactly Buddhist specialties, as you know."

"Is that what you're looking for?"

"Maybe. I just want to know that Jordan will be all right, somehow. That he'll find his way."

My answer was evasive. There was a deeper, more personal reason for my reluctance to visit the lama. It had to do with the Buddhist belief in reincarnation. In an irrational but irresistible way, I truly believed I'd meet my brother again—that I'd find the new being he had become. But what if suicide really did overturn the apple cart? My brother's selfish, destructive act might have cast the germ of his consciousness so far down the ladder of rebirth that I would never see him again, during this lifetime, in any recognizable form. If his mental state at the instant of death was angry, or selfish, he might not be reborn on this Earth at all. He could end up in the realm of hungry ghosts: pathetic, emaciated creatures who can never satisfy their gnawing appetites. The fact that I didn't believe in ghosts, hungry or otherwise, was immaterial. Hearing such news from the Rinpoche might be too much for me to bear.

Grace and Clarice returned, and began collecting their things. "You know," Grace said, "you should come over soon and see my pictures from Nag Baral. They're the best photos I shot since Shivaratri."

"What about the revolution itself?"

She shrugged. "We can talk about that later."

My shoe was off. I put my foot on Grace's ankle and curled my toes. "If it's not too late, I can come over now."

"Sure," she said. "Why not?"

THE EVENING WAS crisp, and foggy enough to seem mysterious. Coal and Clarice rode away on their Baja motor scooter, helmets winking as they passed beneath the amber streetlights near the Royal Palace. The fall of the king had given the palace a clumsy, uninhabited look, like a back-lot prop from an old Basil Rathbone film. Grace and I unlocked our Hondas. A pack of dogs slept in a tight circle near a sewer along the curb.

Durbar Marg seemed alien and forlorn. There were no rickshaws. A few taxis waited, their engines muttering, outside the main gate of the Annapurna Hotel. The ragtag street urchins who usually haunted the sidewalk outside the fancy restaurant were nowhere to be seen. It had never occurred to me that even beggars had to obey the curfew. Where had they gone?

"Look over there." Grace raised her chin, pointing toward the southern end of the boulevard, where the statue of King Mahendra stood vigil behind a trampled fence. Tumbleweeds of barbed wire were piled in the middle of the street, forming a semicircular nest. As we watched, armored personnel vehicles drove up from a side road and parked by the statue. Soldiers jumped into the street and set up a machine-gun post. They worked in silence.

"Do they do this every night?"

"Every night, since the lynching on Kalimati. You missed all the fun."

I'd read about the incident in the *Los Angeles Times*. Two weeks after the revolution, bands of hooligans—*mandaleys* in local slang—had roamed through the city. They'd smashed windows, burned shops, and created general havoc, giving the impression that the interim government couldn't maintain order. When the Nepalis learned that these thugs were mercenaries, on the Palace payroll, they mobbed the mandaley hideout. Six of the thugs were dragged out onto the street. The crowd beat them to death, tied their corpses to a pushcart, and wheeled the bloody mess toward Singha Durbar.

We revved our bikes and took off. Grace led the way. It was 8:45, and the streets were all but deserted. Clumps of army troops monitored the intersections, the tips of their cigarettes neon in the dark. Russian-made machine guns squatted on the platforms of their ATVs. As we approached Nag Pokhari a couple of soldiers, no older than twenty, watched us ride by. "Good night!" they yelled in English. "I love you!"

Every dog in the neighborhood began to bark as Grace opened her gate. We locked our motorcycles in the front yard. Grace filled an aluminum dekshi with water the minute we entered her flat, before she even took off her scarf.

"Chamomile or peppermint?"

"Half of each."

I looked around the apartment, remembering the mandalas and cane furniture, the subliminal smell of Grace's lair. It was such a comfort, being back in Kathmandu.

"Any requests?" She stood at the bookshelf and looked through her tapes. I came up behind her, slid my hands under her scarf, and kissed her neck through the cloudy pashmina. One dog, a hoarse metronome, continued to bark in the distance.

Grace turned around. "Did you bring any condoms?"

"You're so romantic. To tell you the truth, I didn't expect to end up here. Is that a deal breaker?"

"It means we can't fuck." She slid her hands to the small of my back and looked up at me with real excitement. "You can look at my slides, though."

31

Grace Under Fire

GRACE MELTED BUTTER and cracked two eggs into a nonstick pan from which the Teflon surface had long ago been scoured. She even had a toaster, big enough for bagels (should any materialize), bequeathed to her by a departing U.S. intelligence officer. During the night the wind had changed, clearing out the pall of dust. We could see the tip of Langtang from her kitchen.

Before bed we had in fact spent a solid hour standing at the light table, looking through her portfolio of images. They led right up to, and ended one day before, the revolution. After the last slide—taken through a burning tire at a mass demonstration in Patan, on April 5—Grace turned off the switch. "That's it," she shrugged.

"Come on." This seemed a strange kind of teasing.

"I'm not kidding."

"I know you were there. I saw you on CNN, remember?"

"I was there, alright," she said. "Can we talk about it in the morning? It's kind of a long story."

Now it was morning, with the smell of hot butter and toast, and a bar of sunlight on the wall behind me. Grace took a kettle off the second burner and filtered coffee into a thermos. "There's only powdered milk . . ."

"That's fine. Listen, I want to hear what happened on April 6. How'd you end up in the hospital?"

"I was pretty much everywhere," Grace said. "But the Curse caught up with me."

"Not that nonsense again."

"Yep." She filled my mug and positioned the thermos between us. "With a vengeance."

THE AFTERNOON OF April 6 had felt different from the start, the morning unusually warm and hazy. The mountains were barely visible, brushed like tentative clouds against the northern horizon.

All of the shops and galleries along Durbar Marg were closed, their windows hidden behind the corrugated metal shutters that had been rolled down the previous evening in anticipation of the next day's bandh. There were no bicycles in sight; not a single taxi patrolled the streets. Every now and then a bewildered dog would cross Durbar Marg, loping cautiously across the normally crowded boulevard to join his companions in the parking lot of the Annapurna Hotel. Employees and tourists, meanwhile, had gathered in the five-star hotel's posh lobby. They watched apprehensively through the double glass doors as Durbar Marg filled with soldiers.

The situation was ambiguous. That morning, a few thousand demonstrators from Kathmandu's northern suburbs had seethed down Lazimpat and paraded, chanting prodemocracy slogans, past the western entrance to the Royal Palace. They'd milled past the high iron gates without incident, then continued peacefully down the broad boulevard toward Ratna Park.

But those marchers soon joined forces with larger and livelier demonstrations that originated in Asan Tole, Bagh Bazaar, Bhaktapur, and Patan. By afternoon over a quarter of a million Nepali citizens had massed on the Tundhikhel Parade Grounds, waving flags, punching the air, and roaring their approval as Ganesh Man Singh hailed them from a hastily erected podium.

Grace had jogged up Tridevi Marg toward the palace, alone and on foot. A point-and-shoot Minolta, two Canon bodies, and a lens case bounced against her rib cage. Her canvas vest was loaded with film.

It had taken her twenty minutes to get from her Hadigaon flat to the head of Durbar Marg. As she arrived on the scene, she mouthed a brief prayer of thanks. Her personal nightmare had not come to pass. They had not started the revolution without her.

HALF AN HOUR earlier, making the trek downtown had been the furthest thing from her mind. She'd been drinking Darjeeling tea and editing her Patan slides when the phone rang. Grace ignored it for eight rings, then peevishly snatched up the receiver.

"Hello?"

"If you got yourself an answering machine, like every other professional in this town, you'd be doing all of us a big favor."

Christ. Larry Prince would only be calling for one of two reasons: to request an inconvenient favor, or embarrass her with another one of his endless, and endlessly futile, romantic propositions.

"Grace, dear? Are you still there?"

"I'm really busy. What do you want?"

"Well fuck you too, sweetheart."

"Sorry." She hadn't meant to sound so harsh. "It's been a rough day. I ran out of toilet paper, and all the stores are closed."

"You're out of *Rising Nepals*?"

"Ha, ha, ha. Listen, I really am busy. What's up?"

Suddenly there was a lot of noise on the line. "Well you're going to be even busier!" Prince shouted. "There's a huge fucking demonstration at Tundhikhel, I mean *huge*, and they're trucking shitloads of soldiers over to the palace. This may be it. People are yelling for blood. Listen . . ." He held the phone away from himself for a second, angling it toward the crowd. Grace heard an oceanic roar. "So get your gorgeous ass out here. I gotta go."

"Where are you?"

"At the little clinic above Shiva Photo. Great angle on Tundhikhel. I think the crowd's about to head toward the palace. Can you make it?"

"Are you kidding?" She felt like a rookie being called off the bench.

"Great. Listen. Don't take your bike. You'll be safer on foot. Make sure your hair's showing, so they know you're a foreigner. And bring a wet handkerchief, in case there's tear gas. *Kay? Haus, haus. Ek mahina!*" He shouted to someone in the background. "Grace, I gotta go."

"I'll call you tonight," she said. "And thanks." But he had already hung up.

She'd pulled on her All Stars, locked her flat, and run through Naxal, hanging a right at the Durga Temple and continuing past Nag Pokhari. The Jai Nepal cinema, hawking a garish Bollywood epic, lay to her left. On her right was the vast compound of the Royal Palace, concealed behind a high brick wall. As she approached the corner of Durbar Marg the long wall opened, and the palace appeared beyond a high metal gate.

The manicured lawns in front of the pretentious mansion swarmed with Gurkhas, police, and Royal Nepal Army soldiers with AK-47s slung over their shoulders. There were tanks—*tanks!*—in the palace parking lot.

Durbar Marg was Kathmandu's poshest thoroughfare. Looking down the street, widened and paved for Birendra's coronation in 1973, she saw a similar scene at the base of the avenue. Hundreds of police troops waited in full riot gear. All of them held clubs. Many carried rifles, or tear gas grenade launchers, as well. It was incredible. Just yesterday she'd had lunch right down the block, at the Annapurna Coffee Shop. Today the place was a war zone.

She brought the Minolta to her eye and took half a dozen shots of the khaki-clad battalions as they maneuvered in front of the palace gates. Then she grew bolder and moved to approach the soldiers. Most of them were just kids and—as she'd expected—eager to please. They posed for the pretty *bideshi* journalist with their rifles braced across their chests, booted feet perched rakishly on the treads of their ATVs.

But there wasn't much happening here. She should probably try to find Larry Prince. Reaching the Tundhikhel Parade Grounds would mean another long walk. Kathmandu wasn't all that big, but it was amazing how long it could take to get from point A to point B without a bicycle.

It was a straight shot, at least. Down Durbar Marg and around the bronze statue of King Mahendra, past the Clock Tower, and boom. Hopefully, she'd get close enough to the band shell for some photos.

Grace waved to the soldiers and walked away from the palace, trying not to think about the arsenal of weapons trained on her back. The troops along Durbar Marg watched her with suspicion, but no one questioned her progress. She felt like a mouse, tiptoeing past a dozing cat. Suddenly a terrific roar erupted to her right. Her heart leaped into her throat before she recognized the sound: a heavy corrugated shutter, rolling down over the storefront of the Tiger Tops office. The metal shield hit the sidewalk with a reverberating crash.

She reached the Mahendra statue and crossed Jamal. A Thai Airways jet roared overhead, providing a surreal note of perspective. Regardless of what was happening in Kathmandu, the world was attending to business as usual. Grace walked on. To her left was Tri-Chandra College; above it, the Clock Tower chimed. *Tin bajay*: three bells. The lonely tolling made the fine hairs on the nape of her neck stand on end.

At the next intersection, a smoldering bus lay on its back like a squashed cockroach. Its windshield was smashed, the folding doors torn from their hinges. This was often one of the busiest corners in the city; now it was nearly deserted. A single cold store was open. Two soldiers in armored vests stood in the doorway, drinking Fantas.

She stopped then, intuitively aware of a change in the atmosphere.

At first it had sounded like white noise: the rush of wind through a bamboo forest, or the fading drone of an airliner. But this was something else. These were voices. Not just one or two, but a hundred, a thousand voices. Grace stopped, stood, and listened to the noise swell, as relentless as an approaching tsunami.

The rally at Tundhikhel must have ended. Now the demonstrators were on the move, saturating the broad avenues that led to the palace. Grace saw the front ranks: a vast thunderhead of humanity, pressing relentlessly toward the fragile zone of calm she presently occupied.

Like an image coming into focus, the sound sharpened. What had been an abstract roar resolved into rhythmic chanting. It got louder and louder until the wild electricity of the moment shot adrenaline into her veins and made Grace want to scream with excitement. A million people were marching toward her: students and shopkeepers and smartly dressed office workers with their fists in the air; women carrying signs and babies; street urchins, taxi drivers, teachers and lawyers and doctors. They were all chanting together, at the top of their lungs.

"DEMO-CRACY! *JAI NEPAL!* DEMO-CRACY! *JAI NEPAL!*"

Grace paused in the middle of the empty street, dropped to one knee, and twisted a telephoto lens onto one of the Canon bodies. She engaged the motor drive; the film advanced with a healthy purr. Her other camera, a Canon loaded with color, was good to go. She tilted both cameras toward her lips, swallowed, and puffed the dust off their lenses.

Grace shot off half a roll before the prow of the crowd reached the Clock Tower. Jumping up on her toes, she saw no end to the demonstration. People continued to surge out of Tundhikhel park, filling Durbar Marg and streaming down Kantipath and Jamal like fresh lava.

She'd been backing up steadily as she took her pictures, and now she wheeled around to look behind her. The Royal Palace loomed in the background, cartoonlike, a comic book fortress rising above a sea of soldiers. The army was advancing now, moving toward the demonstrators in impenetrable rows. Grace was right in the middle.

Well howdy, she thought. Bricks and tear gas canisters could start flying past her head any second. She assayed the situation. The approaching mob was spreading out; some demonstrators were finding higher ground, clambering onto the roofs of nearby buildings. Kathmandu's single mosque, a squat and unremarkable building with a small dome on top, was just a few meters away. She snapped on her lens caps and ran for it.

Two weeks ago, *Smithsonian* had asked Grace to take some pictures inside the mosque for a photo-essay on coming-of-age rituals. It was a no-go; the Islamic leaders had refused to let her inside. Now she was being pulled onto the roof of the forbidden temple by a pair of teenage boys in black pants and knock-off Ray-Bans. But her sense of victory was soon replaced by panic: The mosque was even more dangerous than the street. Every spare foot of standing room was filled, right up to the roof's unguarded edge. The crowd seethed, and she nearly lost her balance. In a matter of seconds people would start falling off, dropping onto the crowds below.

This was getting her nowhere. Grace writhed through the craning, sour-smelling crowd until she reached the rear of the mosque. From there she managed, with much knee-scraping and bumping of her camera gear, to shimmy down a ceramic water pipe and drop into a fetid alley behind the building.

A dozen middle-aged men wearing short-sleeved sports shirts stood near a dilapidated brick wall, smoking cigarettes. They'd watched her descend in silence and were visibly disturbed by her invasion of their illusory vacuum. Grace barely glanced at them; she guessed that they were travel agents or airline reps who'd been forced to close their shops along Durbar Marg and now hoped to wait out this latest disturbance in the safety of this litter-strewn purgatory.

"Good God . . . Grace, is that you?"

"Hunh?" She scanned the group. A tall Nepali man with a narrow, worried face and gray eyes stepped out to meet her. Her mouth dropped open. "Kunca?" She'd have been less shocked to see him in Missouri. "What are you doing here?"

Mainali shrugged, offering a sheepish smile. "Well, you know, Grace, I'm a journalist as well."

"Oh my God. I am so sorry." Somehow, it had never occurred to her that Nepali journalists would cover their own revolution.

"How did you end up here?"

"Actually I was interviewing the president of Yeti Travels about the pilots' strike. We heard the crowd coming. I tried to get back to my office, but the police chased me back. So I ran in here." He fished into his shirt pocket for a Marlboro and offered it to Grace. She shook her head. "Sorry, I forgot. All you healthy Americans. Rhoda won't let me do this at home. Not even in the garden." He lit the cigarette and inhaled with relish. "So. What's the report from above?"

"Pretty scary. It's a major mess out there. There's a ton of people, and about three hundred troops. Lots of guns. Things look peaceful, but it's heading for a showdown. I wouldn't be surprised if it gets ugly."

"Do you think we're safe here?"

"I have no idea. Maybe . . . but I doubt it. Listen . . ." She pointed ahead. "This road at the end of the alley—it leads back to the Mahendra statue, right?"

"Yes. But the whole street is blocked. You can't get out that way."

"I have to try."

They walked to the end of the alley. She could see the statue, a silent sentinel in the middle of the Marg. A single soldier stood on the sidewalk, guarding the entrance to the intersection. His fellows had moved ahead.

"I've got to get out there," said Grace. "Will you help me?"

"How?"

"I'll duck into that doorway. You walk out a little way and call the soldier. Be *very* polite. Ask him anything. Ask him when you can go home to your pregnant wife. While you're distracting him I'll run out there."

Kunda balked. "What if he shoots us both?"

"He won't shoot us. He's as scared as we are."

There was a short silence. "Rhoda would kill both of us if she knew about this."

"Maybe." Grace suspected that what she was asking was inexcusable. She also knew where this afternoon could take her, if she was brave and lucky. Kunda, it seemed, was reading her mind.

"When you collect your Pulitzer," he said dryly, "kindly remember to thank me." He stepped out of the alley and began walking toward the sentry, hands visible and by his sides, calling out in the friendliest tone he could manage.

"*Oh bhai! Hajur, bhai!*"

Clever, Grace had thought. It's tough to shoot someone who's calling you his "little brother." The soldier turned, allowing Kunda to approach. He greeted the teenager with a respectful namasté, positioned himself so that the soldier's back was turned toward Grace, and launched into a series of animated queries. Grace could see the soldier nodding his head. She hurried past, moving on the balls of her feet.

SHE REACHED THE intersection and walked quickly toward the statue. Now she could see the line of police and army troops, massed in the street alongside Tri-Chandra College. They were positioned with their backs toward her, shoulder to shoulder, blocking the throat of Durbar Marg—which led directly to the palace.

Facing the troops, filling the avenue with the chaotic energy of spilled mercury, was the crowd. The size of the demonstration was beyond comprehension; it was the largest group of human beings Grace had ever seen.

Violence was surely imminent. Death might even be waiting. But Grace felt only a dizzy and almost suffocating pleasure. She was totally alone, in what felt like a kind of bubble: fearless, exhilarated, ready. The rhythmic chanting crackled in her ears like the hypnotic beat of a rave. Her collarbone and pelvis vibrated with almost erotic tension.

This, she knew, was *It*: the singular, epochal instant that photojournalists dream of experiencing. She checked her cameras, lifted the color-loaded A-1, and drank in the air. Nothing, no matter how long she lived or how many things she saw, would compare with this moment. This was history. She was standing in the middle of it. It belonged to her.

A lenticular cloud hung in the sky beside the sun, opalescent. Three birds flew from a tree and swooped above the police line, then veered back to rest under the cement eve of the Norling Restaurant. A blue plastic bag skipped across the empty street and grazed Grace's sneakers. The time was exactly ten minutes until four.

There was no word or warning. One moment the police and demonstrators were facing each other in a tense but peaceful stalemate; the next, all hell broke loose. The soldiers raised their lathi sticks and charged into the crowd, clubbing everyone within reach. The jubilant chants fractured into shrieks of panic and screams of pain. Dull pops could be heard above the melee as canisters of tear gas were fired into the air, exploding on the ground into white clouds of sickening vapor.

Grace jumped onto a curb, held a camera high above her head, and shot haphazardly. So far, she'd been safely behind the action. But now a second phalanx of soldiers, which had been waiting at the head of Durbar Marg by the palace, was advancing down the avenue. In a minute, she'd be the meat in a rather unsavory sandwich. She darted across the street, wheeled around the Mahendra statue, and was about to take cover in a doorway when a canister of tear gas fell and exploded not ten feet away.

She had just enough time to recall Larry's warning about the wet handkerchief when a drift of gas hit her. Grace cursed out loud and began to retch, hands cupped against her face. She ran blindly, weaving toward the middle of the street, as the advancing soldiers swarmed toward her like black locusts.

Grace veered sharply right, thinking it would take her back toward the statue, but she was too late. Something struck her violently across the back, knocking the wind out of her. A square-faced, grimacing soldier had grabbed her camera and was trying to yank it from her neck. "Press!" she screamed. He raised his arm to club her again, but she crouched down and drove her shoulder into his chest, knocking him off balance. As he tried to recover she twisted and shot upright, kneeing him in the crotch. He howled and fell away.

She could see again, but there was nothing to focus on. Pandemonium reigned. The crowd had retreated, but pockets of protestors had broken through the police line and were heaving rocks through the few unprotected windows along Durbar Marg. Soldiers were grabbing whomever they could get a hold of—women, children, anyone who had stumbled—and beating them senseless.

Grace's camera strap had snapped. She had to fix it. The Woodlands Hotel was only a few meters away; it might be open. She ran through a small archway into the hotel's courtyard and ducked behind a carved wooden pillar next to the glass doorway. The vinyl strap had broken close to the camera body. It should be simple just to tie it off in a knot . . .

She barely had time to complete this thought before the nearby door was jerked open. A viselike hand gripped her elbow, pulling her sharply into the Woodlands' blacked-out lobby.

"Go! Hide! Now!" A middle-aged man with bloodshot eyes and clenched teeth shoved her toward the reception counter, waving the back of his hand at her. "Go! Go! Down, down, down!"

Grace knew better than to question the order. She dropped onto all fours and scampered into the protected nook between the reception counter and wall. A few seconds later there was a huge commotion: A group of soldiers burst in, demanding to know where the foreigner had gone. "*Dekhina! Aundaina! Ma lai tha chhaina!*" The manager was pleading ignorance, covering for her. The soldiers barked again. Grace heard smashing sounds, punctuated by pleas and denials from her unexpected ally.

When the soldiers had left, the manager fetched her. Grace stood up and surveyed the lobby; all the potted plants had been demolished.

She spent a few seconds wondering what would have happened if they'd caught her, but decided this wasn't a productive line of thought. At this point, she had two choices: She could hide in the hotel lobby until the demonstration was over or take her chances on the street. It was no choice at all She thanked the manager, promising to return and pay the damages. He wagged his head, certain he'd never see her again. Then she dashed from the Woodlands and through the courtyard, emerging into the mad swell of a full-blown riot.

Grace quickly made sense of what she'd missed. After its initial retreat the mob had surged forward again, driving the troops back toward the palace. The sidewalk outside the hotel was littered with chunks of cement and broken glass. Shoes, eyeglasses, topis, and rubber thongs lay across the street like jetsam, abandoned by demonstrators who had run for cover during the initial charge. Grace stepped in a dark puddle, and shuddered with revulsion as she tracked blood down the street.

Almost all of the women had retreated. This part of Durbar Marg was now controlled by hundreds of men and students, broken into small, adrenalized packs. Bricks and bottles sailed through the air, not quite reaching the retreating soldiers. A few tear gas canisters landed nearby, but the wind favored the demonstrators. The mob was gaining confidence again, congealing and advancing.

A few teenagers had uprooted some street signs, and were using the posts to smash anything within reach. Grace ran beside them as they converged on the traffic circle showcasing King Mahendra's statue. The boys jumped the wrought iron fence and began tearing the monument apart. It was a well-received enterprise. Within moments they were joined by scores of other demonstrators, who bashed the statue's pedestal and uprooted the sickly plants surrounding it.

As she snapped photos, Grace saw a familiar face. Jason Craig, the *Newsweek* stringer, was right beside her. She grinned. "Nice party, hunh?"

"It's sure to piss off their parents," he replied. They laughed together, enjoying the surreal absurdity of their vocation. Jason ducked away, angling for a silhouette shot, and his spot was immediately filled by a burly, red-haired man. A press badge linking him to a Norwegian news organization was pinned to his shirt. They exchanged a quick greeting, the brisk nod of professionals facing the consummate test of their skills.

Up the road, the soldiers were regrouping. Grace turned her attention back to the statue. A handsome teenager wearing a pink shirt and a broad black sash climbed onto the pedestal, holding two flags—representing the Congress and Communist parties—between his teeth. He stepped on King Mahendra's foot and boosted himself up high enough to grab for the Royal Scepter. It pulled out with ease, and he jammed the rebellious flags into the hole in Mahendra's bronze right hand. He faced the cheering crowd, holding the scepter aloft.

Grace had time to take a single photograph before the boy's head exploded, showering bits of brain and skull onto everyone nearby.

There was an immeasurable moment of transcendental silence. Then it shattered like a cathedral window, and the universe was a mosaic of gunfire, screaming, and utter, empty terror.

Grace ran without stopping, clawing pieces of flesh and bone off her face and hair and shirt. Her cameras smacked against her chest. She could see nothing but the endless tunnel of the street in front of her: Jamal. The dull crack of gunfire seemed to be coming from all directions.

Bodies lay bleeding in the streets, some with horrific wounds. She tripped over a trampled, wheezing dog. Another Westerner, the red-haired Norwegian, ran alongside her for a few seconds, vanishing as suddenly as he had appeared. At any moment, she might discover what it felt like to be shot. She imagined a single, lightninglike blow; her whole life flying across her vision; the pavement rushing toward her face; a cold and fading ache.

At the end of Jamal Grace veered left, glancing up Kantipath toward the Yellow Pagoda Hotel. Soldiers were kneeling in the road in front of the British Council, their rifles raised, picking off demonstrators as they fled randomly through the streets. She ran south, zigzagging toward the familiar landmark of Bir Hospital. Her breath wheezed in her throat. Dry-mouthed and panicked, she vaulted the low garden fence and lunged through the swinging doors of the emergency room, hitting the far wall so hard that it knocked the wind out of her and she fell to her knees.

HER FIRST THOUGHT, as she recovered her senses, was that she'd landed in one of the hideous hell realms described in the ancient Buddhist texts. A choir of agonized cries echoed all around her, punctuated by hoarse commands and the rhythmic, withering screams of wounded children. The sharp smell of disinfectant penetrated the corridor, barely masking the stench of sweat, shit, and urine.

Packs of Nepali men and women were shoving through the doors and rushing down the hallway, carrying dead and wounded civilians in from the streets on makeshift stretchers. Most of the victims were children: a teenager with a crater in his chest, a schoolgirl with her leg blown off. There were no more rooms; the casualties were being arrayed in long rows in the corridor, their bloodstained clothes the only insulation between their bodies and the cold and filthy floor. Emaciated pariah dogs, smelling the fresh blood, had snuck in from the shady alleys of Indrachowk to lick at the crimson tiles.

Grace pressed herself against the wall in shock. A wave of nausea threatened to overwhelm her. After a moment it receded, and she remembered why she was here. She was a witness: the only journalist on the scene. If the world was to know what had happened here today, she'd better start doing her job.

Her lens caps had disappeared in the fray. She wiped the dried blood off her UV filters and got to work. She was kneeling in the bloody corridor, photographing the rows of prone bodies, when a doctor in a blood-splattered white coat hurried toward her from down the hall.

"You! Miss! *Tapai lai kasto chha?*"

"I'm all right," Grace called back. "I'm fine!"

"Then for God's sake help us!" She recognized the doctor from somewhere. UNICEF? Peace Corps? No, the strike at the Teaching Hospital, two months ago. This was Mishra, the man who'd organized it all. Excellent! She changed her aperture as he knelt down to lift a wounded woman beneath her knees. The motor drive whirred efficiently. "What are you doing?"

Mishra appeared stunned. "Put that down! Take her shoulders! We have to get this person to surgery."

Grace should not have hesitated; she should have refused Mishra and continued fiercely with her own work. It was as important as his. The pictures she was taking were critical documents, and a part of Nepal's history. She was about to tell Mishra that she, too, had urgent skills; that people were relying on her as much as they were relying on him.

But that would be a lie. Teenage girls, rickshaw drivers and students, mothers and children were lying on all sides of her, bleeding to death as she took their photos. It was one thing to be in a refugee camp or war zone, where suffering became an abstraction. These were people she knew, in a place she loved.

"I'll help you," she said.

He nodded at her gear. "Your cameras will get ruined. Put them in my office, at the end of the hall." Mishra pointed. "Hurry."

Grace craned her neck. She wanted her gear in sight. "Is there anywhere else?"

The woman in Mishra's arms vomited blood and her head lolled to the side.

"*Move!* People are dying while we think about these bloody cameras!"

She ran off guiltily. Mishra's office seemed official enough, and reasonably secure. The drawers were crammed with files. She loaded a fresh roll of color film into her point-and-shoot Minolta before slipping the strap around her neck. Then she wrapped her cameras in her photographer's vest, and covered the bundle with Mishra's sports jacket. She closed his door and jogged back down the hall.

Grace was squeamish about hospitals; she had once fainted while giving blood. Somehow, this was different. A hard-wired survival instinct had kicked in, vaulting her into a realm of dispassionate duty. She and Mishra moved the woman onto an empty table in the madhouse operating room, then returned to the corridor for a porter with a shattered collarbone. When he'd been relocated they returned for the next casualty. Grace sucked in her breath: It was the red-haired Norwegian who'd run beside her down Jamal. He'd been wounded through the neck, and his blood flowed onto the hallway floor. Mishra pronounced him dead on sight.

She rifled through his money belt for some identification. A spent cartridge slipped from his shirt pocket and bounced once on the floor, where it rolled in a tight semicircle. He had intended it, no doubt, as a souvenir. Mishra picked it up with two fingers.

"Bastards," he hissed. "These are hollow-point bullets. They expand on impact, which is why the wounds are so hard to treat. They are shooting to kill, not to wound."

"How do you know?"

"Look at him." Mishra tilted his chin at the corpse. "Neck, chest, and head wounds. They're aiming for the heart, not the legs."

THE CASUALTIES KEPT coming in. By now the corridor was full, and there was no more room in surgery. In a desperate bid at triage Mishra began treating victims in the hallway, recruiting bystanders to assist him as he sliced away torn and bloodied clothing, meted out tetanus shots, and sutured wounds.

There was a brief, strange lull as a small phalanx of soldiers muscled into the lobby. They made their way grimly back to the surgery room. For a panicked instant, Grace thought they'd come for her. But they surveyed the bodies and shouted at Mishra. He shouted back, silencing them. It seemed they were looking for someone; they moved from room to room, their commander barking orders until his voice was lost against the background din.

Grace was handed a kettle of iodized water and told to "prep for the surgeon," whatever that meant. She made her way between the victims, loosening their clothing, offering words of encouragement, and sponging grime and blood away from the places where stitches would go.

It was nasty work. Within minutes she was covered with blood. Her shirt and pants were soaked through. Flies lit in her hair, on her face, on the unused Minolta, and on the backs of her hands. She looked, she imagined, like a casualty herself. She shocked herself with the impious notion that she should save these clothes. The outfit would be great for Halloween: the photojournalist from hell.

The idea was funny and distracting, but when she finally stood up and saw her reflection in the hospital's glass door, something inside of her gave, and she nearly passed out. Death was all over her, like a second skin. She tore off her mask and scrubs, throwing them into the nearest corner. They were set upon by dogs. For an unmeasured moment she stood still, panting in the middle of the crimson corridor in her jeans and a sweat-stained bra, her sleek hair streaked with blood: a vision of Durga among the dead.

There was shouting, much commotion, and the doors to the emergency room burst open. The entire area was instantly awash in brilliant light. It was the CNN news crew; Grace had spoken to them in Patan, less than a week ago. The camera panned the scene, jerking to a stop when it found the half-naked, blood-spattered white girl who reigned over the carnage like a feral homecoming queen. The correspondent looked at her, too startled to comment, and tilted his head on the brink of recognition.

Grace stood unmoving, a primal sense of danger tickling the vertebrae of her neck. *Look away.* But the moment passed. She managed a wan smile.

"Hi, Mom," she muttered. Then she felt a hand on her arm, and Mishra led her away.

"Never mind," he said. "Your mother will never see. They will edit you from the broadcast. And even if they do not, there is no need to worry. Everyone will understand."

"Understand what?" She hadn't a clue what he was saying.

Mishra's thin smile appeared completely out of place in the floodlit, blood-mottled hall. "That you are just another Westerner who has lost her shirt in the East."

Grace stared at him for a few seconds, then began to laugh. She found she couldn't stop.

"You had better go now, I think." Mishra took the blackened sponge out of her hand and wiped it gently across her stinging cheeks. Pink rivulets ran down her neck. "Try to get home and wash up. You can wear the clean shirt hanging in my office."

Grace calmed down. "What about the soldiers? The shooting?"

"Over. Finished. They have called a curfew, but you have until seven to get home. It is nearly six." He took her hand. "Please, go. You have helped us so much. You may come tomorrow and take some pictures. Thank you. Really. Thank you from all of Nepal."

She nodded and, quite spontaneously, embraced him. Mishra laughed and self-consciously squeezed her exposed body, patting her rhythmically on the back.

The television crew had moved on, and the fever pitch of activity resumed as Grace made her way down the crowded hall. The stench of ammonia, striking her anew, was dizzying. There was less moaning than before; most of the wounded civilians lining the corridor were by now either stabilized or quietly dying. She stared straight ahead as she approached Mishra's office. Her only desire was to cover her body, return home, and sleep.

Grace found Mishra's shirt, hanging on a twisted hook behind the door. She removed a Cross pen from the pocket and set it on his desk. And then her whole spirit seemed to drop through her feet, through the floor, to the bottom of the Earth.

Her vest and cameras were gone. The bastards had gotten them, after all.

GRACE CARRIED OUR plates to the sink.

"I'm sorry," I said.

"It's okay. It actually is," she answered. "Maybe it's sour grapes. But I decided that if I was going to take something home, I'd rather it was knowing I'd saved a kid's life than having great pictures of someone's head being blown off."

"Well, that's exactly what we were talking about after Shivaratri. And you followed through. I think what you did was amazing," I said. "I'm proud of you."

"Thanks, Dad."

"That's not what I meant." What did I mean? I walked up behind her and put my hands on her shoulders. "I love you," I said.

The words hung suspended. "Really?" Grace turned on the faucet and squirted detergent into the sink. "I'll believe that," she said, "if we're waking up together a month from now."

32

Word of Mouth

L ARRY PRINCE WAS one of the World's Most Difficult People. He'd lived in Nepal more than half of his thirty-seven years, moving to Kathmandu as a vagabond teenager. Those were the days of the Cowboy Raj, the epoch of rickshaws and hashish, just before Birendra's reign. Prince had led treks into perilous mountain sanctuaries, and was one of the first photographers to visit Tibet after the Chinese opened the occupied country to foreigners. He'd seen death and magic up close. Such distinctions might have been envied and admired, if he didn't wear them like a feathered hat. Pushy and self-promoting, he kept a running record of favors delivered and favors received.

So why did I love this guy?

"Because I'm brilliant, hilarious, and singularly well informed," he reminded me over lunch at his favorite Thamel pizzeria. "Not to mention well connected. And I'm also quite generous—to my friends. But don't cross me. *Please*. Because I'm quite capable of making your life here exceedingly difficult, if not impossible." He signaled our waiter and demanded a bowl of crushed chili flakes. "Do you happen to remember—it was exactly seven months ago—when Brian Leary, that stringer for *Gourmet*, was hauled out of his flat and given forty-eight hours to quit the kingdom?"

"I do." I certainly remembered wondering what a writer for *Gourmet* was doing in Nepal.

"Mmm hmm. Well, I trust you won't repeat this. The week before he left, Mr. Leary had made an indiscreet comment to the American ambassador about my brief—*very* brief—liaison with the vice-consul's cook. As a result, I was not invited to Thanksgiving dinner at the embassy. And as a result of that, I was not able to confirm an arrangement with a certain Marine Corps helicopter pilot, who had agreed to fly me up the Arun River for some shots of the new dam project. As a result of *that*, I had a little chat with my friends at Police Headquarters. And as a result of *that*—oh my!—poor Mr. Leary suddenly found himself persona non grata in Nepal.

"On the other hand, of course, there are," he lowered his eyelids, "*conservatively*, two dozen people who wouldn't even *be* in Nepal right now, had I not interceded on their behalf. So you see, I'm not all-powerful. But I do have some influence. Limited, but effective. Fortunately, I happen to like you."

Some people despised Prince so heartily they couldn't be in the same room with him. I found him endearing. His behavior was clearly an act: a carapace protecting a tender core. I knew how to humor him, but wasn't afraid to call his bluff. This afternoon, though, he had me over a barrel. During my week of research I'd been fishing for details, dusting for the fingerprints that would mark this revolution as peculiarly *Nepali*. And no one else (no other English speaker, at least) followed local politics as closely as he. So I sat patiently across the table, notebook in hand, as he showed me a selection of his photos.

There were more than a hundred images, all taken during the first ten days of April. Prince had been everywhere. It seemed he'd performed supernatural feats: hovering in the air above seething mobs, filtering through army roadblocks, impervious to bullets or lathi charges. This was the single quality that, despite his social retardation, saved him from complete ostracism: He was a first-rate photojournalist.

"Amazing work," I said. "You've produced one of the most important documents in this country's history."

"Thank you. I happen to agree."

"I think the hardest thing for me to believe is that, after so many months of waffling, the opposition leaders finally figured it out."

Prince stared at me, a cartoon figure of wide-eyed disbelief. "You don't think for a minute that April 6 was *planned*, do you?" A piece of fuzz, some kind of airborne seed, clung to his bearded chin. "Oh no. No, my friend. The whole thing happened purely by accident. Incredible, but true."

"How can that be?"

"I'll tell you exactly how: on one condition."

I leaned forward to flick away the fuzz puff. "What might that be?"

"You have to credit me."

"Sure. What would you like me to call you? 'Pizza gourmand'?"

"You can write, 'Larry Prince, longtime Nepal resident and one of South Asia's foremost photojournalists.' That's concise. Do we have a deal?"

"Please continue."

"Yes or no?" He refilled my beer.

"More or less. Now tell me your story."

"Very well. First of all, do you remember reading that a couple of days before the April 6 Massacre—on April 2, in fact—there were huge demonstrations in Kirtipur and Patan?" I did. "The papers said there were thirty thousand people in Patan, but there were easily twice as many. I was there for *Asiaweek*. It was incredible; much more moving and energetic than anything I'd witnessed in Kathmandu. Now, up until then the Palace—and by that I mean the king himself—had been *hearing* about the demonstrations. But he hadn't actually *seen* any of them. So the home minister dispatched a helicopter to take videos of the crowds and bring them back to show the king. Are you following me so far?"

"Of course."

"Good! So. The helicopter flew off. A Royal Nepal Army colonel spent a good hour collecting footage of the crowd. They were hovering close to the ground; people could easily see what they were up to. Finally, they left. Buzzed off. But there was one small problem with their strategy: a problem that nobody had even considered, much less taken into account." Prince paused.

"And what might that problem be, O wise and beneficent one?"

"Oh, come on. You're supposed to be a smart guy."

The House Special arrived, a mélange of vegetal ingredients. There was also some meat: A dead bee lay near the center of the pizza. When I showed the waiter, he groped for it with his fingers, contaminating half the pie. "For Christ's sake!" Prince slapped the boy's hand away. "We'd rather eat the bee." I was about to weigh in with a quip of my own when I noticed the kid's T-shirt: *Don't take life so seriously. Nobody gets out of it alive.*

"So?" Prince was back to his riddle. "What's your best guess?"

I thought for a few seconds before shaking my head. "The colonel fell out of the helicopter?"

Prince rolled his eyes. "I'll give you a hint. How do you say 'filming videos' in Nepali? What's the *verb*?"

"Come on, Larry, I don't know. I didn't even realize there *was* a verb."

"That's it!" he proclaimed, smacking his palm on the table. "*There isn't.* They use our Western idiom: *shooting.* Within two days of the Patan demonstrations, news had gotten around—by word of mouth, as usual— that the police had been *shooting* into the crowd. The fact that they were shooting *videos* was omitted. All people heard was that the army was firing, from the air, at unarmed demonstrators. That was the last straw. It broke the stalemate. It got Kathmandu's middle-class masses off their asses. People poured into the streets, outraged. And the rest"—he raised his beer glass— "is history."

We clicked our glasses together. The story, true or false, spoke volumes about the way news travels in Nepal. The country's information network, after many centuries, still relied heavily on rumor: a nationwide game of "telephone."

Prince pulled a stenographer's notepad out of his satchel. He thumbed to a specific page and pushed it toward me. "Every one of these," he said, "was taken seriously at some point during late March or April."

I looked at his notes:

LARRY PRINCE'S TOP REVOLUTION RUMORS

- *Kathmandu's water supply: poisoned by mandaleys.*
- *King sold Nagarjun Hill, used $$ to buy Sikorsky helicopter.*

- *Indian troops seen massing in the Terai, near Nepal's southern border.*
- *Chinese troops seen massing in Tibet, on Nepal's northern border.*
- *Thousands of disappeared demonstrators buried in mass grave near elephant ride at Gorkhana Park.*
- *Queen and royal heir, Prince Dipendra, have prepared an official document declaring king insane.*
- *A military coup, masterminded by king, to occur on the new moon.*
- *King placed a satellite call to Sylvester Stallone, asking for advice on how to respond to the mass demonstrations.*

I laughed long and loud as I copied these absurd theories into my own notebook, well aware that every one of them might have been true.

MAHESH REGMI, THE firebrand publisher of the *Nepal Press Digest*, was less amused.

"What these rumors demonstrate," the sixty-one-year-old journalist reflected later that day, "is a crisis of confidence that will come back to haunt us, even if democracy does take hold."

I'd known Regmi for years, and considered him one of my most reliable sources. His weekly *Digest*, a collection of tidbits cunningly arranged to highlight social irony and governmental hypocrisy, was Nepal's answer to "Harper's Index." Unlike other activists, Regmi had managed to stay out of prison. He did so by keeping a low profile; his genius lay in the art of quiet subversion.

We met in his office. I sat on a metal chair; Regmi reclined on a green velour couch. The room's two wooden desks were piled high with reports, local newspapers, and stacks of cloth-bound books bearing soporific titles like *Land Tenure and Taxation in Nepal*. The first time we met, I'd asked Regmi how he could possibly read such books. He dryly replied that he had written them.

Regmi was cautiously pleased by the recent turn of events, but curled his lip when I brought up a much-debated hypothesis: The Nepalis had compromised their prospects for true, irreversible freedom by failing to hang the king.

Regmi sighed. With his pop-bottle glasses and toaster-shaped head, he looked a bit like Jean-Paul Sartre. "I'm rather skeptical of all-out revolutions," he said at last. "They tend to bring all-out anarchy."

Nepal still needed a king, he insisted, if only to hold the fabric of this maddeningly diverse nation together. "I don't like this king personally," Regmi confessed. "He really is a fool. But we can make him harmless without removing him."

"Yes, but why take the chance? It worked in Romania . . ."

"Not so fast." Regmi wagged a finger at me. "This brings us back to that list of rumors provided by your friend, Mr. Prince. It's why the 'crisis of confidence' I mentioned is so dangerous. Birendra may not be the world's most charismatic monarch. But he has been sanctioned, by time and tradition, to fill that seat." He lit a cigarette and raised his eyebrows. "Tell me. Do you think a Sherpa villager would ever accept a southern Tharu as king? Or that a middle hills Gurung would accept a Magar? What is it the Arabs say? *The enemy you know is better than the enemy you don't know.* Keeping Birendra in the palace may seem like folly," Regmi concluded, "but removing him opens Pandora's box."

"But how can liberation be gained if the old system, with its class values and tradition of subservience, isn't dismantled?"

Regmi leaned back with a puzzled expression, disappointed by my naïveté. "An awful lot is heaped on that word: *liberation.* But liberation, as you must have discovered by now, is not a final condition. It is not a state of affairs, in either politics or in personal life. And it's certainly not something that follows automatically from a revolution. It is a *process*—and it usually creates as many issues as it settles. Like democracy! Okay, we have democracy. What are we going to do with it? Okay, we're liberated. What are we going to do with ourselves?

"There's the sense that democracy is a magic wand that will make all of Nepal's problems disappear." Regmi swept his hand between us. "Not so. Nepal's economic problems are intractable. No one will be able to solve them locally. To do so will require a partnership with India and China, and God knows what they will demand in return. There also remains the unsettling fact that, as people in Romania and Eastern Europe are discovering, right after a revolution, things can get worse before they get better. *Much worse.* And there's no guarantee they're going to get better at all!"

Though I agreed with Regmi's cynicism, the idealist in me hoped otherwise. I wished that Nepal, freshly revolved, might somehow become an exemplary republic: a jewel of life and liberty in the arrhythmic heart of South Asia.

"Whether things get better or worse is up to the people," I spouted. "Democracy is meant to be *of the people, by the people, for the people.* Whether or not it works depends on one thing alone: whether or not the people participate."

Regmi squinted at me, trying to decide if I was joking. When he finally spoke, his voice was wreathed in smoke-rings of sarcasm.

"Oh, really? And is everybody participating in American democracy?"

"No, but everybody is supposed to."

Regmi carefully extinguished his half-smoked cigarette, wrapped the remainder in a scrap of paper, and tucked it into his jacket pocket. "Well, then! That is what we shall do, as well. We shall also have a democracy where everybody is *supposed* to participate."

33

Why Westerners Love the Ocean

W E SAT TOGETHER cross-legged, on a Tibetan carpet patterned with dragons and coins. Two narrow bolts of yellow light rose from the floor and shot through the holes in a tattered curtain. The dais was covered with pomegranates and tangerines: offerings to the lama. There were other people in the room, but I didn't see their faces. I kept glancing at my brother, watching his reactions, wondering if he was taking it in.

The teaching was profound, and I remember thinking to myself, *This is amazing.* I had been certain that Jordan was dead, and now it turned out that it was all a sham; he was alive, and here we were, together, in the Rinpoche's audience room. When Chokyi Nyima paused to consult his translator, I turned to whisper something to my brother, something about the way I had spent my time when I'd thought he was dead, but he was craning forward with an intent look on his face and held up a hand to silence me. I fell back, chastised, remembering that he understood Tibetan.

Chokyi Nyima turned back to the small assembly and raised his eyebrows. "Any other question? No? Finished?"

Jordan held up his hand. The Rinpoche nodded, and my brother cleared his throat. "How much wood would a woodchuck chuck, if a woodchuck could chuck wood?"

I flushed with embarrassment, but Chokyi Nyima took the query in stride. "Three bags full," he replied.

The extraordinary thing was, I recognized this as the right answer.
My brother concurred. He nodded once, a slight smile on his lips. Then he
turned to me.

"Thank you for bringing me here. I'm afraid I can't stay."

This made no sense. We were living together near Nag Pokhari. His
toothbrush and Drakkar Noir were in the medicine cabinet. He had nowhere
to go, no home I knew of.

"Where are you going?" I asked. And then I understood, as one does
in dreams.

"I've got a small place." He chuckled softly, and raised an eyebrow.
"It's not half bad. Know that your efforts, which I would have dismissed as
nonsense two or three months ago, were of some use." His tone changed.
For the first time in many years, I heard a softness in his voice. "You saved
all my letters?" I nodded. "Do you remember how we used to dare each
other to dive into the biggest waves at West End Beach?"

"Of course I do. God, that was ages ago. And we would sing in the back
of the car, on the way home." I stalled for time. "And do you remember how
we used to go into the bathroom and piss together, making an *X*? You're the
only one who remembers these things. Deb wasn't born until I was *nine*." I
was talking out loud, but no one in the room seemed to notice.

"Do you hate me? I was so mean to you sometimes. We fought really
hard. We'd punch and kick each other, and I think I really hurt you a few
times. Do you remember? Do you remember when I called from California
and asked you to describe Mom's new husband, and all you said was, '*How
he loves meat!*'? That was so great. You're so funny. You're the funniest
person I ever knew. I love you, man. I love you so much."

"Walk with me to the door."

We stood up and stepped over people's legs, making our way toward the
long hanging curtain that separated the foyer from the altar room. Jordan
parted the cloth. We stepped onto cool marble and clasped hands. Blue sky
bloomed all around us. I didn't know what to say.

"*Kali shú.*" He pronounced it expertly.

I placed my palms together. "*Kali pei.*"

He inclined his head and parted. I watched him vanish down the stairwell.

Oh God, I suddenly realized, *he left without his shoes.* I turned around to pick them up from the shoe pile, but stopped short. There was nothing there. The corner was empty. All our shoes were gone.

CHOKYI NYIMA OFTEN talked about the meaning of "emptiness." Everything, from a statue of the Buddha to one of our eyelashes, is composed of atoms; and atoms are essentially formless. The closer we look, the more ambiguous their existence appears. Even on the subatomic level, change is continual. One can neither step into the same river, nor observe the same atom twice, a fact that indicates that matter, for all its apparent stability, is not very different from time.

The amazing thing is that it all carries on. You and I will die, but the party won't stop. Empty or not, the stuff of the world will remain: railroads and lakes and highways, chocolate chip cookies and papayas, tapered candles and birch trees, dinosaur bones and pianos, tortilla chips and the pyramids. We shuffle around the globe, encountering a few hundred thousand of the world's five billion people during our stay, then take our leave, turning planet Earth over to the next shift. The lights stay on. Music continues to blare from taxi radios, and kites sail over Kathmandu.

The whitewashed dome of the Boudha stupa radiated fresh prayer flags, undulating in a warm breeze. A few pilgrims made their rounds. Although the shrine was unusually quiet—compared to the last time I'd seen it, at Lhosar—another holiday was in the offing. Next Wednesday would be Buddha Jayanti, the full moon of Buddha's birth, enlightenment, and death, all celebrated on the same day. The morning pujas would be held at Swayambhu, then the festival would move to Boudha. Sometime in the afternoon, a geriatric elephant would circumambulate the plinth with an image of Buddha on its back.

Before I'd left Kathmandu in early March, Chokyi Nyima had issued a clear directive: *Next time you come Nepal, you see me first thing. Understand?*

I had broken my promise. Though I was eager to see the Rinpoche, my knees weakened at the thought. Time and again, I'd avoided opportunities to visit Boudha. The longer I waited, the more difficult the pilgrimage became.

Ten days after returning to the kingdom, I overcame my trepidation.

I led my motorcycle around the cobbled kora, slogged down the dusty road to the monastery, and climbed the familiar stairs. It was before eleven; the Rinpoche should be in. I hoped he was alone.

Entering the foyer, I beheld a large and chaotic shoe pile. There was a teaching in progress, possibly a week-long class. I took a few deep breaths before letting myself into the crowded altar room. The Rinpoche spied me immediately and clapped his hands together.

"Oooh! Giraffe! Back from the zoo!" He beckoned me toward him. I approached, knelt, and presented a silk kata. "You got here when? Today? Just now, yes?"

Lying seemed a poor idea. "No, Rinpoche. I've been here for a few . . . for two weeks." His eyes narrowed, and I came to my own defense. "I had some very bad news in America. Can I talk about it with you after the teaching? Privately?"

"Hmmm . . ." He looked into my eyes, one at a time. "Sure, sure. But today is very busy. See me after. Okay?" He wrapped the kata around my neck, slapped his palm on my skull, muttered a prayer, and pushed me away. "You sit now," he commanded. I moved to the back of the room, crossed my legs, and leaned against the wall.

"Okay. What we talking?" Silence. "Nothing? What? No one remember? Oooh, maybe all getting old."

A German woman with stringy blond hair waved her hand. I'd seen her on the kora, ticking off prayer beads on an antique malla. She fingered them now, rocking forward and back in an agitated manner.

"Rinpoche, some weeks ago I bought a Tibetan calendar, one of those books that gives all the holidays. Inside it talks about the 'Four Great Festival Days.' I see that the Buddha's birthday, next week, is one of them."

The Rinpoche nodded. "Yes? And? Your question?"

"Well, according to this calendar . . . On such days, the karma you generate by your actions, good or bad, is multiplied . . ."

"Millions of times. *Billions* of times," Chokyi Nyima completed her sentence.

"Yes. *Yes!* Rinpoche, this frightens me! I think I must stay in bed the whole day, because I am afraid of what I might do!"

"No no no." Chokyi Nyima shook his head mischievously. "Not enough to stay in bed. Because even if you stay in bed, how do you know your *mind* won't 'do'? Remember, if we check well, we notice: Each day—each hour!—our mood changes.

"Certain special times," he explained, "are connected with special mental power On such days, if we think something is good, the good feeling might multiply. Meditation may come more easily. When we think of this day as a suggestion, for controlling our thinking, it makes sense. But we must not let the idea of a 'bad day' take over our minds. Otherwise, bad things will definitely come! So occupy yourself with good thinking. Just relax . . . and let mind balance." He glanced down hopefully. "It's good enough, what I say?"

"Not really," the woman sighed. "I still think we must have a lot of problems on that day."

"'*We*'?" Chokyi Nyima declared. "*You* bought the calendar!" The room erupted with laughter. The Rinpoche waited for us to settle down.

"But one thing more to say. Very important." There was immediate silence, as if a crocodile had slid into our pond. "Listen carefully: *Impermanence. Suffering. Emptiness. Egolessness.*

"Understand? This is what Buddha taught. This is what you study. This is what you practice. Everything else is dogma, and superstition. Okay?"

I stared at the Rinpoche. With a few simple words, he had laid bare the core of Tibetan Buddhism. None of its rich, papal trappings—the gilt statues or silk robes, prayer flags or skullcups, bells, bones, or whistles—need distract me again.

The man sitting beside me, a young American with a billy goat beard, waved his hand. "Rinpoche . . . the world's a mess. Why isn't Buddha around right now?"

"Ha!" Chokyi Nyima slapped his knee and straightened his back. "Did you hear the question? Very sharp! Why doesn't Buddha appear right now? Hm?" He scanned the room, but there were no takers. "Does Buddha have no power, or what?" Nobody would touch that one, either.

"Okay," the Rinpoche said. "I explain. Buddha's power is always same. Buddha's kindness and compassion are always same. But these appearances seem to change. Like moon! The moon is always the same size and color. Yes?" We nodded, able to agree on this. "But different type of vessel or lake, with different types of water, create a different type of reflection. Understand? Some water is very clean, very clear! Makes a very good reflection. Some water is dirty, muddy; then the moon is not so clear. Is this a problem with moon, or with water?"

"*Water . . . water . . . water . . .*" The word tumbled through the room, as if from a chorus of desert rats.

"In every age," the Rinpoche continued, "only one Buddha appears. Why? Because the world can absorb only one Buddha at a time. But even when Buddha doesn't seem to be present, the Buddha's activity in the world is still amazing, seeking liberation for all beings. And we need to be connected with this activity. Because *any* connection, even a bad one, will lead to liberation. Even if you punch the Buddha! At that time you will create very bad karma; maybe you will need to suffer a little bit! But even the connection of punching a buddha, or bodhisattva, will eventually cause you to liberate!"

"Really?" This from an impish Israeli woman. "So if I punch you now, will that help me later on?"

"Not necessary!" Chokyi Nyima laughed. "Better, I think, you meditate. It takes less lifetimes that way! Otherwise, you may be reborn as an ant . . . or a worm . . . or as Gadhafi . . . isn't it?" He peered gleefully around the room.

"But what I tell you is true. Buddha said, 'Whoever is related to me, in a good way or bad, at the time of their death I strongly wish them to liberate.' It's very interesting," he mused. "This kind of teaching exists only in Buddhism. No other."

His cordless telephone chirped, and Chokyi Nyima took the call. From his casual tone and comments about a clinic, I guessed Dr. Dan was on the line. I hadn't seen Dan since February; he'd been visiting the Hospital for Tropical Diseases in London, researching a new strain of intestinal parasite.

The conversation ended. Chokyi Nyima drew his eyebrows together. "That was my doctor friend," he confirmed. "A good man, but very confused. He cannot relax! Mind always busy! Marry this woman, or that woman? Maybe marry soon, maybe never marry? Maybe want child, maybe not want child? Maybe stay in Nepal, maybe leave Nepal? Hmmm? Hmmm?" He scanned the assembly.

"Mind is very funny. Very funny! You know? Without too much choice, it is quite peaceful; with too much choice, it becomes crazy. This is one of the problems of developed countries. Too much choice, and too much suffering. Too much worry, and too much fear. Some years before, in Paris, I went to a restaurant. Even I had a hard time. The choice was too much. Two hundred and fifty things on the menu—all cheese!" A monk approached with a thermos, but Chokyi Nyima waved him off.

"So many times, Western people are thinking, 'Oh, I'm free! So free!' Always talking about freedom. But it's not really true. Western people, if you examine well, are not very free. Many rules, many laws. You must do this, you must do that; you need to buy this, you need to buy that. They always need to choose. They always need to *judge*."

The Rinpoche looked out the window, toward the saucer-shaped stupa of Boudha. "I think," he said, "that I now understand something. I understand why Western people love the ocean. Because the ocean is the one thing, really, that you cannot judge. The ocean is the one you cannot change. Even if you judge, ever if you complain, it makes no difference. Even if you worry—'Oh, wave too small, wave too big, water cold, water hot, big shark coming'—no difference! I think this must be why Western people feel so relaxed near the ocean. It is the one thing, the only thing, they cannot change."

THE RINPOCHE USUALLY stayed at his dais after the teaching, distributing medicinal pills and red blessing cords. Today he stood up as soon as the session was over, moving directly toward an adjacent room. I followed nervously.

"Rinpoche, you mentioned we could have a few words . . ."

"Now is not so good. What's problem?"

I couldn't rush into it. Chokyi Nyima sensed my discomfort and gestured to the carpet-covered couch against the wall. We sat down together.

"Rinpoche. I don't know if I ever spoke to you about my brother. My younger brother, Jordan."

"No." He straightened his robes and thumbed the beads on his malla. "Never mentioned. Some problem? Sick?"

"Rinpoche . . ." To my annoyance, tears were pooling in my eyes. "My brother was a great man. He was a scholar. He was a philosopher, and a student of language. He was also a fine athlete. And a very kind man." The Rinpoche nodded. I wondered if my use of the past tense, in referring to Jordan, had showed him where this was going.

"But he was also very depressed. Very unhappy about his life. I don't know why. During the past few months, while I was here working, and visiting you, he sent me letters. He told me about his troubles. That was why I went home: to see if I could help."

"So? Result?"

"I was too late, Rinpoche. Two days after I returned home, my brother killed himself. With a gun."

"Two days!" The Rinpoche's eyes widened. He reached over and put a hand on my leg. "Ohh. Very bad. I'm sorry." I nodded. "You spoke to him? Tried to stop him?"

I shook my head. "We didn't speak. I'd only been home two days." Mercifully, the Rinpoche said nothing. "It was on the weekend, right after my birthday. He was waiting for me to come home, so I could be with my mother. Rinpoche, he had planned to do this for a long time. I don't know . . . I don't think I could have stopped him." But even as I said the words, I knew they were untrue. Had I reached Jordan the day I got home, the world might be a different place.

"Rinpoche, I must speak with you about this. I don't know what to think about my brother—how to balance the goodness of his life with the way he died. I know you're busy. But I need your help."

The Rinpoche studied my face with an almost stern expression, as if he were reading my palm. Then he opened a drawer in the low table in front of us. He pulled out a pen and pad. They had been taken, I couldn't help but notice, from the Mandarin Oriental Hotel.

'Write your brother's name," he instructed. "You have picture, also?" I did a wallet shot of Jordan in upstate New York, standing self-assuredly beside a horse. Chokyi Nyima studied the photograph intently, as if to see through my brother's facade. "Tonight I will put his name and picture on my prayer wheel. I will also make a special blessing in my meditation. But right now, no time for answers. Can you come Friday? In two days?"

My heart sank. "I'm so sorry, Rinpoche, I'll be on trek that day." But I'd waited two months and could wait a few days more. "Will you be here next week?"

"Mm. Buddha Jayanti coming. Very busy time. Many pujas. Like Lhosar! But maybe Friday after. Okay?"

"Yes. I'll be here."

"No, not here. At that time I stay at Nagi Gompa. North of the valley. You know?"

"Yes, Rinpoche, I've been up there."

"Good. You come that day, ten o'clock. We talk brother. Okay?"

"Very well. Thank you, Rinpoche."

He nodded, tucked Jordan's picture into his robe, and cloistered himself away.

A single pair of shoes lay outside the altar room entrance. I slipped them on and left the monastery.

34

Milk and Cookies

O N AN OVERCAST Thursday morning, Grace and I took a taxi down Ramshah Path, veered around the statue of King Tribhuvan, and hopped out by the ornate iron gates leading into Singha Durbar, Nepal's parliament compound. We passed our credentials to a sober Gurkha guard, who motioned us inside.

The government building is an overcooked neoclassical architectural omelet, a high-cholesterol Rana-epoch monstrosity stuffed with white columns, ovoid archways, frothy fountains, and a generally unconvincing air of grandeur. As with all official Nepali buildings, from the government ministries to the university, any illusion of elegance vanishes the moment one steps inside.

Our appointment with Nepal's new prime minister was at ten. Though we'd arrived thirty minutes early, there was plenty of time to panic as we lost ourselves in the labyrinthine corridors of the durbar. Up one flight of steps, down two; through a rotunda, down the hall, and smack into a dead end; around the corner, under a tree; I felt like a hapless photon, trapped in a cruel video game. At length we spied an open door, which led into a room that fit the description I'd been given on the phone. Inside were a threadbare couch, a wooden desk, and a closed door, separating the waiting area from the inner sanctum. We sank into the couch and waited to see what would happen next.

Out in the hallway, *biscoot* wrappers, cigarette butts, and dust bunnies swirled in a vortex. The carpet in the reception room appeared to have been freshly peed on, and the head of a deer, or some similar creature, regarded us sympathetically from the wall. The wooden desk was bare, though in the layer of dust veneering its surface some local sly had finger-painted the word *puti*: vagina.

"Classy place," Grace observed.

The door to the inner office creaked open, and a slight, elderly man wearing a yellow darwa-surwal and neat brown vest approached. We rose to our feet.

"Hello . . . I'm Jeff Greenwald, a writer with the *San Francisco Examiner*. This is Grace Modena, my photographer." I extended my hand. He gripped it warmly while his eyes grazed upon Grace with undisguised lust. I felt like waving my hand in front of his face. "Sir? We have a ten o'clock appointment with Prime Minister Bhattarai?"

"I am Rajdoot," he declared. "You are German? French? Israeli? English?"

"We . . ."

"Yes, yes, yes, yes, yes. The PM's office, I will show you. But please, you will first take tea?"

I glanced pointedly at my wrist. "We're already running a bit late."

Rajdoot wagged his head and without another word led us out of the room and back into the maze of corridors. Pointed at long last to our elusive destination, we were relieved to enter a clean, carpeted waiting room with a handsome leather sofa and polished brass fittings on the doors. It was easily the most elegant official habitat either of us had seen in Nepal.

A middle-aged secretary accepted our introductions. "Please take a seat. The prime minister will see you in a moment." He pushed a button on his desk. A servant entered, carrying jasmine tea in china cups.

"This is more like it." Grace tightened a butterfly screw on her tripod and tested the grip. "Got your questions ready?"

I nodded and leafed through my pad. "Everything from the Tibetan refugee situation to the new tourist visa regulations."

"Really? Wow . . . maybe he'll grant me a permanent visa on the spot. Can you imagine? Full-on residency, with no money-changing requirements?"

"You're aiming too low. I'm going for honorary citizenship."

The door to the prime minister's office opened, and we were summoned inside.

The room was large, oddly windowless, and appropriately ostentatious, lined with teak paneling and acres of maroon wallpaper. A tiger skin lay upon the floor, the dead cat's jaw agape. Portraits of the king and queen hung above the enormous desk, their expressions as glazed as doughnuts.

Krishna Prasad Bhattarai stood to greet us, his engaging smile revealing horrible teeth. Silvery hair gushed from beneath his black topi like spun fiberglass. His hand, when I took it, felt dry and fragile.

Bhattarai was a remarkable man. Every moment of his adult life had been dedicated to the Nepal Congress Party, including the fifteen years he had spent in prison for prodemocracy activities. A notorious bachelor, he'd lived with his sister for the past two decades. We had met for the first time in February. I'd visited the NCP office during a strike and found "K. P.," the party's secretary general, sitting on the floor of the litter-strewn room. He had somehow avoided arrest and was drafting a formal letter demanding the king's resignation. It was a heartbreaking scene: a political pygmy, shooting pumpkin seeds at a rogue elephant.

And now this unassuming, congenial loner was prime minister of Nepal: a "caretaker" position he'd assumed only three weeks ago. He seemed stunned into docility, like a teenager who'd been tossed the keys to an aircraft carrier.

Bhattarai motioned us toward the overstuffed chairs facing his desk. As he eased back into his own seat, Grace and I exchanged glances. There was something . . . *off*. The massive desk, the office, the corn-fed faces of the king and queen seemed to dwarf the prime minister, who didn't know what to do with his hands. Except for a blotter, two phones, and a pen set, his desktop was empty. As for the tiger skin, it seemed as appropriate in Bhattarai's domain as it might have in PETA's headquarters. I was struck by the feeling that none of this was real, that Grace and I had landed in one of those dreams in which a long-anticipated event falls horribly short of one's expectations.

The prime minister must have sensed our discomfort. He smiled lamely and stretched his lanky arms into a broad shrug. "I am only filling a seat!" he declaimed.

I smiled, charmed by what I took as humility. It took a full half hour to realize that he had spoken the absolute truth.

The interview was tragic. Despite his enthusiasm, Bhattarai had no grasp whatever of the issues of the day. It was as if his whole political life had been spent in a vacuum, wrestling with political concepts that would never be put into use. Most of his responses to my questions were vague and uncertain. Others were so misinformed that publishing them locally would cause widespread panic. When I asked, for example, about the Congress Party's plan to create jobs for the thousands of young Nepali men and women who would graduate from Tribhuvan University during the next decade, Bhattarai waved his hand as if shooing away a fly.

"Most of our unemployment problem is solved," he observed, "by people going off to work in India or the United States."

His responses to questions regarding Tibetan refugees ("We will tell the Chinese that the Tibetans are harmless people, and that we will not allow them to attack China from Nepali soil.") and Nepal's future prospects ("The one thing I am sure of is, I will remain unmarried!") were patently absurd. My biggest shock, though, came when I asked him about the rumors that the king and queen had transferred millions of dollars from Nepal to their Swiss bank accounts. Bhattarai peered at me quizzically.

"I also hear these stories," he allowed. "But I don't understand: What could be the source of such income?"

Was he lying? Or just totally, unforgivably naïve? At that moment, I realized that Larry Prince was right: The revolution had stopped short of its goals. Demonstrators should have stormed the palace and placed the royal family in chains, demanding an unflinching investigation into years of corruption, smuggling, and human rights abuses.

Instead, cowed by the monarchy, the new government had floundered with protocol. Their waffling—deciding whether, and in what capacity, the

king should stay on—had given the royal cronies time to secure their hold-
ings and destroy all evidence.

It came as no surprise. Centuries of fear and conditioning had left their
scars. The Nepalis were simply unable to confront their king. Where this would
lead, no one could say. But it seemed unlikely this new government would fulfill
Virgil's immortal goal: "To establish peace under the rule of law." Hamstrung
by tradition, Nepal had snatched defeat from the jaws of victory.

GRACE AND I had been granted thirty minutes. As our time ran out, I tried
to wrap things up. Our host would have none of it. He rang a bell; a servant
entered with a tray of tea, milk, and assorted cookies. Settling back in his
chair, a Nilla wafer in his fingers, Bhattarai sighed with contentment and
allowed his wandering eye to bivouac upon Grace. He smiled. She smiled
back and kicked me with the side of her shoe. Taking the cue, I pitched a
final question.

"Um, Mr. Prime Minister? The previous administration was rather
inhospitable to foreigners—to nonofficial visitors, at least—who wished to
spend extended periods of time in Nepal." Bhattarai gave a low whistle and
nodded sympathetically at Grace, whose afflicted expression recalled the
girl in William-Adolphe Bouguereau's *The Broken Pitcher*. "Some of us," I
continued, "for example, Ms. Modena and myself . . ."

"Grace," Grace said.

". . . like Grace and myself, have dedicated our professional lives to
Nepal. We would like your permission, sir, to stay here as long as we wish:
without having to follow arcane visa restrictions, leave the country several
times a year, or change large sums of money each month. Is there any way
that you might grant us this privilege?"

Bhattarai leaned forward, placed his palms on his desk, and drummed
lightly. It made a rich, hollow sound. I would have bet money there was
nothing in the desk but a pencil, three paper clips, and a plastic spoon. The
prime minister threw himself back in his chair.

"Yes, why not!" he cried jubilantly. "You are welcome! We welcome
beautiful girls also! You are all welcome! Most welcome!" He grinned at
Grace, displaying Halloween teeth. "Are you married, my dear?"

"Nooo . . ." She giggled girlishly.

This was the critical moment. The point was to get a letter, an official document signed by Bhattarai, to show the authorities at Immigration and the Home Ministry. At the moment I started to speak, however, the telephone on Bhattarai's desk began chirping. He held up his hand for silence, answered ceremoniously—"Bhattarai speaking"—and listened intently, blocking his other ear and squinting. He muttered something in rapid Nepali and replaced the receiver without saying good-bye.

"Affairs of state. *Key garney*: what to do?"

"Problems with the king?" Grace commiserated.

"No, no. An incident in Pokhara. Some crazy thing. No, don't worry about the king. That is finished. He will remain head of state, this much is of course true, but only if he behaves. Otherwise . . ." He made a slicing gesture across his throat.

I tried to recapture lost ground. "Mr. Prime Minister . . ."

But Bhattarai rose to his feet, and we were compelled to follow. "Thank you very much," he said. "A pleasure to see you. Come and visit anytime." He circled his desk, accosted Grace, and seized both her hands. "You, especially, are welcome. You are *always* welcome, my dear."

Outside of Singha Durbar, under the now blazing sun, Grace waved to flag a cab.

"So." I felt relieved to be out of the oppressive, impotent ministry. "You plan to come back for that visa?"

"I'd consider it, if his teeth were better."

"Offer to pay for his dental work. It'd probably cost less than what you're paying for a black market visa."

A taxi pulled up. We scooted into the back. The driver looked at us in the rearview mirror. "*Kahaa janee?*"

Grace looked at me. "Where *are* we going?"

"Let's get some lunch." I leaned forward. "*Nanglo Café janchau.*" The driver wagged his head. Grace wagged hers in imitation and grinned at me. I suddenly wanted to make love with her, as soon as possible. "What are you doing this afternoon?"

"Not a lot. I've got to pick up my slides at Lotus before five."

"Today is your didi's day off, right?"

"Yeah, she works Tuesdays and Fridays. Why?"

"I don't know . . ." I felt strangely shy. She reached over and held my hand, still radiant from our charged encounter with the prime minister. "You just look so adorable this morning. And I have to spend tonight at home."

"That's right," she looked sullen. "When are you flying to Lukla?"

'At six in the morning. Ugh. And I still have a million errands to do."

The trek was a bold and crazy idea, inspired by my longing to spend some time in the mountains. Hiking in the Khumbu would be a tonic. I'd get good interviews, I hoped, with the Sherpas and hill tribes, the village folk who made up most of Nepal's population, but whose perspectives on the revolution had been ignored even by the local media.

"When are you getting back?" Grace asked.

"In five days. Next Tuesday. May 8."

"Wow. Short trip. Wish I could come."

"Me, too. I was thinking, we've never trekked together."

"That's true. It could be great." She paused. "Or it could be a disaster. Literally."

"It wouldn't be," I said. But I'd certainly considered it.

A CORD OF smoke rose from the incense burner on Grace's dresser. Bells, horns, and shouts filtered in through the window. Outside, the leaves of the nearby trees were powdered with beige dust. Grace snored a little, her arm thrown across my chest.

Our lovemaking had evolved, become more intimate and bonding than it had been in February. But I sensed that she was wary, unsure of how completely to forgive me for my silence during March and April. The fact remained: I hadn't called, or written, or turned to her after Jordan's death. But I had kept my parting promise: I'd come back. That counted for something.

I looked at the clock and took a long breath. My to-do list was a nightmare; I hadn't even rented a sleeping bag. Very soon, I'd have to extract myself from her embrace. But not yet. I looked at Grace. The sense that we belonged together seemed to illuminate me from within, like a phosphorescent tide. It was thrilling, unanticipated. My memories of our courtship had been derailed by my departure, Jordan's death, Carlita, the revolution. But here in her Kathmandu flat, watching her ribs rise and fall through the skin of her back, I could imagine a future. There was a shape, a kinetic whole, we could make together.

I kissed her on the neck. She didn't wake up when I rolled out of bed. A few minutes later I was dressed and slipping my daypack over my shoulders. The bedroom door made a thin, creaking sound. Grace rolled onto her side, pulling a pillow over her head.

"Sweet dreams," I whispered, and closed the door as quietly as I could.

35

Promises

H OT WATER CAN be the ultimate luxury—and at 50 rupees for five minutes, it was also the bargain of the century. I washed my hair under the black bladder of a solar shower, pulled on a pair of shorts, and checked out of my guest house in Namche Bazaar. The Sherpa settlement had mushroomed since my last visit, six and a half years earlier; every house now had dangling electric bulbs, and even the more modest lodges offered pizza and brewed coffee.

I hiked up the well-worn trail that winds above the village and stopped for breakfast in Kunde, beneath the sacred mountain called Khumbila. The trek from there—which passes through Khumjung and drops to the Dudh Koshi ("Milk River") before climbing fourteen hundred vertical feet to the far ridge—is one of the most beautiful in Nepal. I made my way carefully down the slick flagstones, drinking in the staggering views of Ama Dablam to my right, the gleaming face of Lhotse visible a few days up the valley.

The long climb was even slower, but I enjoy uphills. After an hour of sweat and steady breathing I reached the crumbling remains of the Tengpoche Gompa. The charred walls, recently destroyed by fire, stood in silhouette against the sky. Mount Everest was visible above the ridge to the north, its pyramidal tip appearing much lower than the surrounding mountains. I ate a bowl of *thukpa* and slept well, despite the thinning air. When I awoke, the soaring hump of Ama Dablam was bathed in golden light.

A half day of trekking brought me to Pangboche, nearly thirteen thousand feet above sea level. The village is set on gray moraine; a group of
children on the outskirts played catch with round stones, pitching them
back and forth with unnerving force. The Imja Khola ran nearby, hoarse
and lively, iridescent with powdered mica. At this elevation Nepal feels like
another planet: an alien world bereft of trees, greenery, or much in the way
of oxygen.

Pangboche is the Nepali equivalent of Roswell. The local abbot led me
into his gompa and displayed (for a small price) the village's famous relics: a
finger bone and conical scalp, with a few tufts of hair, alleged to have come
from a yeti. (If true, I noted, the yeti was a redhead.)

The point of my trek was to gauge political awareness in a region far
from the Kathmandu Valley. How were the overthrow of the king, and the
prospect of democracy, playing in the mountains? Though my ability to
communicate was limited, it wasn't hard to enlist local teachers or guides
who spoke English. With their help, and my own improving command of
Nepali, I'd spoken with dozens of people, in tea shops and on the trail, from
adolescents to the elderly, from householders to porters. Their replies to
my questions were direct and basic. Democracy meant freedom of speech,
government accountability, education, and the availability of decent jobs. It
meant that people could steer their own destinies. Most of the Nepalis I met
were fascinated by the concept. Most—but not all.

On the way to Pangboche I'd met a group of schoolboys and asked
what they expected from the new order. They were all around fifteen years
old. Their "leader," Anil, was a tall youth with gazelle-wide eyes. In perfect,
clipped English, he pronounced democracy a curse.

"Because of democracy," Anil said, "hundreds of people in Kathmandu
have been beaten and killed."

"You are aware," I replied, "that the Royal Palace and the police were
the ones who did the killing."

He shrugged. Killing of any sort was an absolute, and anything that
provoked it, for any cause, should be demonized. I turned to his friends.

"Is there anything that could make you respect democracy?"

There was a lively debate, which Anil summarized. "We need schools. We need electricity. We need medicines. Every year many crores of rupees come to Nepal, but we never see the result. If the new government cares about us, they must give us what is promised. Otherwise, what difference between the old and the new?"

One of Anil's companions was a thin boy with sad eyes and a shocking hare lip. A bright silver button, an inch in diameter, was pinned to his jacket.

"Is that his third eye?" I joked.

"Oh, no, no!" Anil frowned earnestly, answering for his friend. "That was a picture of the queen."

I inspected the button closely. Before the recent turmoil, buttons emblazoned with portraits of the king or queen, posed on a mint-green background, had been popular. This was the right size and shape, but no trace of an image remained.

"What happened to her?"

"The queen took all of our country's money, to buy a house and car. Also, she tried to kill the king. So yesterday he rubbed it in the dirt, to take the picture away. It took more than one hour," Anil added with pride.

THE LONG MILES on the trail were an empty canvas. I filled them, painting with uninhibited strokes. Sometimes I'd converse with my brother, forgetting for the moment that he would never see these snow-runneled mountains, the mica-lined rivers, or the lammergeiers soaring overhead. Sometimes I bantered with Grace, or fantasized about where our path might lead. Every so often these internal dialogues became so cluttered that I had to stop, my head spinning, and ground myself. Even this wasn't easy. The sky was deep blue and highly reflective, as if it had just been waxed. It was a state like infancy: Every sight, every component of the landscape, was infinitely interesting, helplessly distracting. Once, gazing to the south, I saw what looked like a brilliant vajra, moving steadily eastward. Was this a visitation? A sign from Padmasambhava? I watched it for five full minutes before realizing it was a commercial jet, its windows glinting in the sun.

The ground was dry and cracked, covered with stones, boulders, bones. Shadows were razor-sharp, uncompromising in the rare atmosphere. The sun itself was impossible to look at. I averted my gaze with fear and humility, understanding for the first time the unbearable brilliance of a star.

A few hours beyond Pheriche I stopped. I stood still for a moment, and turned slowly around. The landscape was miraculous, but my time was too short. I could go no further.

There was a small tea shop on the route back toward Tengpoche, and I sat down for a glass of chiya. Another guest sat at the other table: a local man, in his early forties, with the square face of a samurai warrior. He spoke the easy, idiomatic English of a Kathmandu professional. After a casual greeting, I joined him at his table.

He introduced himself as Norbu Sherpa, an officer with Sir Edmund Hillary's Himalayan Trust: a charitable foundation created by the soft-spoken New Zealand climber who'd scaled Everest in 1953. Norbu had worked for the Trust for four years, but knew Sir Edmund since childhood. "I was raised in Khumjung and went to the first school he built." He had just spent a month touring the Khumbu region with a fact-finding group of his own. The Trust, he told me, was keenly curious about the repercussions of the recent revolution.

"It will be quite difficult for the multiparty system to bring its message here to the Khumbu," Norbu said, confirming my suspicions. "In 1960, when Nepal had its first experiment with democracy, there was violence and looting by right-wing reactionaries. As a result, the older generation associates democracy with anarchy."

He took a pen from his pocket and sketched a map of Nepal on the back of an old *Newsweek*. "The young people—the ones who attend university, and who fought for this change—no longer live in the mountains, in the villages, with their extended families. They have moved to the cities." Norbu drew large circles around Nepal's big population centers, with arrows radiating in from Nepal's northeast and northwest hills. "Even *I* live in Kathmandu, nine months of the year. For that reason, we have to be very cautious."

I didn't follow his reasoning. "Cautious in what respect?"

"Cautious about pretending we understand this place—even if we were born here. The people in this area know that we've changed. They know we identify ourselves with the cities, not the hills. They know that we no longer share their problems. So they don't trust us fully."

Norbu's proposal was simple, and sensible. Educated people from the urban centers would be funded to return to their home villages, for two or three months at a time, and work on social projects: building water systems, improving irrigation, repairing the monasteries, staffing health posts.

"A genuine effort must be made to win the people's faith and prove to the older generation that democratic leaders are good leaders. Because these next few months, before the first round of elections, are the most important of all. This is the phase where the new leaders will make it or break it. This is where democracy must be about *showing*, not just telling. The people here have had enough of promises. If the democratic leaders *show* they can run the country better than the king, the people will support them. Wholeheartedly.

"This coming monsoon," Norbu told me, "when people come back home for their social and religious festivals, we will return to the Khumbu again. We will come in a big group: not to promote our political beliefs, but to mix with the people. Slowly, slowly, we will help them understand what democracy means, and what it can do for them."

It was midafternoon by the time we parted company. The mountains seemed to be sublimating before my eyes. Plumes of mist boiled into the air, swept away by the jet stream in thick white banners. It was shirtsleeve warm in the sun, but the air held little heat; as the clouds thickened, the mercury plummeted. I pulled on my fleece and continued down the trail to Tengpoche, hoping my comfortable bed was still available. A bit of comfort seemed well earned. I'd gotten my story, and felt I was back in the swing of things.

Later that night, I bundled up and went outside. Tiny satellites crept between the stars. Was Nepal now my home? I'd loved the place for years, but had never felt this sense of commitment before. If we put our resources together, Grace and I could afford a nice compound—a house with a garden, kitchen, and rooftop view. The monsoon was only two

months away. It was a good time to look for houses, when so many expats
went on home leave.

"What do you think, Jord?" As if everything I did, from this moment
on, was on his behalf as well as mine. "Is she a keeper?" I grinned. "Am *I*?"
But the night sky was silent, and the constellations unreadable.

36

Grace Before Lunch

G RACE HAD NOTICED it the moment she'd awakened, just after dawn: something odd with the world. She remained aware of it all morning. It was as if a polarizing filter had been placed over the sun. But while the daylight appeared somehow muted, sounds seemed magnified: the neighbor's rooster, a breaking bottle, a herd of distant cows. The buzz of an airplane, spilling in from the east.

She'd noticed this phenomenon as a girl, on camping trips with her family. Every year, during spring break, they'd pile sleepily into a Dodge station wagon, the rear well packed with coolers and pillows, tents and Coleman sleeping bags, Monopoly and Risk, her father's sleek white telescope. She and her sister Jen in the backseat, competing to spy red silos or Oklahoma license plates. They'd drive for hours, grinding in the slow lane past the luminous farms of Kansas, over the Rocky Mountains, into the stark pink of New Mexico or southern Utah. Sometimes they'd end up in Capitol Reef, or Canyonlands; sometimes in Bryce or Death Valley. Grace would crawl out of her tent at dawn, while her father was studying the morning star through his Celestron.

"C'mere, Gracie, look at Venus today . . ." He'd known she was there without taking his eye off the lens. "Look at that . . . just a tiny crescent . . . just like the moon. But it's a whole world. Can you imagine that?" She'd peer through the 'scope, indulge him for a minute or two, then wander off toward the outhouses. There'd be frost on the rocks, sometimes a fox or a

rabbit. A jet glinting noiselessly overhead. The air seemed to ring. Grace
would stop amid the silence, amazed by the stillness of the planet, the sense
that she'd caught the world unawares.

A small cloud blocked the sun, casting her flat into sudden shadow.
Suddenly, Grace knew what she was feeling. The monsoon was coming.
Not right away, but soon. The first storms might even arrive this month.
The Himalayan spring was ending, even in the mountains. The last rhodo-
dendrons had bloomed.

Almost a year ago, during her first summer in Kathmandu, Grace had
welcomed the monsoon. It had filled her with a sense of liberation; it made
her want to sing and dance, to strip off her clothes and run into the street,
her face turned toward the sky, like a woman she'd seen in a *National
Geographic* story. There was something miraculous about the monsoon,
something divine—as if the deluge, transported by thunderheads from the
Bay of Bengal, might cleanse her soul. It was an organic cycle, a rhythmic
purge, another proof that God was female.

After a week of nonstop rain, though, her enthusiasm had dissolved.
The lanes had become a stew of mud, garbage, and cow shit. Cars and
trucks hove down the streets in a frenzy, chasing up curtains of filthy water.
Taxis were scarce. She'd arrive home soaking wet, to a flat full of mosquitoes. Nothing dried out; even her bed smelled of mildew. And there was
nothing to do. Most of her friends had left town, fleeing the floods in favor
of Thai beaches, pilgrimages to Tibet, visits to friends and family. She'd
been mired, alone, hugging her knees as the sky emptied and thunderclaps
pounded her windows. An exile, marooned in a dark, dank cell.

Not this year. No way. It was still May: the perfect time to decide where
to go. Where to go, and who to go with.

South India. She'd never been. Lou Tanner had gone last year; he'd flown
to Madras, bought a Royal Enfield, and drove it around the horn of India:
down to Kanyakumari, and up the west coast to Goa. Two weeks ago he'd
drawn her a map, peppering it with the most fabulous place-names she'd ever
heard: Mamallapuram, Tiruchirapali, Thanjavur, Ooticamund. The South
Indian temples were like baroque wedding cakes, he'd said, their gates covered with hallucinatory sculptures of gods and goddesses, animals and mythic

beasts. There was drumming everywhere. In one temple, Lou had heard a
regular, explosive, popping sound. In a dim room behind the main altar,
he'd found its source. A parade of pilgrims was smashing ripe coconuts onto
the ground, symbolically shattering their prideful minds. And the beaches!
He'd found a virtually unknown paradise, shaded with palm trees, near a
fishing village south of Kovalam. "Just don't try to swim in the morning," he
warned. "The locals shit on the beach and wait for the tide to carry their crap
away." Grace had grimaced, but Lou shrugged. "No place is perfect."

She was dying to go—but not alone. The subcontinent was a vast
unknown, a dizzying kaleidoscope of images and archetypes, urgings and
maledictions, abstract advice. Gorgeous, maddening, overwhelming. There
was one thing everyone agreed on: It was a tough place to be on your own.
The friends who'd had the best times had gone with their partners.

She had little sense of her relationship, or its future. There was the magazine story, with its deadline. Then what? What plans did they have, once
the article was done? The memory of their two month separation, without
so much as a postcard, still rankled. She'd known he was leaving, she had
accepted that, but she had also expected some contact. Was it asking too
much, to stay in touch with your lover?

With that thought, Grace felt a sudden shock; a sharp, painful sense of
what it must have been like for her own friends, after she'd disappeared in
the wake of Dean's accident. She'd had a regular Tuesday date with Alison,
bargain night at the movies, religiously honored even when Alison was pregnant. Or Sunday mornings, when Vanessa would invite Grace for brunch,
the *New York Times* spread like a bacillus culture all over the living room
floor, bowls of yogurt and strawberries on the coffee table. It had never
occurred to Grace to wonder, until now, how Alison or Vanessa had spent
those Tuesdays and Sundays, the weeks after she'd disappeared.

Granted, he had a better alibi. But two months! He hadn't spent every
hour in mourning. He'd seen his ex-girlfriend. He'd flown to New York,
visited friends, eaten at restaurants, gone to movies, shopped for CDs. He'd
bought a jean jacket.

"I thought about you every day." That's what he'd said. Thursday
night it had sounded romantic; now Grace rolled her eyes. Was he thinking

about her now, trekking in the hills? Was he devoting even a moment to wondering where their relationship might be in, say, another two months? Or a year? Grace couldn't visualize it. She tried to imagine the two of them in India—on a beach, at sunset—but it was a reach.

She ground up some coffee, put on the kettle, and picked up the magazines scattered around the flat. Generally she liked Saturdays, the Nepali day of rest. It had taken a while, but she'd finally learned how to treat them like Sundays. No newspaper, sad to say, but a good time to catch up on her reading. And how the mags piled up. She'd better make it through this stack. Larry Prince had flown back to town yesterday, after a meeting in Bangkok, and he'd promised her the latest issues of *Cosmopolitan*, *Traveler*, *Aperture*, and the *New Yorker*. That should hold her until the rains came.

She was sitting at the kitchen table, drinking coffee and leafing through a three-month-old *GEO*, when the doorbell rang.

Her friends knocked, knowing that she hated the buzzer. Three kinds of people rang the bell: her landlord, fruit sellers, and kids from the school library, who made frequent rounds to collect used books. The fruit man had come in the morning, and her landlord was in Beirut. Grace left the kitchen, tied on a green sarong, and picked up the small stack of paperbacks by her bed: *Winter's Tale*, *O Jerusalem! To Kill a Mockingbird*, and *Tess of the D'Urbervilles*. She was barefoot, wearing an ankle bracelet. Her toenails were pink. The bracelet jangled as she trotted down the stairs.

"Who's there?"

"Grace!" She recognized the loud voice. "Open up. It's Larry."

Larry? It was out of character for Prince to bring her magazines over to her. He'd been by only once before, for her housewarming party.

"Oh, shit! Sorry, I need the key." She ran back upstairs, found the key to the deadbolt, glanced in the mirror, and ran down again. The books were still under her arm. She heard Larry talking to someone and opened the door. Then time stopped, and the books fell to the ground, and the ringing in the air became a roar.

"I brought someone by," Larry said, grinning.

"Oh, Grace," Vanessa said, and rushed forward, folding her up in her arms.

THAT HAD BEEN this morning. Eleven hours ago. Her world had since transformed. Now Grace stood in the center of her bedroom, facing the empty walls. They looked anemic, naked. Her calendar, and the postcards taped to the wall above her dresser, were gone. The Kalachakra mandala and the Tara painting, rolled into tubes. Her books, the ceramic cups, the bronze rice paddles from Patan, all packed away. Tomorrow she would strip the bed, fold the futon, and hire a minivan to take her things to Rhoda's. Then to the Yak and Yeti, to meet Vanessa.

The flight to Bangkok was at one o'clock. Three hours later, they'd touch down in Bangkok. Just for a night, before flying on to Phukhet. He'd be there, waiting at the airport: Dean Ishimuro, PhD. Walking with forearm crutches, but snorkeling without them.

The whole plan, of course, had been Vanessa's. She'd known intuitively what Grace needed. It was her idea to come here and coax Grace home: just for a month. If she wanted. There was no pressure, Vanessa said. She could decide in Phukhet. But they'd bought her a ticket home.

Grace surveyed her luggage: a suitcase, duffle, and two camera bags. Not to mention the daypack, filled with slides, prints, and unprocessed film. That was the only souvenir she was bringing home: film. No singing bowls, no Tibetan carpets, no masks or prayer wheels or marionettes. Just two years of images. The story of her life, as seen through a viewfinder.

Grace walked into the kitchen and poured herself another glass of wine. The dishware, luckily, belonged to the landlord. That was another thing to do tomorrow: bring the milk and cheese downstairs. The food, and her key. Her hope was to come back in September, after the monsoon. But that was a million years from now—and who could guess what these next months would bring? It was ironic: Going home had become the ultimate adventure.

A wave of weariness swept through her. She dropped into a chair and picked up the current issue of *Traveler*. Unconsciously she glanced at her fingernails—and the memory of that Kansas City salon, where she'd stolen the article about Nepal, crept up on her like a sneaker wave. Then it hit her, all at once: everything she had been, and was now, and might never be again. The life she loved, and the love she was letting go.

37

Wheel of Misfortune

T HE MORNING OF May 9 began as they usually do: in bed. Coming back from the mountains was a shock, and I was in no hurry to face the city streets. There was also the elevation change, from the thin air of the Khumbu back to Kathmandu. Not a huge difference, but enough to reoxygenate my cells and saturate my body with a sense of well-being. I'd slept deeply, dreaming of a spaceship the size of Mount Everest. No, Mount Everest *was* the spaceship. It had lifted off and soared, a sun-blocking behemoth, moving across the sky and above the rivers with the maneuverability of a biplane. Vast chunks of ice dislodged from its flanks, thundering down around me. They littered the ground like landlocked icebergs, their blue tips scraping the sky. The immense mountain-ship, stripped of its snowy coat, appeared as naked and black as a cinder cone.

I pulled my legs out of bed. Buddha Jayanti, the full moon of Buddha's birth, was a day to think good thoughts. Chokyi Nyima's exchange with the German woman stuck with me: The karmic effect of everything I did today, good or ill, would be multiplied billions of times.

Grace was nowhere to be found. My post-trek fantasy of luring her out for a bowl of borscht at the Red Square had come to naught. I tried her again: still out. Was she aware of the day's potential? I envisioned her in Pharphing, hanging a string of prayer flags. Or near the gate of Pashupatinath, scratching a sacred cow between the ears.

FIVE HUNDRED RUPEES in coins jangled against my hips, weighing me down like ballast, as I stepped through the Boudha gate. It had drizzled before dawn, and the cobblestones steamed like boiled potatoes. Fresh prayer flags cantered in a light breeze. I entered the kora and tied my windbreaker around my waist. Before I could put my hands together for a prayer, a leper approached, clasping a tin plate between withered stumps. I placed a coin on the tray and returned his smile. Buddha's birthday is a banner day for beggars; devotees and pilgrims arrive with a Christmas spirit, eager to practice generosity and pay off a bit of their karmic debt.

I surveyed the scene. It was just as I'd expected. Beggars, cripples, sadhus, homeless mothers, trash pickers, orphans, toothless anis, and hobbling monks formed a receiving line around the stupa's circular plinth. The kora had became a kind of "merit mill." Devotees circumambulated with the shrine on their right, the beggars to their left. The opportunities for karmic advancement were astronomical. I did the math: a poor farmer offering a single ounce of rice could return home transformed, having accumulated merit equivalent to dispensing 1,250 tons of grain.

My own plan was equally simple. I'd walk around the stupa and give every beggar one rupee. The multiplied merit gained by this gesture would be dedicated to Jordan.

There were scores of beggars, but their numbers seemed manageable. Most sat cross-legged along the shallow drainage canal that encircled the shrine. Flat metal plates and offering bowls rested on their laps, or on the stones before them. They'd appreciate my one-rupee coins; the customary offering was only a few paisa, or a spoonful of rice. Though it didn't seem like much, one rupee was real money in Nepal, where the average per capita income was about $3 a week.

I took a fistful of coins from my pocket, joined the kora, and began dispensing alms.

It began well. I made eye contact with every beggar I encountered. There was an uncommon bond, on this day, between giver and receiver. Even the most downcast ragpicker, by accepting my charity, became a partner in a mutually beneficial transaction.

Once I'd gone a quarter of the way around the stupa, though, the ring of beggars seemed to have thickened considerably. Up to that point I'd been dropping a rupee in each bowl, exchanging a glance with the recipient before moving on. Suddenly, I was confronted by a multitude of outstretched hands. My transactions were no longer with people, but with palms. Some were small and plump, others as seasoned as catcher's mitts. Some held mallas draped over grimy wrists or showed long, narrow fingers wrapped in narrow gold bands. Some hands had no fingers at all. The paddlelike stumps, mapped with abbreviated lifelines, shook at me with force.

A third of the way around the kora, I realized that my store of funds would not suffice. The number of beggars had multiplied exponentially. But I continued moving clockwise, dispensing coins as quickly as I could.

Then a terrible thing happened. *I recognized a hand.* It was a woman's palm, with two gold bands and a tribal tattoo. I recognized her face, too. She'd been among the first beggars in line.

The truth became clear: I was being had. In my zeal to hand out rupees, I'd fallen for an obvious ruse. The more mobile beggars were accepting my charity, backing out of line, and racing ahead to find another opening. No wonder the line was getting thicker! With my every step, more beggars leap-frogged forward to take up new positions. Some had probably gotten two or three rupees by now.

On the heels of this discovery came a righteous anger. I stopped in my tracks. The offending beggars, for their part, realized instantly that I'd worked things out. A fracas ensued as the "virgin" beggars—those with legitimate claims to a rupee—shouted at me in protest, rattling their bowls. But the two-timers, unwilling to reveal themselves, followed suit. King Solomon couldn't have told them apart.

I stood paralyzed with confusion, my clothes tugged from all directions, when two policemen arrived. At first, I was grateful for the escort. They led me along the kora, fending off the career beggars and directing my philanthropy in plain English: "This one okay. This one also, yes. Can give. Him, no! No! No good man! This one give. This woman, no! Bad!"

But even the police couldn't stop the most desperate souls from elbow-
ing their way back in. By the time I reached the halfway point, the scene
was dismal. My self-appointed bodyguards were literally clubbing beggars
away—and the question of whether or not I was still "gaining merit" from
this exercise deserved serious consideration.

It was time to cut my losses. Just ahead, a twisted leper raised his hands.
The stumps of his legs rested on worn-out tire treads. I pulled every last coin
from my pocket and showered him with rupees. They covered his plate and
rolled in all directions.

There was a moment of suspended calm, followed by a mad scramble.
Further up the line, luckless indigents howled abuse at me.

As I fled the stupa, the fearful German woman at Chokyi Nyima's talk
seemed prescient: I should have stayed in bed.

AFTER THIS PHILANTHROPIC fiasco, it seemed a good idea to balance my karmic ledger. Just beside the Boudha gate, several Tibetan-owned shops sold
block-printed prayer flags. I bought a string of fifty, reclaimed my motorcycle, and rode the eighteen winding, potholed kilometers to Pharping.

The trip was arduous, but it was a pleasure to put the city streets behind
me. I parked on the side of the road, at the edge of the rice paddies that
surrounded Urgyen Tulku's farmhouse. A woman stood in the lama's yard,
reaching toward the limb of a tree, and for a thrilling moment I thought it
might be Grace, but it was only a housekeeper, rescuing a cat.

Across the road was a small temple. The unassuming shrine is the site
of a much-loved miracle, still in progress. For centuries, an image of the
elephant-headed Ganesh, carved from a stone outcropping, welcomed visitors on their way up the hill. About twenty years ago, though, the Hindu
pachyderm got some Buddhist company. Just above Ganesh's head, in the
same stone face, a second sculpture began to emerge. The "self-arising
image" depicted Tara, the protector goddess of the Kathmandu Valley. In
1979, when I'd first visited Nepal, the palm-sized image had been rough and
abstract. Now it showed amazing detail. Tara's head and arms were clearly
defined; her legs were poised and smooth. I studied the image carefully. Was

someone carving it surreptitiously, sneaking in after hours with tiny chisels and steel wool? There were no signs of tool marks; even the freshest features looked ancient. It was as if the Tara had always been there, tucked into an alternate dimension, waiting for this particular decade to emerge.

I bought three candles from the blind ani who sat, spinning a prayer wheel, in the corner. These odd little temples were like magic lanterns; you stumbled across them and made your wishes. But what to pray for? The last time I'd made a wish, I'd asked for the inspiration to write about Jordan. Today, though, with the factor of forty billion added in, I might be more ambitious.

And so I prayed for insight. Not to be all-knowing, but merely free of confusion. I prayed that I might depart Nepal, when that day came, with more understanding than I had when I'd arrived: of Grace, my brother, and myself.

Outside the temple, a dirt pathway switchbacked up and out of sight, to a grassy knob surrounded by ancient trees. It was a strenuous climb, but the view of the valley was magnificent: On clear days one could see the ethereal peak of Langtang, and west to the Ganesh Himal. Today, unexpectedly, the sky had filled with clouds, and the temperature was dropping. By the time I'd hung my string of flags, the wind had come up. The thousand lines of lung ta webbing the hilltop vibrated frantically, beating like hummingbirds' wings.

Rain began to fall. A few fat drops at first, with the promise of more to come. I hurried down the hill and gunned my Honda. For the first ten minutes of my ride the wind howled, testing me with stray drops. Then the sky opened. I had no raincoat. Within seconds I was soaked, riding face-first into the first real downpour of the year. A stream of water flew up from the bike's rear wheel, skunk-striping my back. The road turned slick, and every pothole became a pokhari. I gritted my teeth, drenched to the skin, and tried to remember that rain was a *good* thing.

It took more than an hour to reach Ring Road. I entered Kathmandu by way of Kalimati, at the peak of rush hour. The last time I'd been here—with Coal and Clarice, in the middle of a bandh—the horrendous road had been empty. Not today. Horns blasted at me from every side. Taxis raced by, raising curtains of muck. But Buddha Jayanti was still in progress, and I dared not complain.

This was my karma—and it was no picnic.

38

Mike's Breakfast

T HE NEXT MORNING was blindingly clear. Rooftops steamed. The clouds boiled away at first light, revealing the snow-dusted ridges of Gosainkund. I envied the travelers who were just setting out for the mountains, weeks of trekking ahead of them. The rhododendrons would be radiant. Even the stunted plants on my deck were glistening, cleansed of soot and dust. For the first time in weeks, birds wheeled through the sky.

On an impulse I swept the cobwebs off my Hero bicycle, pumped up the tires, and rode into town: past Snake Lake and the cinema hall, down Durbar Marg, and along the narrow lane parallel to the Yak and Yeti Hotel. Hidden up the street was Mike's Breakfast, an oasis of sunshine and calm. I took the table next to the birdbath and ordered a small pot of freshly brewed coffee. Mozart's clarinet concerto played from speakers hidden in the poinsettia trees. The waiter brought me *The Rising Nepal*. It was filled with tedious news about political appointments and constitutional referendums, nothing with any bite. The paper was hedging its bets, reluctant to throw its full support behind the revolution. It was hard to blame them; the tide might turn again. I looked around, hoping Grace might show up. Her absence had become mysterious.

At quarter to nine, Coal and Clarice appeared. I waved them over. It was banana pancakes all around—except for Coal, who ordered his usual grilled liver and onions.

Their own Buddha Jayanti experience, at Swayambhunath, was on par with my Boudha fiasco. The temple plinth had been mobbed, Coal said. There was barely room to stand. By midmorning the resident macaques, teased to the point of madness by Nepalis of all ages, decided they'd had enough. They leaped en masse from the trees and rooftops, grabbing the offerings on the shrines and snatching food from the hands of their human tormentors. They focused their wrath on tourists, who lacked the moxie to smack them away. More than one bideshi lost her daypack; another was bitten and now faced a series of painful rabies shots. Clarice, Coal explained, had panicked, opening her *jolla* and throwing their lunch—yak cheese sandwiches, apples and all—at the grimacing primates.

"I did *not* panic," she insisted. "It was Buddha Jayanti. One best not be stingy."

Our food arrived: fragrant flapjacks and a gray slab of liver. I didn't understand how Coal could eat water buffalo liver, much less for breakfast, let alone in Nepal.

"Perfection," he announced, pouncing on his cutlery and chewing each bite with pleasure. "I'm in a fine humor this morning. Sex with my wife, a run with my dogs, a brilliant idea over tea. I tell you, it doesn't get any better."

"What's your brilliant idea?"

Clarice didn't look up from her plate. "It's a hare-brained scheme. I won't let him do it."

"When we're thick with rupees you'll eat your words." A waiter brought a dish of sour cream, which Coal spooned over his potatoes. "Where's your sense of adventure? I wouldn't be surprised if the king himself volunteered to . . ."

"He wants to open a scuba diving school," Clarice announced. "Ask him where."

"Where, Coal?"

"Why, right in your own neighborhood. Your veritable back garden. Nag Pokhari!" I stared at him.

"Where else? It's big enough, it's conveniently located, and there's that small Ganesh temple, perfect for storing compressed air tanks."

"Coal . . ." I refreshed his coffee. "You're a genius."

"You see?" He turned to Clarice, vindicated. "I'm telling you, it would be a sensation. Imagine the sign: a noble cobra, clad in a mask and snorkel. Coiled below, three words: *Snake Lake Scuba*. It's an amazing place, really. Very mysterious. Are you aware that no one knows how deep it is? It may be part of a vast, subterranean aquifer. There's a rumor it joins an underground cavern, stretching clear to Pokhara. Pokhara! Can you imagine? And if what they say about the nagas is true . . ."

"The whole place," I said, "will be lined with gems."

"Exactly."

"Butchering the goose," Clarice warned, "for the golden eggs."

Coal sawed his liver. "Don't be silly, my dear. We would leave their *nagmanis* untouched."

"Best you do," she said. "Else they may go for yours."

There was a short lull in the conversation. Clarice looked at me briefly, furtively, as if she were about to say something, then turned her knife over a few times.

"Which reminds me," said Coal, clicking a pen and jotting something on a paper napkin. "Must fax Beijing for those jade buttons."

"My God," I blurted. "I forgot. You're off to China, aren't you?"

"That's right," Clarice nodded. "On Monday. For a full bloody month."

"A month? Seems like a long time."

She said pointedly, "It does to me as well."

"How will you entertain yourself?"

"Oh, I'll see the sights," she shrugged. "Some friends from Africa are living in Hong Kong; I may spend a week or so there as well."

"Kathmandu won't be the same without you guys in town."

"Ah, well. Sorry." Coal addressed me theatrically. "You'll be on your own. Footloose in Kathmandu."

"I'm sure Grace will console me."

Coal and Clarice looked at each other. Coal put down his fork. "Listen, old chap. There's no easy way to tell you this." He cleared his throat. "Grace is gone. She's left Nepal." I looked at him dumbly. "It's true. She flew out Monday, on the Bangkok flight."

"Bangkok?" The information was huge and smooth, like a mutant apple; I couldn't get my teeth into it. "You mean . . . on assignment?"

Clarice was fishing in her daypack. "No. She's on her way back to America. Michigan, I believe."

"Missouri," Coal corrected.

It wasn't sinking in. I sat limply, a rhinoceros on my chest. Clarice found what she was looking for. "She left you a letter." I took the envelope. It was a padded six by nine, made of *lokta* paper, with a lump in it. The eyes of Buddha were block-printed in the upper left corner.

"Someone came to see her," Clarice said. "Someone from home. Turns out she'd left a bad situation, and had more or less disappeared from sight. She made mention of an accident, whilst she was driving. It happened two or three years ago. She's been on the run, dodging her friends, ever since. Can you believe it? Nobody, friends or family, knew she was here."

"Then . . . how did they find her?"

"That's the amazing thing," said Coal. "They saw her on CNN and sent someone over to fetch her."

"Did she say . . ." I struggled for the simplest words. "Is she coming back?"

"Don't know," said Coal. "We saw her but once, and briefly."

The back of my face, behind my eyes and nose, seemed to be liquefying. Clarice reached over and put her hand on my arm. "It's extraordinary, isn't it, the hidden worlds of people. Any people. All people. The people you think you know."

"Except for us, of course." Coal speared a potato and loaded it with onions. "We're just as we appear, old chap. What you see is what you get."

I SAT ON a wooden bench at the edge of Nag Pokhari. It was the same place we'd met on Shivaratri, in February.

For a long moment I simply sat, holding the envelope, conjuring Grace. Her hazel eyes and girlish giggle. Her earlobes and hips. Just a week ago, I'd held her. Abruptly, everything had changed. Kathmandu felt pale, bleached of mystery. Nag Pokhari was a lifeless tank. My presence in this place, this *country*, seemed pointless.

The nearby traffic clattered like static. I took a deep breath, and opened the letter. She'd written in red ink. The short, bulbous *i*'s and rounded *m*'s were a surprise; I'd never seen her handwriting before. There were two sheets of paper, and a small plastic canister. I knew instantly what was inside.

Dear Jeff,

Maybe this won't come out so well, I've had a bottle of wine (cheap Australian stuff) and I'm in a state of shock. But I have to write to you.

So what can I say . . . life is weird . . . I never thought I'd be writing this letter. It's midnight Sunday, and I'm leaving tomorrow for Thailand.

I couldn't believe this, and maybe you won't either, but it's true. My friend Vanessa showed up at my door this morning. Dean's fiancée. We were all in the accident together, and I didn't think I'd see her again. A month ago, Vanessa's mom saw me on CNN, and everyone knew I was in Nepal. Vanessa said she'd come here, with no idea how she'd find me. Who did she end up sitting next to on the plane from Bangkok? Larry Prince.

The whole story is beyond belief. Dean was paralyzed from the accident, the doctors said for good, but he's making a miraculous recovery. He's actually walking. Now he's waiting in Thailand with two of our other friends, and he wants to see me. I can't say no.

After Thailand they want me to go home to Missouri with them. It's not just an idea. They bought me a ticket. I have a week to cancel . . . but it's not really a choice.

You are the only one I told about the accident, at least what happened afterwards. You know it was the worst thing in my life, and that I tried to run away from it. I ran to Nepal and didn't look back. I couldn't, it was like my life was out of control and I was hurting the people I cared about the most. I told you this. At first, when I saw Vanessa, I thought you had somehow found them and told them—but of course you didn't, and I'm sorry I distrusted you that way.

So now it all caught up with me. God bless CNN. At first I felt scared (I still do), but now I think it will be good, a liberating experience. It's my chance to make things right. Like you coming back here for your brother. Not exactly, I know, but similar. I can't move forward, with myself or with anything, until I put this to rest. There are so many people I have to see, and apologize to. I know that I still love those people.

A few days ago you told me you loved me. I love you, too. Forgive me for saying this, and maybe I'm wrong, but I feel like this—meaning, our relationship—isn't as important to you as you say it is. Does that make any sense? Because I think I'm the same way. Our work comes first. Maybe you'll decide to leave Nepal in another month, or a week. I don't know. Maybe I'm scared we'll get really close again and you'll leave again and it'll be like last time, when you just evaporated. That hurt me a lot. But I'm not leaving because I'm pissed off, in fact I spent the whole day wondering if I should stay here, and leave for Thailand after you got back. But I can't. I don't trust myself to go. But I have to go—to Thailand and to Missouri, also. And I have to go alone.

All my furniture is at Rhoda and Kunda's. I'll try to come back after the monsoon. Somehow I don't think you'll be here. Coal and Clarice have Vanessa's address and phone number. If you come back to America maybe we can meet in a few months, in California or Missouri. That is if you don't hate me for this. But I don't think you will. I think you'll understand. You understand these things.

I hope and pray you find peace about your brother. I think I know how you must feel. I have so many ghosts of my own.

Please call me when you can. I'll miss you, naga-man.

I love you

Grace

PS—don't run out of film.

I opened the black canister, shook out the roll of Plus-X, and left it, amid the other offerings, on the shrine by Snake Lake.

39

Nagi Gompa

IVE MILES NORTH of Kathmandu, well beyond the dusty ribbon
of the Ring Road, an ancient and enormous statue of the sleeping
Vishnu reclines on what appears, at first, to be a bed of snakes. On
closer inspection, it's a single snake: the cosmic serpent Ananta, king of all
nagas, whose intricate coils represent infinity.

I paused outside the open temple, wondering whether to enter and pay
my respects. But my mission right now was elsewhere, and in a different
spiritual tenor.

The village of Budhanilkantha was quiet this morning. I continued
through, on foot, toward the base of Shivapuri hill. A small group of goats
stood tied to a post. By the edge of the dirt road two boys played with a
top, spinning it on a square of worn cardboard. I stopped for a moment
and watched them. Nepal's unerring gift for synchronicity stunned me. The
metaphor of a top—a simple, wooden top—had crossed my mind many
times during the past few days. The trajectory seemed painfully familiar.
Wind the string, and give it a good toss. For a while, it seems it will spin
forever. But something always intrudes: entropy, gravity, a stray pebble.
The spin becomes a spiral; the spiral decays. Any child can draw a picture of
a top, poised and spinning. But who can sketch out those last few moments:
that chaotic, spastic jig?

I had wobbled through the long afternoons in silence, speaking to no
one. Grace was a snapshot, an apparition, visible when I closed my eyes.

But as difficult as the days were, the nights were worse. I lay in bed wishing I'd stayed in the mountains, where the clarity of the night sky put the size of the world, and the human condition, into perspective. If my trek had been short, it was because I'd had something to come back to. Would I have come back to Nepal at all, I wondered, had I known how events would unfold?

But there was something else I'd returned for, as well: this morning's audience with the Rinpoche.

I left the boys and their top and continued up the road past a thinning array of butchers, tailors, and cold shops. A short walk brought me to the gates of the Shivapuri reserve, with its ramshackle entrance booth. From here it was an hour's walk to the nunnery, on a steep forest trail lined with tattered prayer flags.

NAGI GOMPA SITS on a flank of the valley's northernmost hill, a blur of white buildings poised below the clouds. The forest rises behind it, ascending to the peak of Shivapuri and the source of the Bagmati River. The quality of light, as at Boudha, is wonderful. But here it has a cooler, slightly greenish tint, as the monastery is sheltered by trees.

Half of Chokyi Nyima's face was illuminated by the pearlescent glow of a nearby window. The other half remained in shadow. I shivered, approached, and offered him a kata. There was no joking about giraffes, none of our usual preamble about politics or the revolution. We sat face-to-face, alone in the dim altar room.

"So. Very sad thing. Really terrible, to lose brother. How can I help?"

"Rinpoche, you know that my brother took his own life. I need to understand something. How does Tibetan Buddhism view suicide?"

There was a moment of silence.

"Suicide is very sad, a very painful thing," he offered. "Life is precious, especially human life. We can help and serve so many beings, if we have good motivation. And we can help ourselves—to become a better person, wiser person, happier person. We can even get enlightenment, in this precious human life. We have so much positive power! And that is the reason we need to live, every moment. Very important. We should never waste, we should never damage, our precious human body."

"But do you think it's even possible," I wondered, "for a rinpoche, or a Buddha, to understand the depth of suffering that creates the motivation for suicide?"

"Of course! When Buddha gave his first teaching, it was on *dukka*: suffering. He said, *Please think well. There is a cause of suffering—and there is a method to be rid of suffering*. These are two of Buddha's Four Noble Truths So if someone want to know how be rid of suffering, it's good to know the true cause of the suffering. Not only pills, or drugs, or alcohol, or sex.

"Okay? Some other question?"

"Yes." I swallowed. I'd been rehearsing the question for days, but with the moment upon me I found myself struggling for words.

"Rinpoche, I've come to your teachings and spoken with other Buddhist students. There's a belief that if someone dies without embracing the Buddhist dharma, their human life is essentially—to use your word—wasted. They enter the Bardo without hope of liberation, without any tools for reaching a higher rebirth." Now came the sticky part. "This really disturbs me. It makes the belief in Buddhist practice sound like absolution, like in the Christian church. Without it, there's no redemption. If this is true, everything that my brother did during his lifetime was worthless. I can't accept that."

I looked at the Rinpoche. His eyes were soft, but unwavering. "I refuse to believe it." I continued. "My brother was a marvelous person. Difficult, but extraordinary. Even though he ended his life without any knowledge of Buddhism—in a state of despair—I cannot accept the idea that his life was wasted."

There was a brief pause. Chokyi Nyima coughed briefly, then cleared his throat. "Okay. First I explain the Christian idea, like you said. Then about your brother.

"The Christian idea of absolution is actually quite good. Why? Because if someone can feel really sorry for any negative actions they have done, and believe that the blame for these actions has been cleared away, it is possible they can die peacefully. And even though just thinking away those actions doesn't make them go away—since the karma of those actions will still be there—it does help. There s some definite benefit there.

"In the same way, if one is a Buddhist, one can call upon all the buddhas and bodhisattvas to witness that one genuinely feels bad for anything bad that one has done, and ask for blessings to purify one's state of mind. Again: One can die peacefully."

There was a moment of silence.

"Now about your brother." Chokyi Nyima looked at his lap, smoothing a fold in his robe. He appeared deeply pensive, yet tinged with regret, like a physician compelled to deliver difficult but incontrovertible news. "First, the act of taking one's own life is never positive. There is always some negative consequence, some negative karma from that. There's no way around it. I'm sorry. Sad to say, difficult to hear, but true.

"But this, also, is true. Any positive state of mind that your brother had at any time during his life—any moment of good heart, of open heart—has its own effect. The positive karma generated during a person's life is never wasted. It is never canceled out. No matter how he died, that effect does not disappear. Do you understand?"

I nodded. The Rinpoche's words released a cascade of images, rolling across my inner eye: Jordan at Cornell, inviting a homeless man to sleep in his apartment; Jordan in Manhattan, carrying an old woman's groceries; Jordan on the Santa Cruz campus, signing earnestly with deaf-mutes. *When I sought for truth I could have moved the planets, and the stars. In all I did I kept to truth and courage.* Was it not so? The quest for truth, in my brother's style, had required amazing courage, and might have blossomed into a lifetime of compassionate action. He had certainly been capable of it—until his "abomination" cast him into a pit of self-loathing. His own mind became traitorous. If his noble intentions had soured, turned acrid, it was not the fault of his heart.

Still, something continued to haunt me. It was the tired old theme, rarely questioned, of blaming the victim. I was surprised to hear that even Tibetan Buddhism, with its high premium on compassion, dooms the despairing suicide to a kind of damnation.

"Not damnation," the Rinpoche replied evenly. "We're speaking of karma. Listen carefully; I will explain.

"There are many good qualities of the human mind. But there are also some very bad ones. These include attachment, aversion, and ignorance: stupidity. Just so, the different reasons why one could take one's own life could be out of anger, jealousy, hatred, pride . . . or ignorance. Stupidity.

"Your brother's suicide was caused by stupidity: ignorance of the value of a human life. Thinking that life is too much pain, too much suffering. Thinking that it is better to be dead, because then the pain stops. Thinking that death itself is just a pleasant, oblivious state.

"That is very ignorant. Very *stupid*," Chokyi Nyima said. "Because that is not the way it is. It is not damnation, not superstition, but fact. You cannot liberate yourself from samsara—from *anything*—by running away."

I stared silently through the window. The word *stupid* had never been applied to any aspect of Jordan's life. It was shocking to hear it used so accurately. And yet . . . despite this assessment, I could not imagine a future in which my brother's essence was not only redeemed, but *rewarded*. I had to believe that the universe had found a place for him: a simpler incarnation, where his soaring vision and proud solitude might find their most appropriate home.

Perhaps this news was coming. I looked hopefully at the Rinpoche, but he placed his hands on my shoulders and raised his eyebrows.

"That's all," Chokyi Nyima said gently. "Clear?"

If there are no irrational taboos to be found in Buddhist philosophy, there are no easy comforts, either. I nodded, and bowed my head for the Rinpoche's blessing.

BELOW THE MONASTERY, a dirt road and numerous footpaths led to the labyrinth of rice paddies and thatched huts that marked the limits of Kathmandu. The weather was hot and dry, and a pall of dust hung like a lens over the city. *Grace doesn't live here anymore.* Never had the descent into samsara seemed less inviting.

I stood still for a moment, taking in the view and absorbing the Rinpoche's teaching. Wondering what I would *do* with it. And it occurred to me, in a flash, that I could do absolutely nothing. What was called for now was surrender. Complete surrender, as at Boudha, when I'd turned out my pockets and thrown my coins into the air.

The realization was startling, but true. I had nothing left to give. Jordan was gone. My service to him, of whatever value, had come to an end. Grace had left as well, seeking an urgent redemption of her own. I wished her every happiness, and could offer no more. As for Nepal . . . it would stumble and fumble, without elegance or apologies, toward fulfillment or futility, liberation or anarchy. There was nothing I could do.

My pockets were empty. But the air was warm, and smelled of juniper. I drew it deeply into my lungs.

That was it. That was all. That was what I'd come for.

A steady breeze moved my hair. Cords of prayer flags flapped above the nunnery, their colors bleached by the sun. A group of anis sat on the grass of the monastery's shaded courtyard. Some were sewing; one leafed through a copy of *People* magazine. The scene had a timeless quality, slightly skewed, like Masami Teraoka's paintings of geishas devouring Big Macs and ice cream. On the gompa's roof, a group of monks in high yellow hats blew into long-necked trumpets. There was no puja today; this was evidently a practice session. Long, low blasts reverberated down the valley, like the trumpeting of adolescent elephants.

In a nearby yard, a girl in a tattered dress chased a goat in circles. A black mastiff lay nearby, watching with weary interest. The family garden was protected by a lattice of sticks, flimsy in appearance but no doubt quite robust. Still, its powers of protection were limited; the lettuce leaves within were layered with dust. I squinted at the sky and started down a footpath, wishing I'd brought my hat. And then remembered that I had; I'd stowed it before my audience with the Rinpoche. I stopped in midstride and shrugged off my daypack, kneeling down to fiddle with the zipper.

Behind me, the flank of Shivapuri roared into the sky like a massive green wave. To the east, the long ridge of Nagarjun might have been a mirage; I could barely see it through the haze.

I stood up and shrugged the pack back on, waiting for a dizzy spell to pass. Then something caught my eye: a flash of motion above me. Two shapes were moving against the clouds, far beyond the lines of prayer flags, dipping and swooping at great speed. I stared at the scene for a full minute before my mind made sense of what I was seeing.

In the vast emptiness above the valley, a thousand feet over the irrigated fields and mud-walled cottages, a golden eagle rode a thermal updraft. Clutched in its talons, lashing and twisting, was a snake. At a point nearly level with the clouds, the eagle paused—and dropped its prey. The snake fell toward the Earth. Its ropelike body seemed to move in slow motion, as if falling through water.

The eagle jackknifed in the sky, rocketing downward with incredible speed. It swooped upward beneath the serpent, snapping it from free fall. Now the bird climbed again, wings tipped and wide, lost for an instant against the sun. Again, it released the snake. This time the eagle waited, tempting gravity with cool arrogance. Then it dived again, expertly reclaiming its prize.

I watched the raptor with limp arms, stunned by its virtuosity and grace. There was no cruelty, no pathos in the scene. It was the unfettered expression of *eagleness*: a guiltless display of the bird's singular genius. The serpent, no mere victim, was a partner in this dance. I remembered the mysterious temple at Shantipur—the sacred mandala, written in naga blood, that brought the monsoon rains. This snake had a role to play, as well. Stolen from its hiding place, carried into the light, its sacrifice unlocked the eagle's true nature.

In an instant, I understood. The eagle soared above me. I wanted to call out, but there was no way my voice would carry; no hope that my brother would hear me, above the galloping of prayer flags and the wailing of the monastery horns.

◻ ◻ ◻

For thirty years I had glimpsed Nepal's Royal Palace only through its high gates, or beyond the tall trees that sheltered the grounds from view. But in February 2009, the building and its gardens opened as a public museum. Checking my daypack and passing through security, I felt like a Chinese peasant, entering the Forbidden City after the Qing Dynasty fell.

It was thrilling to approach Narayanhiti and climb the marble steps flanked by statues of horses and mythical beasts. But as grand as the building appears from the outside, the inside is dark and cold, filled with shabby decor that looks as though it hasn't been changed for fifty years. With its small windows, narrow corridors, and stuffed tigers (not to mention crocodile skins and rhinoceros heads), the place has a strange juju. One cannot use the word *comfy* to describe a single room.

There are the usual salons with useless gifts from visiting dignitaries: bronze medallions, filigree peacocks, a crystal paperweight from New York City mayor Edward Koch. The walls are lined with photographs of visiting heads of state, the most humble of them more influential than their host. But the grounds are spacious and quiet; you can hardly hear the horns blaring on Durbar Marg.

The palace—designed in the 1960s by American architect Benjamin Polk—is grand, without conveying any sense of inspiration. I did, however, find myself impressed by the opulent Gorkha Hall, with its soaring,

Gaudi-esque columns and—most important—Ceremonial Throne. Every
king needs one of these, and this one is a beauty. More than half a ton of
silver and 30 tolas of gold (nearly a pound) were used to build the settee-
sized, velvet-cushioned seat of power. Silver elephants support the legs. A
canopy of nine gold nagas shaded the king's head, and thick gold serpents
served as his armrests.

King Birendra's personal office was as modest as the Throne Room was
gaudy. He'd sat behind a large desk, a world globe behind him, a stereo in
a nearby cabinet. The shelves are filled with an odd assortment of books:
Freedom in Exile, by the Dalai Lama; *1001 Wonderful Things*, by Walter
Hutchinson; *Hindu Castes and Sects* by Jogendra Nath Bhattacharya. There
is a picture of Tibet's Mount Kailash on the wall.

Birendra, of course, is no more. On June 1, 2001, the drunk and besot-
ted Crown Prince Dipendra allegedly went insane—gunning down his father,
Queen Aiswarya, and many other figures who populate the background of
Snake Lake. The venue for the infamous Royal Massacre was a separate
building: an older complex of rooms on the grounds behind the palace. That
structure has now been demolished. Only the foundation remains, as if it
were an ancient ruin. Cardboard signs indicate, by number, the overgrown
sites where the murders occurred—including the little garden bridge, still
standing, upon which Dipendra reportedly took his own life. These land-
marks are weird abstractions, and a sobering reminder of how the new government immediately destroyed every shred of evidence that might shed light
on the real motives for (and perhaps the real perpetrators of) the killings.

If one visits Narayanhiti looking for mystery, or an aura of godliness,
one leaves disappointed. There is little sense of majesty at the former palace,
few signs of greatness at any level. One gets the feeling that King Birendra—
though not a cruel or uneducated man—lacked any shred of imagination. I
left with the feeling, which I'd had often during the 1980s and 1990s, that
he was simply filling a seat: hoping to be an adequate king, with as little
effort as possible.

IN THE DECADES since 1990, Nepal's character has changed dramatically.
In 1995 the Maoists, long dismissed as a fringe group, began a systematic

drive to overturn Nepal's political hierarchy—an insurgency that became a full-fledged civil war and would claim some twelve thousand lives. The Royal Palace Massacre, falling in the middle of that conflict, was an almost unbearable tragedy. Though mocked and reviled by many of his subjects during Jana Andolan, King Birendra had ultimately become a beloved symbol of Nepal's unity and neutrality. His grisly murder, ostensibly by his eldest son and heir, threw Nepal into a state of shock from which it has still not recovered.

There have been positive notes, as well. The ten-year Nepal Civil War ended in 2005, with Maoists winning pivotal positions in the government. But Gyanendra Shah, King Birendra's sourpuss brother—who was out of the country during the Royal Palace Massacre—was still in the palace, consolidating his power. This inspired a second "People's Movement," more rapid and peaceful than the first. In May of 2008, Gyanendra was deposed—and the ancient Hindu kingdom officially became the Federal Democratic Republic of Nepal.

At this writing, Nepal's political climate is in such flux that anything I write here may be obsolete in a month's time. A new constitution is currently being drafted, and contentious debates are raging as to how the country will be redistricted and governed.

And it desperately needs good governance. When I returned to Kathmandu to complete *Snake Lake* in early 2010, the city hovered on the brink of chaos. Corruption was rampant, and the valley hung under a pall of smoke and soot from nearly half a million cars, trucks, and motorbikes. An uncontrolled building frenzy saw lovely traditional homes being destroyed (along with countless trees), and ugly cement high-rises popping up everywhere. Drivers swerved madly around children and garbage piles, blasting their horns and obeying no one's rules but their own. I was reminded of ecologist Garrett Hardin's 1968 paper, "The Tragedy of the Commons," which described an all-too-familiar situation: Individuals, acting out of pure self-interest, destroy a shared resource—though their actions cripple their society as a whole.

As much as I still love Nepal, it's hard to visit the once charming valley without thinking about Hardin. Modern Kathmandu appears to be the product of fifty years of selfish choices, one right after another. The situation has reached a point where the journalist Barbara Adams (long a Kathmandu resident, and now an honorary Nepali citizen) believes the country requires a *third* Jana Andolan: a revolution of ethics and morality, to turn back the tide of greed destroying this once mythic setting. I fully agree.

Despite its unabated turmoil, Kathmandu remains the most fascinating and magnetic place I have visited during this particular lifetime. Many of the places described in these pages—the Bead Market, the Boudha stupa, the view of Pashupatinath from the benches above the Bagmati River—are as wonderful as ever. And even in the midst of decay, the Nepalese have somehow maintained a sense of humor, and show wonderful kindness toward the visitor. Twenty years after the revolution, my prayer is the same as it was in April 1990: that the people of this astonishing country find the wise and compassionate leadership they deserve. I continue to believe that Shangri-la is not some imaginary Himalayan paradise, but a vision of the best possible future.

Jeff Greenwald
Kathmandu, March 2010

ACKNOWLEDGMENTS

*S*NAKE *LAKE* WAS a process that included numerous false starts, retreats, and phoenix-like resurrections. A great number of people came to my aid, in infinite ways—from providing creature comforts in Kathmandu to reading raw (sometimes very raw) drafts of the manuscript.

Among my muses and allies in the United States I sincerely thank Christina Ammon, Rob Brezsny, Richard Cember, Jeanie Daskais, Sheila Davies, Sallie Fischer, Miriam Goderich, Maia Hansen, Jane Harmon, Laurie King, Marianne Betterly-Kohn, Usha Lama, Elliot Marseille, Patrice Mulholland, Wes Nisker, Karen Nuñez, Michael Pedroni, Christi Phillips, Alexandra Pitcher, Amod Pokhrel, Suzie Rashkis, Mary Roach, Patty Spiglanin, Joan Walsh, Linda Watanabe-McFerrin. Special thanks and love to the wonderful Kristina Nemeth, snake charmer Laurie Wagner, and my cherished mother and sister: Roslyn Greenwald-Miller and Debra Greenwald.

My community of friends in Nepal has also served as a great inspiration to me. I place my hands together in gratitude to Carroll Dunham, Nick and Chrissie Gregory, James Hopkins, Thomas Laird, Lisa and Ravi Pradhan, the late Mahesh Regmi, the Venerable Chokyi Nyima Rinpoche, Dr. David Salim, and the gifted Alison Wright. I also wish to thank Barbara Adams, Mukunda Aryal, Ian Baker, Kunda Dixit, James Giambrone, Frances

Howland, Thomas Kelly, Frances Klatzel, Lucy Needham, Ray Rodney, Eric and Marcia Schmidt, Ang Rita Sherpa, and Diane Summers.

Michael Conner, a Renaissance djinn and harmonica genius, helped me coax this book out of hiding and into a presentable form. The brilliant and tireless Marcia Williams, who reads (with comprehension!) more books in a month than I do in a year, steered it into the best possible hands. It has been an honor and a privilege to work with Counterpoint Press, and with the legendary Jack Shoemaker. Jack, in turn, had the wisdom to sit me down with Roxanna Aliaga—an editor with vision, skill, and great powers of diplomacy.

Finally I am deeply grateful to Peter Barnes, The Mesa Refuge, and the Ludwig Vogelstein Foundation for providing support during the writing of this book.

ani—a female Buddhist nun.

Asan Tole—the center of the traditional market area in downtown Kathmandu.

bandh—a general strike, or work stoppage.

bideshi—a foreigner.

bodhisattva—an awakened being who qualifies for nirvana, but has chosen to be reborn again and again to help all beings attain freedom from suffering. Bodhisattvas appear mainly in Mahayana and Vajrayana, the schools of Buddhism that flourish in Nepal, Tibet, Mongolia, and Bhutan.

Boudhnath—an ancient stupa and pilgrimage place several miles from central Kathmandu, sacred to Tibetans all over the world. The place-name Boudha (also spelled Baudha, or Bodha) can also refer to the larger community of Tibetan gompas, homes, and businesses surrounding the ancient stupa.

chakra—literally "wheel." The dharmachakra is the Buddhist Wheel of the Law, set turning during the Buddha's first sermon. Vishnu (see below) also holds a chakra, or fiery disk. The word also applies to the seven main energy centers in the human body.

chiya—Nepali tea (as opposed to Indian chai), customarily served with milk and copious sugar.

dal baht—lentil (dal) stew and rice (baht), served with a helping of vegetables and a sour or spicy condiment: the traditional Nepali meal.

darwa-surwal—the traditional Newari men's dress, consisting of blousy pants and a matching shirt fastened near the shoulder, a dark vest, and a traditional brimless hat called a topi.

dharma—the Buddhist philosophical system, including the teaching of Buddha and the practice of Buddhism.

dorje—see vajra.

Ganesh—son of Lord Shiva and his consort Parvati, Ganesh (or Ganesha, or Ganapati) is the elephant-headed god of auspicious beginnings. He is also the protector of travelers, and the remover of obstacles. His mount is a shrew. Ganesh's brother is Kunda, the god of war.

gompa—a Tibetan Buddhist monastery.

karma—literally "deed"; the Buddhist law of cause and effect, holding that any action or thought performed in this or previous lifetimes will have a direct bearing on one's future process of liberation. Karma is sometimes compared to a seed that ripens during successive lifetimes.

kata—a sheer silk scarf, given as a traditional Tibetan greeting to lamas, rinpoches, and other respected persons.

kora—a devotional circuit, usually performed clockwise, around a sacred temple, mountain, or residence.

Lhosar—the three-day Tibetan New Year celebration. Lhosar is also celebrated as a universal birthday for all Tibetans.

lokta—a vegetable fiber used for paper-making. Lokta paper is a cottage industry in some parts of Nepal. Unlike wood, lokta is easily grown and quickly renewable.

lung ta—prayer flag; the literal translation is "wind horse." It is believed that hanging these flags on auspicious days generates karmic merit, and carries one's aspirations and prayers to heaven.

malla—a Tibetan or Hindu rosary, often consisting of 108 beads.

Manjushri—the Buddhist god of discriminating wisdom. Manjushri holds a sutra in one hand, and a sword in the other.

mantra—a sacred formula, written or spoken, used as an aid in meditation practice.

men-drub—literally "liberation through eating." A specially prepared food consisting of ground herbs and relics, empowered by a lengthy ritual and dispensed by high lamas as an aid to liberation.

mudra—a hand gesture displayed by a Buddhist or Hindu deity, conveying a specific message: protection, calming, exposition, etc.

Nag Hrad—"The Tank of Serpents," the ancient name of the Kathmandu Valley, when it was an inland sea.

Nag Pokhari—"Snake Lake," a natural pool just east of Narayanhiti Palace that has been converted into a minor shrine.

naga—a member of the race of sacred snake gods, the original inhabitants of the primordial Kathmandu Valley.

nagmani—sacred, priceless, egglike gems possessed by the nagas, which confer immortality and other riches on their "owners."

namasté—literally "I greet the God within you." The traditional Nepali greeting, offered with the palms pressed lightly together.

-nath—a suffix, designating a site as a place of worship (e.g., Pashupatinath, Swayambhunath).

Newars—the indigenous inhabitants of the Kathmandu Valley, famed for their metal, ceramic, and woodworking skills.

paisa—a Nepali coin, or coins. There are 100 paisa in a rupee. A 50-paisa coin is called a mohar.

panchayat—a political district in Nepal.

Pashupatinath—Kathmandu's most important Hindu temple, dedicated to Lord Shiva, on the banks of the Bagmati River.

rinpoche—literally "precious one." This honorific title is often bestowed upon lamas who serve as the abbots of monasteries, or who are believed to be tulkus (see below).

rupee—the Nepalese unit of currency. In January 1990, the official exchange rate was about 30 rupees to the U.S. dollar.

samsara—the earthly realm of desire, suffering, and rebirth.

Shiva—the enormously powerful and revered creator/destoyer of the Hindu pantheon. Shiva dances with the drum of creation in one hand, and the flame of annihilation in the other. He has myriad aspects: omnipotent lover, pure ascetic, source of the Ganges, protector of animals, etc. In his wrathful tantric form, he is the terrifying Bhairab, while his wife Parvati—herself yet another aspect of his power—becomes the fearsome Kali, or the bloodthirsty goddess Durga.

Shivaratri—the new moon of the Hindu month of Falgun, dedicated to the worship of Lord Shiva. Though celebrated by Hindus across South Asia, the festival is especially lively at Kathmandu's Pashupati temple complex.

stupa—a Buddhist shrine, usually in the form of a dome. Ancient stupas were probably simple mounds, later covered with brick or stucco. Stupas contain holy relics of past saints or buddhas, and are often capped with elaborate finials. Boudhnath and Swayambhunath are the two most revered stupas in the Kathmandu Valley.

sutra—a sacred Buddhist text, usually composed of long rectangular pages that are read horizontally and flipped over.

Swayambhunath—the so-called Monkey Temple, sacred to Buddhists and Hindus alike, atop a high hill near the western edge of Kathmandu city.

tantra—an esoteric and highly complex path to liberation, developed in Tibet during the tenth through fifteenth centuries.

tika—a red mark, often made out of dyed sandalwood paste, applied to the forehead. Tikas—unlike purely decorative bindhis—are applied to both men and women on religious occasions.

tulku—a revered individual who has taken a human rebirth after a previous lifetime as a high lama or buddha. The Dalai Lama, for example, is believed to be a tulku: in his case a direct reincarnation of the previous Dalai Lama, as well as a human reincarnation of Chenrezig, the bodhisattva of compassion.

vajra—a highly stylized lightning bolt, symbolizing in Tibetan Buddhism the indestructible essence and diamond clarity of the liberated mind.

Vishnu—the great preserver of the Hindu pantheon. Vishnu will be incarnated ten times, to save the inhabitants of Earth from demons and other menaces. His avatars have included Rama, Krishna, and Buddha.

ABOUT THE AUTHOR

J EFF GREENWALD IS the author of five bestsell-
ing books, including *Shopping for Buddhas*
and *The Size of the World*. His writing has
appeared in many print and online publications
including *The New York Times Magazine, National
Geographic Adventure, Wired, Tricycle,* and *Salon.*
He lives in Oakland, California.